909
E

EXPANDING HORIZONS

4   Expanding Horizons

1415   1415   1431

Newsweek Books New York

Editor Neville Williams

1434   1445   1450

4 Expanding Horizons

1453

1455

1469

Library of Congress Catalog Card No. 73-81685
ISBN: Clothbound edition 0-88225-064-7
ISBN: Deluxe edition   0-88225-065-5

© 1970 and 1974. George Weidenfeld and Nicolson Ltd
First published 1970. Revised and expanded edition
1974.

Printed and bound in Italy
by Arnoldo Mondadori Editore—Verona.

1477   1480   1485   1492

1494   1512   1516

Contents

Introduction

The hundred and one years surveyed in this volume, from the Battle of Agincourt to Erasmus of Rotterdam, saw the passing of the Middle Ages. There is no single event, no universally accepted date, which marks the beginning of the "modern world." In the sphere of international affairs the fall of Constantinople to the Turks (1453) was certainly a watershed, and yet the French invasion of Italy, forty years on, was no less epoch-making.

Each country emerging from the old Europe keeps its cherished anniversary or looks back on a particular founding father. For France this was Louis XI who brought all the independent duchies, save Brittany, under firm control; for Spain the seminal event was the marriage of Ferdinand of Aragon to Isabella of Castille; for England it was Henry Tudor whose victory over the Yorkist Richard III in 1485 founded a dynasty, and if at the time the Battle of Bosworth seemed no more than just another engagement in the Wars of the Roses, Henry VII was in the event so successful in his dynastic ambitions that the crown of England has remained since then in the line of his heirs. In the city-states of Italy the key figure was Cosimo de' Medici of Florence; in Russia it was Ivan the Great who achieved independence from the Mongol hordes to found a kingdom.

In Western Europe as a whole the legacy of the six or more rulers who succeeded in becoming masters of their own houses, absorbing independent fiefs and achieving natural frontiers in these years, was the nation state. The West would be plunged into a series of dynastic wars (effectively lasting until 1763) during which these nation states hardened. Warfare predominated, and the hope of visionaries that Christian rulers would abandon their rivalries to unite in a common cause against the Turk grew fainter each year.

A narrow interpretation of "the expanding" world in our title might suggest to some the life's work of the Portuguese pioneer Henry the Navigator, for the discovery of Cape Verde and the rounding of Cape Bojador pointed the way to the long sea route round the Cape of Good Hope to India and thence to the Far East. Rather more readers, perhaps, would assign the primacy to Christopher Columbus's first voyage of discovery across the Atlantic. Yet here we are concerned with much more than the discovery of new continents and the interactions of civilizations, for man's intellectual horizons were also expanding, reaching an apogee in the new Humanism of Erasmus. Since such learning was the handmaid of religion, the foundation of the Vatican Library in the middle of the century provided an impetus to scholarship of which the Church can justly take pride. There was a rash of new foundations of universities, colleges and schools, principally aiming at improving standards of education among the clergy. The rediscovery of the main texts of Greek literature and philosophy added a new dimension to classical scholarship, but Desiderius Erasmus had the patient genius to edit the Greek version of the New Testament, no less than the flair for writing the greatest satire of the age, *In Praise of Folly*. But what kind of impact would he have achieved without the rapid development of the art of printing, stemming from the publication of the Gutenberg Bible, sixty years before? Of a truth, in all spheres of human endeavor change was taking place at an unprecedented rate so that the fifteenth century was essentially a formative, transitional age, heralding a new, revolutionary epoch—the maelstrom of the Reformation.

Despite the emergence from the medieval map of clear-cut states (except in the Italian peninsula), the unity of Christendom remained; for ruler and ruled alike the papacy was still paramount, an institution ordained by God, even during the scandalous pontificate of Alexander Borgia. All over Europe there was much rebuilding of churches and money was freely given for beautifying chapels and chantries, naves and chancels. Italy had no monopoly of artistic effort— witness the stained glass of Fairford Church in Gloucestershire or the van Eycks' complex polyptych of the *Adoration of the Lamb* in St. Bavon's Church in Ghent, which formed a pictorial counterpart to the mystical writings of Thomas à Kempis, that were so widely read by the devout.

The cry of Dean Colet, the Oxford Reformer, of Friar Savonarola of Florence, who had inspired him, and of Erasmus the wandering scholar, who reckoned himself the Dean's pupil, was for a reform of the Church from within by the calling of a General Council. This unity of Christendom, fragile enough at times, under the stress of political change *just* survived the close of this volume. Michelangelo's frescoes for Pope Julius II in the Sistine Chapel glorify the fountainhead of Christian experience, since Rome was the universal heavenly city in 1512, as it had been in the age of Dante or of Augustine. The globe was shrinking as rapidly as man's knowledge of the universe was expanding, yet still art and science, like education, remained firmly under clerical control. Volume 5, however, significantly opens with Martin Luther's revolutionary stand at Wittenberg, which signaled a divided Christendom. On various occasions in the century, whether it was John Huss' teaching that led to his martydom or John Colet's preaching at Old St. Paul's, we see flashes of comprehension and apprehension, parting the curtains to reveal the coming drama of the Reformation, though as yet the extreme question about papal authority was never asked. The Humanist outlook, embracing a fearless search for truth and beauty, was indeed already questioning the purpose of man and that search would lead inevitably to dispute with the authority the Church had exercised

beyond the very memory of man.

Two ghosts must be laid. First, that history is no more than past politics; secondly the theory of Sir Edward Creasy in his classic study *Fifteen Decisive Battles of the World* (first published in 1852) that all milestones must necessarily be military or naval actions. Of the sixteen topics discussed in this volume no more than six are primarily concerned with warfare and only four deal mainly with politics. Our theme is the unity of history and so we devote attention to the different facets of man's endeavor that make up that unity. Accordingly we acknowledge the significance of geographical discovery, of artistic creation, of religious thought, or pure scholarship and economic development.

Though each of the sixteen essays in this volume is complete in itself, these separate contributions by different authorities are not presented in isolation, for the unique events with which they deal are placed in historical context through the means of narrative passages, by a single author, that link each essay to its successor. These linking passages provide the volume with a greater cohesion than would otherwise be the case so that without attempting to cover the whole field of world history with the comprehensiveness of a textbook, they do offer a general survey of the epoch— the movements that underlay it, the economic changes that gave it shape, changes in warfare and the developments in the arts that gave the era its unique style.

Principally these links discuss events and personalities that were of great moment in the history of a particular country, but are of insufficient importance to rank as "milestones" in world history, where selection is all-important. Examples are the Teutonic Knights, the consolidation of Hapsburg power, the rise of Islam, the conciliar movement, the growth of professional diplomacy and the fate of minor states such as Poland and Persia, Vietnam and Venice,

Scotland and the Scandinavian realms.

Necessarily the "milestones" do not appear at regular intervals. Indeed, the Battle of Agincourt and Huss' death occur in the very same year, while only two years separate Columbus and Charles VIII. In contrast there are sixteen years between the accession of Cosimo de' Medici and the foundation of the Vatican Library, and eighteen between the French invasion of Italy and the frescoes in the Sistine Chapel. Such a pattern consequently creates some unevenness in the time span assigned to different linking passages. Nonetheless it is fair to remark that no incident of importance nor individual of significance has been omitted. The index provides further consolidation, while the illustrations, maps and charts together complement the text of both essays and linking passages.

With the beginning of the Age of Discovery, Europe ceased to be a Mediterranean continent. There was a shift of emphasis to northwestern Europe and to the development of Antwerp—not merely as the commercial capital of the world but as the center of banking and finance as well. The new capitalism of the Antwerp Exchange and of such great banking houses as the Fuggers of Augsburg is certainly an expansion of the system of medieval credit built up by Jewish money lenders and the banks of Florence. Never before had society been so fluid: careers in the service of monarchs such as Louis XI of France or Henry VII of England were open to talented members of all classes.

Plagues were recurrent and in every country in Europe the disasters of the Black Death remained a vivid part of the folk memory. Even without the threats of pestilence or of bad harvests, which could bring death from starvation to many, life was fraught with anxieties for peers and peasants. John Colet was the only survivor of twenty-two children born into the family of a Lord Mayor of London, who could indeed afford the best medical attention. It was miraculous that so many women survived the rigors of childbirth. Diet even for the affluent was monotonous and, for most, unwholesome. Standards of living were, however, improving and there were rich fortunes to be made out of the new traffic in luxuries—silks from Italy and the spices from the East that came to Lisbon. In spite of the vigorous ports and inland commercial centers, late-medieval civilization was essentially rural in emphasis.

As we pass these milestones, from Henry V of England to Erasmus of Rotterdam, we witness the fall of dynasties, the changing of boundaries and the ways in which individual enterprise is supplanting the chivalric ideal. Vernacular literature takes shape alongside a rejuvenated, universal Latin and a rediscovered classical Greek, and all are disseminated widely by the printing presses. To be young in 1500 was to be in heaven, for there is a new urgency about man's quest for fulfilment as he attempts to explore the unknown, to exploit his environment, and to challenge long-accepted truths. In his unquestionable desire for knowledge as a whole he claims to understand for the first time the purpose of life, to appreciate anew the significance of beauty and to come to terms with reality. In so doing, man is "expanding" his world.

NEVILLE WILLIAMS

The Battle of Agincourt 1415

"The last great medieval king," England's Henry V, rekindled the Hundred Years War with his astonishing victory at Agincourt. There, some six thousand tired, hungry, dispirited English yeomen destroyed a strong, well-rested French army three times as large. Although Henry V was subsequently recognized as heir to the throne of France, his premature demise prevented him claiming his inheritance—and England and France remained separate nations.

Once there was a king who won a battle. And even now, more than 500 years later, the fame of Henry V still stands on the events of one day in late October, 1415. That day saw the flower of French chivalry slaughtered in a large and very muddy wheat field only about fifteen miles from where the stream of tourists now drive on their way between Calais and Paris. The field of Agincourt looks today much as it must have then. Stand on the country road between the villages of Agincourt and Tramecourt and look to the north across the wheat and you will be almost exactly on the line held by the English as they awaited the onslaught of the enormous French army. If they had turned and run, Henry V would have been just another unsuccessful medieval king. But because they held the line and won the battle he has been called "that princely hero who, through the splendor of his achievements, illumined with the rays of his glory the decline of the medieval world." Such is fame.

Henry V was twenty-eight when he fought the battle, a goodlooking man at the peak of his athletic prowess. His father, Henry Bolingbroke, had seized the English throne in 1399 and much of the ensuing years had been spent defending that usurpation. But when Bolingbroke died in 1413 the kingdom was quiet and Henry V could look elsewhere to satisfy his ambitious nature. There was little doubt as to where he would look.

Across the Channel lay France, long claimed by Henry's ancestors as their rightful inheritance. With a king who suffered periodic bouts of insanity and therefore with no strong central government, France was split between two warring parties, each seeking to seize the spoils arising from the king's illness. No time could be more propitious for invasion. While Henry and his agents negotiated to keep France divided and made outrageous demands upon Charles VI, England prepared for war. Orders were sent to leading lords and captains to raise contingents for the army. Many of these men had retinues specifically trained for war, and were eager to serve under so popular a king in what promised to be an exciting and profitable expedition. For medieval war was a business, a business in which booty and ransom money could do much to make life more luxurious or prop up a fading fortune.

The two main fighting elements in the English army were men-at-arms and archers. Men-at-arms were front-line troops who, by the time of Agincourt, were completely encased in plate armor. They must have presented a terrifying spectacle as they strode forward, clad from head to foot in burnished steel, their hips encircled by a jeweled belt from which hung a great sword on the left and a long dagger on the right. But to the French, whose knights were just as well-armed and brave, the real menace in the English army came from the archers. The English longbowmen with their six-foot bows of seasoned yew had dominated warfare for nearly seventy years. Trained at the village butts from childhood, clad in short-sleeved mail shirts and iron caps, they were by this date almost professional soldiers who enlisted for sheer love of fighting, desire for adventure and hope of plunder. They provided about three quarters of the English army of some eight thousand men.

By late July, 1415, the young King's arrangements were completed. Those who might have felt conscience stricken by an unprovoked invasion of their neighbor had been soothed by the leaders of the Church, who declared the war just. Negotiations with the agents of the King of France had broken down, as they were intended to. There are few kings ready to give up their crown, several of their richest provinces and their daughter with a huge dowry, without at least a fight. All this and more Henry had demanded and, once refused, he really had no option but to continue his preparations to take by force what he considered his by right. On August 11, Henry boarded his great ship, the *Trinity*, at Southampton and an enthusiastic crowd watched the gay and colorful fleet set sail.

Their first objective was the Norman town of Harfleur at the mouth of the Seine. This was to be a bridgehead from which the full-scale invasion of France could be launched. But Harfleur offered unexpectedly stiff resistance. Well-protected by its location and its fortifications, the town did not surrender until the middle of September, and by that time Henry's fine army was much reduced by casualties and by sickness incurred in the

Henry V, the last great medieval king of England. He successfully revived his country's claims to the French crown but his early death left insoluble problems for his successor.

Opposite English soldiers lead the Dukes of Bourbon and Orleans captive from the field of Agincourt. Only those of highest rank were taken prisoner and among the enormous French losses were more than fifteen hundred noblemen and knights and four thousand men-at-arms.

13

A contemporary French drawing of a battle scene On the left are the English archers who proved so deadly at Agincourt.

unhealthy salt-marshes surrounding Harfleur. The season was now late. To march on Paris with so weakened an army was unthinkable. But to leave a garrison at Harfleur and sail for home would have been humiliating. By October 5, Henry set his course. Too weak to invade France proper, he would march his army across Normandy to the town of Calais, the other English possession in northern France, thus boosting his morale and reputation without seriously risking an encounter with the French. For the French had been slow to raise a force against him and, although they had now gathered an impressive army, only their advance guard was in a position to hinder him.

So on October 8, Henry led his army, now reduced to six thousand men, out of the safety of Harfleur. The army's speed was determined by foot soldiers and baggage-wagons, and his rate of seventeen miles a day to the Somme seemed to ensure a safe arrival at Calais some three or four days later. But when he arrived at the Somme he found that things had gone seriously wrong. He

had calculated on crossing by a tidal cattle ford at the river's mouth, but on arriving there discovered that the French advance guard, whose numbers were at least equal to his own, had beaten him to it. The ford was staked and heavily defended. He was forced to turn south and march along the west bank of the river until he found an undefended crossing. As his army made its way further into enemy territory it was accompanied by the French on the opposite side of the river. English spirits dropped, food supplies were nearly exhausted and morale was not improved by the weather. The rain poured down and it seemed that the troops were doomed to a wet, unpleasant and not very heroic death through famine and disease.

At last geography played into Henry's hands. By marching across a great bend in the river he was able to get a day's march ahead of the French on the other bank, and on October 19 the whole of his army had crossed the river at an undefended ford. But this success seemed only likely to change the fate of the troops from slow death by famine to

An English fleet sets sail. The English controlled the Channel and were able to ferry armies to and from France without any opposition.

a quick one in battle, for between them and Calais lay the French army, which had managed to join the vanguard by crossing the English rear as they struggled through the rain. Now the French outnumbered the English by at least three to one and their leaders were determined to fight.

Henry went on toward Calais, his soldiers uneasily aware of the presence of the enemy, even though the broken and hilly nature of the terrain prevented the two armies from seeing each other. At last, on October 24, the English crossed the small river Ternoise and climbing the hill opposite saw, as they approached the village of Maisoncelles, the whole French army little more than a mile away in the plain ahead. They were taking up their positions across the high road to Calais and filled a very large field, "as with an innumerable host of locusts."

The site the French had chosen was almost perfect for a medieval battle. It was an enormous open field, sown with winter wheat, about two miles long by one mile wide. At each end was a village, in which the two armies made their headquarters. In the center the two woods of Agincourt and Tramecourt spoiled the field's symmetry, causing it to taper like a hourglass, so that at its narrowest point there were only about a thousand yards between the trees.

Henry v rose at dawn on the day of the battle and heard mass. Confident in God's support he arranged his forces. Being so heavily outnumbered he determined to fight between the two woods, thus preventing the French from outflanking and surrounding him. His men-at-arms were arranged about four deep in three massed groups. Guarding the flanks of each group were archers arranged in a wedge formation, and on the extreme wings of the line, on the edge of the woods, were much bigger contingents of archers. The archers had been ordered to provide themselves with six-foot stakes sharpened at each end, which they were told to set in the soft earth pointing toward the French as a defensive screen.

The French had learned little from the English victories of the fourteenth century. They still saw war as a chivalrous business between knights and scorned to make much use of men from those lower classes from which the English yeomen-archers were drawn. Their men-at-arms were drawn up in three immense lines of battle, one behind the other, with only the third line mounted.

Henry V's patron saint, George of England, in battle with the dragon; from a fifteenth-century stall end.

15

A French manuscript illustration of crossbowmen practicing in the butts. In England these archery butts were a feature of every village and the law compelled every able-bodied man to practice at them once a week.

Their leaders had all pushed their way into the front line, so as to have the honor of being the first to strike the hated English. So massed was their front that there was no room either for artillery or crossbowmen, both of which were present but played little or no part in the battle. Their only concession to tactics was two wings of mounted men-at-arms whose task it was to break up the mass of archers on the English flanks.

The battle started about eleven on the morning of October 25, the sun now shining after a wet night. As the French cavalry on the wings rode forward the English archers planted their stakes and, leaning into their bows, sent flights of steel-tipped arrows into the mass of horsemen moving slowly across the muddy field. Unable to pass the stakes and much damaged by the arrows the cavalry wheeled into the center of the field, in front of the French front line of dismounted men-at-arms who, weighed down by their armor, were in turn struggling across the mud. The confusion of fallen and terrified horses was already considerable, but the French men-at-arms, heads down against the sun and arrows, pressed on and soon struck the English line. The massive weight of this onslaught forced the English back a spear's length, but then they held. The archers threw away their bows and they, too, flung themselves on the French men-at-arms with axe and mallet. The French front line began to fall and then the

The fruits of victory. Henry marries Catherine of France and becomes heir to the French throne. His death two years later condemned his son to an unsuccessful struggle for his inheritance.

A letter written by Henry after the battle, dealing with the question of ransom for those prisoners who had been taken.

A fanciful fifteenth-century impression of Agincourt. The English knights never actually engaged their French counterparts on horseback but waited until the archers had decimated the French cavalry before engaging on foot.

real slaughter began. For the French, who had already converged toward the center of the field to get at the English men-at-arms and away from the archers, now found their second line pressing on their backs, leaving them no room to use their lances or even raise their sword arms. Men who went down could never rise again and soon the center of the field was composed of heaps of armor full of dead or suffocating Frenchmen, over which the virtually unarmored, and sometimes barefoot, English archers scrambled to continue their remorseless killing. In half an hour the battle was decided.

Seeing the fate of their comrades the French rear line started to move away to the north, and the English, now masters of the field, began the grisly job of turning over those heaps of armor to sort the living from the dead, and to claim their prisoners. Despite the English blood-lust many

French were still alive, but most of them were to suffer a cruel fate. For Henry, perceiving movement of troops to his rear and fearing that he might still be surrounded, gave the order that each man should kill his prisoners, these having not yet been stripped of their armor and probably equaling his own army in numbers. His soldiers, their fury now cooled by the thought of so much ransom, refused, whereupon Henry ordered a killing squad of two hundred archers of his own guard to do the dirty work. And so "all those noblemen of France were there killed in cold blood, and cut in pieces, heads and faces, which was a fearful sight to see." The only prisoners spared were those of very high rank, whose ransoms were reserved for the King.

Much of the heaviest fighting was around Henry himself, as the French struggled to reach him or die. Henry, like a true medieval king, distinguished himself personally in the battle, and saved the life

18

of his brother Humphrey. The number of Englishmen killed was small, the most distinguished victim being the King's corpulent cousin, the Duke of York, who commanded the right and is supposed to have suffocated in his armor when he fell. The French losses were enormous, and the roll of the fallen begins with the dukes of Alençon, Brabant and Bar, and continues with ninety counts, over fifteen hundred knights and some four or five thousand men-at-arms. What the total roll of dead at the battle was no one knows, for nobody bothered to count the thousands of those of low station who died.

The English spent the rest of the day stripping the dead of armor and other valuables which they loaded on carts and then, after a night's rest, set off for Calais. The dead were further stripped during the night by the local peasantry and were now as naked as they were born. The English army reached Calais three days later, and after a rest embarked for England.

The news of the victory preceded them and the citizens of the towns from Dover to London exerted themselves to give their royal hero a fitting welcome. The pageant which greeted Henry as he rode into the city incorporated every possible type of medieval show. Symbolic statues and gaily painted wooden towers, banners, trumpets, tapestries and splendid pavilions, cheering crowds and a chorus of beautiful girls singing with timbrel and dance this song of congratulation, "Welcome Henry the Fifte, Kynge of England and of Fraunce."

Perhaps they were being somewhat premature in their congratulations. Agincourt was certainly an astonishing victory against enormous odds and made Henry such a reputation as a fighting king that never again did a French army challenge him in major battle. But Agincourt itself brought little other than fame. At the cost of about a quarter of his army lost by disease he had captured one town and won one battle. Harfleur may have been a useful addition to the English possessions in France, but it was still just one town in Normandy and Henry claimed the whole of France.

Agincourt may have been an isolated battle but by it Henry had once again reopened that great struggle between England and France which is known as the Hundred Years War. The war was to end finally in the defeat of the English claim to the crown of their neighbor, but many historians assert with much justice that the real losers were the French. The war was fought almost entirely on their soil and much of France was turned into a desert, holding back French economic progress for more than a century.

Henry himself, together with his men-at-arms and archers, set sail again for France in 1417. In a brilliant campaign he conquered the whole of Normandy. Military success brought about what the earlier diplomacy had failed to achieve. Henry married Catherine, daughter of the mad King of France, and became recognized as the heir to the French throne. But on August 31, 1422, he died, leaving an infant son, Henry VI, whose heritage was to exhaust a generation of Englishmen, compelled to defend the conquest of his magnificent father, the last great medieval King of England.

PETER EARLE

After the battle, the French prisoners and dead are stripped of their armor. At Agincourt most of the prisoners were slaughtered because Henry feared that his army was about to be surrounded.

Heretic or Martyr?

John Huss of Bohemia, under attack for his theological views, was lured to the Council of Constance where he was summarily tried and executed for heresy. His followers' refusal to recant their views led to the Hussite Wars which they eventually won. But the Hussites fell out among themselves, dooming Bohemia to political instability.

John Huss preaching in Prague. His attacks on the sale of indulgences inevitably brought him into conflict with the Church authorities.

Opposite A portrait of the Czech reformer by Erhard Schoen (c. 1530).

John Huss, said Martin Luther in the preface to his edition of the Czech martyr's letters from prison, was "a magnificent great spirit, who writes and teaches in so Christian a manner, so manfully struggles with the challenges of death, so patiently and humbly suffers everything, and finally so courageously accepts the most fearful death in the name of truth, a good martyr in Christ." Huss suffered that "most fearful death" on July 6, 1415, at Constance in southern Germany. He had faced charges of heresy before the council that had been assembled there for the main purpose of ending the Great Schism in the Western Church, which had resulted at one time in there being three rival, contending popes.

The "truth" for which Huss suffered the heretic's death was a complex of doctrines contained in his writings over many years. But central to all his alleged heresies was the idea that the Church of his time, in its organization, its internal polemics, its toleration of corruption and its concern with worldly wealth, was not the Church that Christ had preached. Not that this was an original idea. Such criticisms had been voiced in Europe for hundreds of years, most recently by John Wycliffe in England. Indeed, Huss found in the English reformer's thought a confirmation of his own ideas and support for their further development. A century later the same ideas were to be found in Martin Luther's dispute with the ecclesiastical authorities. Huss thus stands in a line of men who opposed the ecclesiastical cant and hypocrisy of their time. What lends a peculiar twist to his story is the environment in which it took place, and the fierceness of the religious wars unleashed in his homeland after his death.

Huss' environment was the then imperial capital of Prague, the center of the Holy Roman Empire. More particularly, his work was centered chiefly on the University, founded half a century earlier by the Emperor Charles IV and still bearing his name. Charles had conceived of the University as an imperial, rather than a national, institution, and its members were accordingly divided into four "nations": Bohemian, Bavarian, Polish and Saxon. In all the four faculties—Theology, Medicine, Jurisprudence and Philosophy—German masters and German students predominated, and

effectively controlled all academic affairs. This was to play a significant part in subsequent events.

Nationality disputes and frictions have been a potent factor in social and political change in Eastern Europe, and the interplay between the Slavonic nations and the Germans has been particularly important. In fact, the tensions between Germans and Czechs at the Charles University at the turn of the fourteenth century were a small part of a wider hostility throughout Bohemia, as a Czech national consciousness developed and a Czech literary language grew up. In any case, the artistic and intellectual splendor and secular opulence of the imperial capital made it exactly the sort of place where forward-looking thinkers on all subjects were readily tolerated; but it was equally a place where controversy could all too easily turn into bitter strife intensified by national antagonisms.

This was what happened in the case of Huss. He entered the Charles University in 1391 when he was in his early twenties, at a time when the struggle between the Czech masters and the numerically superior German masters was particularly bitter. The struggle had crystallized into a theological controversy over Wycliffe's teachings, which were disseminated by the much-traveled Jerome of Prague and generally supported by the Czechs. Huss was brought to the forefront of this struggle when, in 1401, he became Dean of the Faculty of Philosophy. In addition, the following year he took charge of the Bethlehem Chapel in Prague, a center of reformist preaching in the spirit of Jan Milič, founded in the same year that Huss had entered the University. Milič, who died in prison at Avignon in the 1370s, was a rich prelate who had given up his wealth and his ecclesiastical offices to preach a kind of primitive folk-Christianity. Preaching at the Bethlehem Chapel was in Czech, and this, coupled with the circumstances of its foundation, made it only natural that it should become a center no less of Czech nationalism than of reformist theology. Long before Huss took over the Chapel, he had a reputation for near-heresy or unorthodox beliefs; now, crowds flocked to hear him, and his fame was said to be equal to that of Milič before him. Like Milič, Huss was bitterly opposed to the opulence of the

A Hussite view of papal worldliness: the Pope with minions at his feet. This contrasts with the picture opposite from the same manuscript.

to unseat him and discredit him with his protectors, the Archbishop of Prague, Zbyněk Zájic and the King, Wenceslas IV. Wenceslas, who had succeeded Charles IV, was anxious to neutralize the influence of the Church because of the approval of Pope Boniface IX for removing him from the imperial throne in 1400. Thus his support for Huss was less from conviction than for political reasons.

Despite this powerful protection, Huss increasingly laid himself open to attack by propounding and developing Wycliffe's teachings, which had already been denounced in Rome as heretical. An abortive attempt was made to have him tried before the Archbishop in 1408. In the same year, however, Stanislav of Znojmo, the leader of the Czech faction in the Faculty of Theology, was forced by the Curia to recant his defense of Wycliffe's attack on the dogma of transubstantiation by which the bread and wine become the body and blood of Christ through consecration. Stanislav's recantation left Huss the leading figure in the Bohemian movement for ecclesiastical reform.

Huss was not a tactful man. For him, truth mattered above all else, and he would speak what he saw as the truth regardless of consequence. It was this that led to his breach with Archbishop Zbyněk in 1409 over the latter's attitude to the Council of Pisa, summoned to dethrone all of the rival popes and introduce some order into the Church. Huss was in favor of this, but the Archbishop felt himself bound by a duty of papal obedience.

After this quarrel, Huss' relations with the Archbishop never quite returned to the same footing, though they were to some extent patched up after the King intervened. But the Archbishop's initial reaction had been to excommunicate Huss, and though he did not proceed with this, the events that followed only widened the gulf between them.

For Wenceslas, angered by the German masters' support for the Archbishop, and anxious as ever to contain the power of the Church, stepped in and reformed the University statutes to give the Czech masters a permanent majority in all academic decision-making bodies. The disgruntled foreign scholars left in large numbers to carry their complaints to Rome, and Huss was elected Rector of the reformed University. But the continuing cool state of relations with Zbyněk stood in the way of Huss' receiving his doctorate for his greatest work, *Super IV sententiarum*, a commentary on the *Sentences* of Peter Lombard. Furthermore, without the Archbishop's support, Huss was more and more at the mercy of his enemies in Church circles. In 1410 they persuaded Pope Alexander V to issue a bull ordering the burning of Wycliffe's works in Bohemia and shutting down the Bethlehem Chapel as a center of dissident preaching. The bull was phrased in terms which left no room for appeal, but Zbyněk had still enough friendship for Huss to allow him time to withdraw gracefully.

higher clergy and denounced it in no uncertain terms. He found a ready audience, for feeling was running high against the Church among the relatively vocal peasantry of Bohemia, who suffered from punishing land-taxes levied by ecclesiastical landlords. In addition, a gulf of poverty divided the lower ranks of the priesthood from the affluent prelates and to cap it all the very authority of the Church had been called in doubt by the Great Schism. Reformist preachers were no new thing in this part of Europe, but Huss stood out as one of the greatest.

The prelates were naturally perturbed at his popularity and lost no opportunity in their attempts

But graceful withdrawals, even for tactical reasons, were not in Huss' nature. With a great deal of academic support behind him, he attempted to make a formal appeal to the Pope. At this, the Archbishop repudiated him and had Wycliffe's books publicly burned. Again, Wenceslas mediated and extracted from Zbyněk a promise of support for Huss in the coming investigation by the Curia. But upon the Archbishop's death shortly thereafter, the center of opposition to Huss shifted to Rome, well outside the King's sphere of influence.

For the moment any heresy charges were shelved, but in 1412 the issue was revived by a dispute over the sale of indulgences in Bohemia. These particular indulgences were issued by the antipope John XXIII to finance his campaign against Gregory XII. Huss was on shaky ground in attacking this abuse, for Wenceslas was financially interested in the sales and forbade all criticism. Three students who attacked the sale of indulgences were even publicly executed. There was, not unnaturally, much anger among reformist theologians as well as great popular indignation. But their sale continued.

It was at this point that Huss spoke out, denouncing indulgences and publicly supporting certain of Wycliffe's theses which even the forward-looking Prague Faculty of Theology had rejected. He also proclaimed what to Rome must have appeared an extremely dangerous principle; he said there was a law of Christ superior to the law of the Church, and that believers did not have to obey papal commands that conflicted with this law of Christ.

This, of course, was the ultimate in heresy—a refutation of the doctrine of papal succession to Christ. Huss was saying in effect that believers did not have to follow the dictates of a man seen by the Church as Christ's plenipotentiary on earth. Accordingly, in 1412, a papal legate solemnly pronounced Huss' excommunication, and Wenceslas sent him away from the city until the affair had been forgotten. In the country, however, Huss continued writing and preaching much as before, believing that he would now be left alone by a Church whose days were numbered because of its disunity and corruption.

This was not to be. The Council of Constance, summoned in 1414 to discuss the unity of the Church and the possibilities for reform, also had on its agenda the problems of the heresies then current, including—prominently—those uttered by Huss. Thus it came about that Huss was invited to Constance to "justify himself before all men." He did not have to attend, and indeed, at first, he was reluctant to trust his accusers' assurances that he would not be harmed. He was no doubt strengthened in these suspicions by the fact that Wenceslas' half-brother, the Emperor Sigismund, in whose domains Constance lay, had designs on the crown of Bohemia and was in league with Wenceslas'—and Huss'—opponents. In addition, it could hardly have been a secret to Huss that the Council, though primarily aimed at ending the confusion

Christ washes the feet of his disciples.

caused by the Great Schism, intended formally to condemn a large number of his and Wycliffe's theses as heresies. And for heresy, canon law knew only one punishment—death by burning.

A group of noble Bohemian supporters of Huss negotiated a safe conduct for him with Sigismund, and on these terms Huss eventually agreed to go to Constance. He suspected he might be walking into a trap, but he wanted to spare Bohemia the

23

"crusade" threatened against it by John XXIII in case of his non-appearance. In the event, his suspicions were well-founded. He left Prague before the promised safe conduct arrived, and what did come was a document amounting to no more than an ordinary passport, with no assurances as to his safety. Shortly after his arrival in Constance, Huss was arrested on Sigismund's orders and handed over to the Bishop of Constance for imprisonment in the castle of Gottlieben. Largely because of the influence of powerful supporters in Bohemia, he was accorded three public hearings at the Council, in which he sought to refute at least some of the charges against him, but he was not allowed to present any coherent case in his own defense. He could, of course, have recanted publicly and perhaps have secured a reduction of his sentence to life imprisonment. But even that was by no means certain. A majority of his inquisitors saw him simply as a dangerous heretic who must be destroyed at all costs. In any case, Huss was not the man to compromise, even in the situation in which he found himself. He was sentenced to be burned at the stake, and the sentence was carried out with indecent haste outside the city. His ashes were scattered into the Rhine to prevent the Czechs preserving them as relics. Jerome of Prague suffered the same fate, and went to his death calmly, reciting from Socrates and the Early Fathers.

Opinion in Bohemia was outraged when the news came in from Constance. A condemnation of the Council's treatment of Huss, known as the *Protestatio Bohemorum* and signed by 452 Bohemian and Moravian noblemen, was sent to Constance. It described Huss as "this good, just and Catholic man who persistently rejected all errors and heresies." Though he did not join in signing the document for fear of antagonizing Sigismund, Wenceslas was angry at the course events had taken in Constance. For a short period, Bohemia, despite the existence of a relatively small papal faction, seemed to have achieved a remarkable unity, to have "come together into one," as Huss had urged in a letter written from prison in Constance less than a fortnight before his death. Preaching in the spirit of Huss continued, and "Utraquism"— the giving of communion under both kinds (*sub utraque specie*), that is, bread and wine, by reformist preachers—underwent an upsurge. The University of Prague formally declared Huss a martyr and

announced that July 6 would be a permanent day of remembrance for him.

But within this apparent Bohemian unity, the sectarian spirit continued its work, which was to culminate—twenty years after Huss' death—in one of the major tragedies of Czech history. The Hussite movement had been divided, often on quite minor theological points, even before Huss' death. But in the wave of feeling that turned into a great popular movement after 1415, the split became apparent. The main division was between the moderate urban intellectuals and burgesses of the so-called "Calixtine" faction, who emphasized the Utraquist view (of frequent communion as a prerequisite to salvation), and, on the other hand, the militant Taborites—named after the biblical Mount Tabor, as they also called their assembly mound in south Bohemia—who rejected the Mass as well as all the sacraments except baptism and communion, and who exercised the greater popular appeal.

Charles VI of France, protagonist of conciliar reform, discussing Church unity with Wenceslas of Bohemia.

Opposite right The Emperor Sigismund, in whose domains Constance lay. His designs on the crown of Bohemia led him to ally with the opponents of Huss and his royal protector, Wenceslas.

Opposite left Huss judged and condemned for heresy at the Council of Constance. Despite a promise of safe conduct, the Emperor had arrested him and handed him over to the Council.

25

Opposite Huss burned at the stake and his ashes being collected for scattering in the Rhine. His death outraged opinion in Bohemia and contributed to the rise of Czech nationalism.

Jan Žižka, brilliant Hussite leader, at the head of the peasant army that defeated the imperial forces.

Below The Pope judging heretics: an orthodox view of papal authority and divine retribution.

Tensions between the two factions grew, coming to a head in 1419 partly because of Wenceslas' attitude to the movement. In that year, a Calixtine procession in Prague, enraged by a stone-throwing incident, stormed the town hall in the city's New Town and threw the mayor and councillors out of the windows. Under the strain of this incipient revolt, Wenceslas had a stroke and died.

In the aftermath, fighting broke out, particularly between the largely German papal faction in Bohemia and the Hussites, who wanted at all costs to prevent Sigismund from succeeding to the Bohemian crown. After much destruction of life and property by both sides, Sigismund managed to reach Prague and have himself crowned in 1420, but no sooner had he done so than he suffered a shattering defeat by a peasant army led by the Hussite nobleman Jan Žižka, blind in one eye, but a brilliant military leader.

The Hussite wars and a seemingly endless series of imperial "crusades" against Bohemia went on for another fifteen years, with the various factions fighting in ever new permutations with one another. In 1421, an assembly of Bohemian nobles and burgesses, together with some more reluctant Moravians, confirmed the so-called Prague Articles as the theoretical basis of Hussitism and voted to depose Sigismund. The Moravians were reluctant to take such drastic action because they had not been so affected by the movement as the neighboring Bohemians. In fact, in Bohemia Hussitism took on ever more fanatical forms. Žižka on one occasion even had to execute fifty or more of the wilder fanatics from his ranks as an example.

After Žižka's death from plague in 1424 the leadership was taken over by Prokop, a former priest who equalled his predecessor in military skill, especially in the techniques of mobile warfare, using wagons in much the same way that tanks are used in modern times. Under him, the Hussite reputation spread and became so fearful that by the early 1430s the established rulers were prepared to come to some agreement with the Hussites. With some initial reluctance, Pope Martin v agreed to a plan conceived at the Council of Basel in 1431. But Sigismund was determined to have a victory and proceeded to invade Bohemia with a large army. It was only after he was routed decisively by the Hussites that agreement was reached, under the Basel terms, on four theses containing the main points from the Prague Articles.

So the Hussites had their victory. But in the very hour of victory, the movement turned on itself. In a bitter battle between Utraquists and Taborites at Lipany in 1434, Prokop himself and most of the leading Taborites were killed. This battle ranks, with a whole catalog of other disasters, as one of the great, melancholy tragedies that fill Czech history—all the more so because it was a kind of national suicide. It increased, rather than helped to diminish, the political instability that was to bedevil Bohemia for many years to come.

MICHAEL MONTGOMERY

The condemnation of John Huss was not the main object of the Council of Constance. Far more important in the minds of those taking part was the continuing papal schism, and it was the great achievement of Constance to end it. The authority of the medieval Church and its whole structure depended on unity. If men could choose which pope they would support, the moral power of the Church was threatened. The problem was that no ecclesiastical machinery existed to deal with a papal schism. Papal condemnation was of no value—each pope simply anathematized and excommunicated the other. Because of the strength of the conciliar movement, it was generally, though not universally, accepted that popes were subordinate to councils; and it was increasingly felt that it was not necessary that a pope summon a general council. The conciliarists of the University of Paris, of whom Pierre d'Ailly, the King of France's confessor and later Bishop of Cambrai, was the most significant, thought that the best way of dealing with the legal problem of how a council should be summoned was to ignore it. The conciliarists suggested that the kings of Europe should withdraw their obedience from both popes and themselves summon a general council which would have the task of electing a new one.

Charles VI of France was persuaded to withdraw his support from the Clementine (Avignon) Pope, Benedict XIII. The Emperor and Henry IV of England stopped making financial contributions in support of the Urbanist (Roman) Pope, Gregory XII, and added their voices in favor of a council. Most of the cardinals from both obediences summoned a council to meet at Pisa in 1409. Neither

Pierre d'Ailly, leading Conciliarist of the University of Paris.

Benedict nor Gregory recognized the Council of Pisa, and both decided to hold councils of their own; Gregory at Cividale in north Italy, Benedict at Perpignan, near Avignon. But Pisa received almost universal recognition from bishops and princes. Some 500 bishops, including most of the cardinals, gathered together, declared that both popes were deposed and selected in their place Peter of Candia, Archbishop of Milan, who became Alexander V.

Pisa did not solve the problem, it worsened it. Since neither pope recognized the council's authority, both could ignore its rulings and instead of two rival popes there were now three. The problem was not made easier by the death of Alexander, whose honesty and reforming zeal had given cause for hope. His successor, the Neapolitan adventurer, John XXIII, lacked both these and almost all other qualities, almost certainly succeeded in becoming Pope only by bribery.

The pressure for an end to the

Schism continued. The Parisian doctors were pressing for thorough-going reforms, and the kings of Europe were anxious to have only one supreme pontiff. The King of the Romans, Sigismund, forced John to summon a council at Constance and to offer his resignation. When the Council met, Gregory also resigned and Benedict was abandoned by almost all his supporters. This left the field free for the election of Odo Colonna as Martin V in 1417 and the Great Schism was at last ended. Martin succeeded in overcoming the demand for reform of the Church "in head and members" by agreeing to hold regular general councils. The decretal *Frequens* laid down that a new council should be held five years after Constance finished, that another should be held after seven years, and that thereafter there should be a council every decade. In the event of a further papal schism a council should immediately be summoned.

The Holy Roman Empire

The King of the Romans, Sigismund (1368–1437), was conspicuous neither for military nor political ability, despite the decisive part that he played at the Council of Constance. He had become Marquis of Brandenburg on the death of his father, Emperor Charles IV, in 1378, but showed little interest in this territory, and sold the Neumark (the most recently acquired part of this territory) to the Teutonic Knights in 1402. He lived for most of his life in Hungary, which he much

preferred to Brandenburg. His wife became Queen of Hungary in 1382, and Sigismund was elected King in 1387. In 1396 he led a crusading army against the Turkish-occupied city of Nicopolis, but lost his entire army of 90,000 in battle. As a result, Hungary was laid open to the danger of Turkish invasion, and Sigismund's authority was seriously impaired.

Because of the weakness of his position in Hungary, Sigismund tried to extend his power in Germany. His ineffective brother Wenceslas, King of the Romans, appointed him Vicar-General of the Empire. When Wenceslas was deposed by the electors in 1400, Sigismund expected to be elected in his place (and had helped in the deposition, with this in mind), but was disappointed. It was not until 1410, that Sigismund was elected King of the Romans, and he was only crowned Emperor in

The Emperor Sigismund dictating a letter. He was the leading spirit of Constance.

1433. In 1419 he was elected King of Bohemia, although owing to the Hussite difficulties he never had much power there. He was regarded with distrust even by most of his Hungarian subjects, who disliked his ambition, his betrayal of his brother and his inability to govern effectively. As a soldier, too, he failed to make much mark, being defeated in every war in which he took part—by the Turks, the Venetians and the Bohemians.

Poland, Lithuania and the Teutonic Knights

The death of Louis I, King of Hungary and Poland, in 1382 led to civil war in Poland, which was brought to an end in 1385. The legitimate heiress was Jadwiga of Hungary, whose husband, Ladislas II (Jagiello), Grand Duke of Lithuania, became King of Poland in 1386.

The Rival Obediences of Western Christendom 1378-1417

The Roman line	The Conciliar line (Pisa 1409)	The Avignonese line
Urban VI (1378–89)		
Boniface IX (1389–1404)		Clement VII (1378–94)
Innocent VII (1404–6)		Benedict XIII (1394–1423)
Gregory XII (1406–15)	Alexander V (1409–10)	
	John XXIII (1410–15)	

Schism resolved at Council of Constance (1414–17) with election of Martin V (1417–31)

By uniting Poland and Lithuania, Ladislas reduced the threat that the Teutonic Knights had presented in trying to seize Lithuania by a policy of bribery, terror and assassination. The excuse that their only interest in Lithuania was to Christianize it was removed, for the Lithuanians accepted Catholicism. But the Knights decided to attack the Christian Kingdom of Poland with the same vigor that they had previously reserved for the pagan Grand Duchy of Lithuania. In 1401 Ladislas surrendered the Grand Duchy to his cousin Witold (1350–1430), but the alliance between the two countries remained close and in 1410 at the huge Battle of Tannenberg (Grünewald), Ladislas and Witold decisively defeated the Teutonic Knights. Although the Poles were unable to follow up this victory effectively, it ended the domination of northeast Europe by the Teutonic Knights. At the Treaty of Thorn (1411) the Knights agreed to pay Poland a large indemnity as well as hand over a province and a city to Lithuania.

The support of Poland allowed Witold of Lithuania sufficient freedom to be able to attack the Mongol "Golden Horde," bringing him the Ukraine. He also protected Lithuania's access to the Black Sea by strengthening his fortifications along the Dnieper. In 1413 Witold and Ladislas signed

Ladislas II, King of Poland.

the Union of Horodlo, which once again brought their countries together, although Lithuania's autonomy was guaranteed. The Union also brought the many Lithuanian nobles who had become Orthodox Christians into the Western Church.

During the rest of his reign Ladislas was not seriously threatened by the Teutonic Knights although the Emperor Sigismund tried to make an alliance with them in an attempt to partition Poland. By the time of his death in 1434 Ladislas had made Poland into a powerful, well-defended state. After his death the achievements were nearly lost by his son, Ladislas III (1434–44), whose incompetence was only equaled by his lack of interest in Poland.

The rise of Burgundy

When Philip the Bold of Burgundy died in 1404, his son, John the Fearless, made a bid to gain complete control over King Charles VI. He was opposed by the King's licentious brother, Louis of Orleans, with whom Queen Isabella was openly living. Each mustered armies, fortified his Paris "hotel" and prepared for civil war. The disaster appeared to have been diverted in November, 1407, when the Duke of Berry persuaded John of Burgundy to visit Louis of Orleans, who was ill. But three days later assassins hired by Burgundy killed Orleans as he lay in his sick bed.

Burgundy was then forced to leave Paris despite the support of most of the citizens. A monk even preached a sermon justifying the murder of a man so evil and debauched as Orleans. Unable to return to Paris however, Burgundy assisted his brother-in-law, the Bishop of Liège, in suppressing a rising in his episcopal city. During the early years of the fifteenth century the quarrel between the supporters of Orleans (who were known as Armagnacs, because their new leader was Bernard of Armagnac) and those of Burgundy intensified. John of Burgundy was eventually given permission to return to Paris, but in 1413 he was again told to leave the city.

Despite the tension within the family, Burgundy continued to support the French crown during the resurgence of the Hundred Years War. He was still, however,

banned from Paris. In 1418 the governor of the city, in defiance of orders, allowed Burgundy to return. The Duke promptly made himself master of the city, relying on the support of the populace. During the following months he attempted to secure an alliance with the party of the Dauphin (the future Charles VII) but before this was concluded, Burgundy was murdered. It is not known who was responsible but the new Duke, Philip the Good, blamed the Dauphin and threw his support behind the English. In 1420, by the Treaty of Troyes, Philip recognized England's Henry V as Charles' legitimate successor. The alliance was sealed by the marriage of Philip's sister to one of the English commanders, the Duke of Bedford, and the English soon found that they could rely on support from the Burgundians. France's days as an independent monarchy seemed numbered.

Henry V

The Treaty of Troyes, which the French were forced to accept because of Burgundian pressure, virtually ceded France to Henry V. By its terms he was to marry Catherine, daughter of Charles VI, to govern France as regent during his father-in-law's lifetime, and thereafter to succeed him as King. Although Paris and the north rejoiced at these arrangements, in southern France the Dauphin continued to be recognized as the true heir. As the thirty-five-year-old English ruler prepared to embark on a third expedition to France in 1422 he suddenly died, leaving a nine-month-old infant to succeed him as Henry VI. The Treaty of Troyes was immediately jeopardized.

The English Parliament appointed the infant's uncle, John, Duke of Bedford, as Protector of England, but when Bedford also became regent of France he handed over power in England to his brother, Humphrey, Duke of

Effigies of John the Fearless, Duke of Burgundy, and his wife.

Gloucester. Difficulties with England's Burgundian allies and dissensions in the council between Gloucester and his uncle, the highly influential and enormously wealthy Cardinal Beaufort, hindered Bedford's progress in the field.

Cardinal Beaufort

The leading political figure in early fifteenth-century Europe was Henry Beaufort (1375–1447). The illegitimate son of John of Gaunt, Duke of Lancaster (1340–99), Beaufort was educated at Cambridge and Oxford. He quickly became powerful both in Church and State, becoming Chancellor of England in 1403 and Bishop of Winchester in 1404. His opposition to Henry IV in his quarrels with his son, the future Henry V, led to the loss of the chancellorship and of the chance of succession to the throne.

After Henry V's accession he again became Chancellor. However, he quarreled with the King in 1417 and after resigning the chancellorship attended the Council of Constance, where, after himself being a candidate for the papacy, he was chiefly responsible for the compromise by which Martin V was elected Pope. Martin wanted to make him a cardinal and legate *a latere*, but on the insistence of Henry V, who was jealous of his success, Beaufort refused this offer. After Henry V's death in 1422 Beaufort became Chancellor for the third time, and effectively ruled the country until 1426, when he quarreled with the Duke of Gloucester and resigned the chancellorship in a fit of pique.

He left England, was appointed a cardinal and legate to Germany, Hungary and Bohemia. He led an unsuccessful anti-Hussite crusade, but returned to England in 1429. The rest of his life was spent in domestic struggles with the Duke of Gloucester and in amassing a large fortune. By the time of his death he was probably the wealthiest man in Europe, and certainly the wealthiest in England. Despite his great ability, his achievements were limited. Because he was never likely to become King of England, he was never in a position to carry out his policies in the state; and largely because of the jealousy of Henry V he was unable to become pope.

29

The peasants of southern France believed that she was a saint, and followed her into impossible battle; the English insisted that she was a witch, and ultimately burned her at the stake. Footsoldier and foe alike were certain that some supernatural force guided the peasant girl from Lorraine who called herself Joan of Arc. No mere mortal could have rallied the vanquished troops of the deposed Dauphin as the Maid had done—nor could any commander alive have led such a motley force against the English siege troops that surrounded Orleans and routed them in less than a week as the Maid had done. Joan's "voices" saved France and restored the Dauphin to the throne, but they doomed her in the process. As she went to the stake on May 30, 1431, a penitent onlooker exclaimed "We have burned a saint!"

On February 12, 1429, a French army led by Jean d'Orleans, natural half-brother of the King's cousin, Charles d'Orleans, was ignominiously routed by a mere supply train of the English army. The Bastard of Orleans' humiliating defeat left the King despondent, the court stunned and the French citizenry thoroughly discouraged. It seemed that nothing could halt the English army's advance; Orleans, cornerstone of the kingdom and the gateway to central France, appeared doomed. The country braced itself to face the final English onslaught—but as it did, word began to spread through the French countryside of an extraordinary girl from Lorraine who claimed that she brought the King help from God.

Like most of Europe, fifteenth-century France was still suffering from the aftereffects of the Black Death, and according to contemporary chroniclers Charles VII's kingdom had not yet recovered its former strength. In France as elsewhere, there had been a rash of popular risings following in the wake of the plague, and these recurrent civil disturbances had further undermined the precarious French monarchy. France, therefore, was unprepared to counter the English invasion when it came; the young Dauphin's troops could offer only token resistance to the invasion launched by their former allies.

In 1340, nearly a century earlier, the King of England had openly proclaimed himself King of France. Intermittent fighting had ensued, but by the end of the century peace had been reestablished. In 1392 the unhappy King Charles VI of France had become so unbalanced that he could no longer rule his kingdom effectively. Like the regular reappearances of the plague, Charles' insanity recurred intermittently after 1392, but the internal weaknesses of his kingdom did not become fully evident until the night of November 23, 1407. On that fateful night the King's brother, Louis d'Orleans, was assassinated by John the Fearless, Duke of Burgundy. In the political vacuum created by Charles' incapacity, the royal princes engaged in a bitter struggle for power—their feuding soon developed into civil war.

In an attempt to restore order to the faction-torn country, several rival claimants asserted their uniformly dubious claims to Charles' throne. Among them was King Henry V, scion of the Lancaster dynasty, which had recently seized the English throne from the last Plantagenet, Richard II. On August 14, 1415, Henry V disembarked on the beach of Saint-Adresse near Le Havre. Less than three months later his small expeditionary force brought an imposing French army to its knees on the field of Agincourt. In a battle that almost defies description, the English lost some four or five hundred men, the French almost 7,000. The nobility of France was decimated. Thousands fell on the battlefield and nearly fifteen hundred others were taken prisoner and transported to England. Among the captives was Charles d'Orleans, leader of the "Armagnacs" and foremost opponent of Henry V's French ally, John the Fearless, Duke of Burgundy. (After Agincourt, Henry's "Burgundian cousin" made it clear that his interests enlisted him on the side of the victorious young King of England.)

Henry began the methodical reconquest of Normandy, an ancient English possession, in 1417, and a year later Paris was delivered into the hands of the English and their Burgundian allies. The luckless Charles VI of France became a mere puppet and his son, the Dauphin Charles, barely escaped a Burgundian plot to take him prisoner. The Dauphin attempted to secure support for his projected campaign against the English through negotiations with Henry's wavering ally John the Fearless, whose immense territories stretched from Burgundy to the North Sea. On September 10, 1419, the two met on the bridge at Montereau, a village located at the junction of the Yonne and Seine rivers in northern France. The interview—and the Dauphin's ambitions—were cut short when one of the Dauphin's overzealous followers assassinated the Duke of Burgundy. The Duke's murder drove his son Philip

Joan and her banner; a marginal drawing from the *Register* of Parlement.

Opposite Joan of Arc; a symbolic painting from Antoine du Four's *Lives of Famous Women.*

Charles VII, the weak Dauphin whom Joan made King of France; by Jean Fouquet.

the Fair into firmer alliance with England, and the Dauphin was obliged to abandon Paris and take refuge south of the Loire.

The notorious Treaty of Troyes, signed on May 21, 1420, officially recognized England's claims to the French crown. Henry v sealed the pact by marrying Catherine, daughter of Charles vi of France, and the French crown was officially entailed upon him. The Dauphin was formally excluded from the succession, and his mother, Queen Isabella of Bavaria, further discredited his candidacy by encouraging suspicions about his legitimacy. The University of Paris, which had played a major part in drawing up the Treaty of Troyes, warmly welcomed the handsome young English King, and a gold coin, struck by Henry to win the confidence of the French merchants, was symbolically named *le salut*—the salvation.

Two years later a brace of events occurred that no one had foreseen: Henry, who was in the prime of life, died suddenly on August 31, 1422—and two months later, on October 21, Charles vi followed him. The succession was left to two rival claimants, the Dauphin Charles and Henry and Catherine's nine-month-old son, the infant Henry vi. In accordance with the provisions of the Treaty of Troyes, the crown of France rightfully belonged to the infant King. To secure Henry vi's claim, his uncle, the Duke of Bedford, assumed the title of Regent of France, subdued Normandy and the Ile-de-France and established the court at Paris. Disowned by his mother, the Dauphin could lay claim to no more than the southern half of France, and he became known by the derisive title of King of Bourges.

In 1428 Bedford judged that his hegemony north of the Loire was sufficiently well-established and he undertook a major offensive against the Loire-side city of Orleans. Bedford's target was a city of primary strategic importance, for it controlled the roads to the south. Its capture would enable the Regent to link up northern France with the English fiefdom of Guyenne (Aquitaine) in the southwest of France.

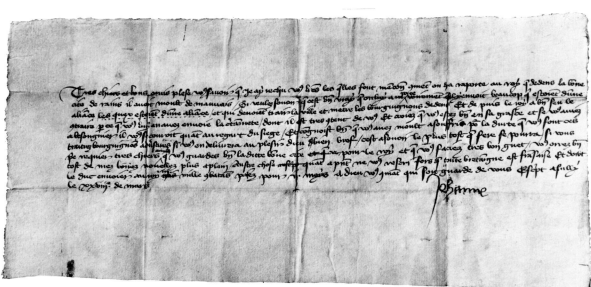

A letter from Joan to the people of Reims, March 12, 1430.

Joan of Arc at the court
of Charles VII.

○ Directly controlled by English
○ Burgundian territory
○ Anglo-Burgundian territory
○ Lands loyal to
Anglo-Burgundian alliance
○ Controlled by French
monarchy
○ Fiefs of France
○ New French territory

France 1420

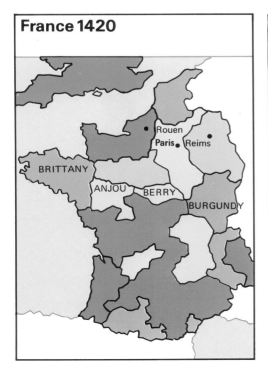

Rouen
Paris Reims
BRITTANY
ANJOU BERRY
BURGUNDY

Campaign of Joan of Arc 1428-31

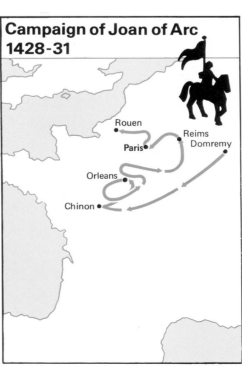

Rouen
Reims Domremy
Paris
Orleans
Chinon

France 1453

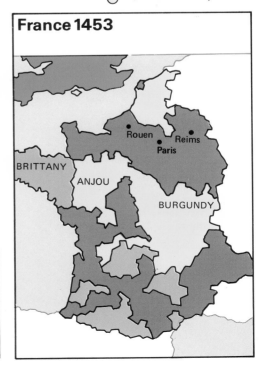

Rouen Reims
BRITTANY **Paris**
ANJOU
BURGUNDY

Philip the Good, Duke of
Burgundy, England's major
French ally.

Below The castle of Chinon, commanding the confluence of the Loire
and the Indre, captured from the English by Joan.

The siege of Orleans, therefore, was mounted with deliberation. Bedford's commanders, employing a strategy that had proven effective ten years before at Rouen, encircled the town with a temporary barricade to prevent egress. The population, completely surrounded by allied troops and undermined by famine, could expect no help from the Dauphin, who was without resources, without initiative and moreover without much confidence in his own cause. It was at this point that the peasant girl from Lorraine first sought an audience with the Dauphin.

After keeping Joan waiting for two days, the King finally consented to receive her. By all accounts, the peasant maid's first words to her sovereign renewed the Dauphin's flagging hopes: "Fair Dauphin, I am called Joan the Maid. The King of Heaven sends you word by me. You shall be crowned and consecrated King in the city of Reims, and are to be the viceroy of the King of Heaven, who is King in France." Furnished with arms and a small company of men—all that the Dauphin's utmost efforts could raise—Joan set out for Orleans, and on April 29, 1429, she succeeded in getting a relief convoy into the beleaguered city. She entered to the tumultuous acclaim of the townspeople, who "felt as if the siege were already raised," according to an eyewitness.

Astonishing as Joan's feat was, it was less dramatic than the events that followed. To the astonishment of the Dauphin's supporters and the stupefaction of

The coronation of Charles VII at Reims.

Below Joan leads the French attack on Paris.

Bottom The capture of Joan of Arc by Burgundian troops at Compiègne.

the allies, the siege of Orleans was raised after only three engagements. On Wednesday, May 4, the English fortifications at Saint-Loup were taken and the Loire-side gate to the city was liberated. On May 6, a skirmish took place on the opposite bank of the Loire—and when it was over, the English had lost the fortifications of Les Augustins. A day later the fortifications of Tourelles—which guarded the approach to the city's main bridge—were also taken. The left bank of the Loire was now open; Orleans had been relieved.

Realizing that his cause was lost, the English commander raised the siege a day later, on May 8, 1429. Joan forbade her men to pursue the enemy or to engage in further combat, for May 8 was a Sunday—a day of truce. The brief campaign was over; in less than eight days, a city invested for more than six months had been liberated.

The Dauphin and his advisers were uncertain as to the best way in which to utilize their unanticipated victory. Their quandary produced a temporary lull in the campaign, and Joan was forced to intervene. She urged Charles to advance upon Reims, where, the maid insisted, he would receive the consecration of his kingship.

From a strategic point of view, the march to Reims—deep within the Anglo-Burgundian zone—was extraordinarily daring, and it was undertaken in circumstances of the utmost improbability. The first English fortifications on the Dauphin's invasion route had to be taken by storm, but Joan's troops were equal to the task: Jargeau fell on June 10, Meung on June 15, and Beaugency two days later. The first decisive encounter of the campaign took place on Saturday, June 18, when the French King's army clashed with a force led by Bedford's commanders Talbot and Falstaff. The unpremeditated engagement was a stunning victory for the Dauphin: the English lost two thousand men and Talbot was captured, while French losses were negligible. (Some

contemporary chroniclers speak of two French deaths, others of three.) Continuing northward virtually without opposition, Charles reached Reims and was crowned there on Sunday, July 17.

Such a reversal of circumstances was all but unparalleled in the annals of history and it is not surprising that the highly superstitious English at once suspected that their opponents had been aided by supernatural forces. In a letter written at the end of July, 1429, Bedford himself called Joan "a hound of the Evil One," and the University of Paris was not slow to express a similar view. A year later Joan was captured by a Burgundian force at Compiègne, and, while the spineless Dauphin stood by, the Maid of Orleans was ransomed by the English, imprisoned and subjected to a farcical ecclesiastical trial at Rouen. In the course of that inquest, the simple dignity of Joan's replies disconcerted the most able of her interrogators, and their charge of sorcery could not be made to stick. In the end, it was on the very minor charge of wearing men's clothing that the chief prosecutor, Pierre Cauchon, succeeded in having Joan condemned. Cauchon, a member of the University of Paris who had been made a bishop for his active part in drafting the Treaty of Troyes, ordered the Maid's death.

Before she was led to the stake on May 30, 1431, Joan repudiated the confession that had been tormented out of her, and as the flames leaped around her an observer exclaimed, "We have burned a saint!" Less than two years after the coronation ceremony at Reims, the hostility of the English, the opposition of the universities and, above all, the defection of her associates had conspired to martyr the Maid of Lorraine. The Dauphin, now Charles VII, hastened to dissociate himself from the peasant girl to whom he owed his crown, and truth about the trial and condemnation of Joan of Arc was not established until almost twenty years later.

On November 10, 1449, eighteen years and six months after Joan's death, French troops entered Rouen, freeing the city after thirty years of English occupation. During those years the resumption of Anglo-French hostilities had turned to Charles' advantage: in 1430 the Duke of Burgundy had been forced to surrender Compiègne, and in 1435 he had been obliged to sign a separate peace treaty with his cousin Charles. A year later Arthur de Richement, the Constable of France, entered the liberated city of Paris, and within a decade tentative overtures of peace were being made. That new atmosphere of amicability was officially acknowledged through the marriage in 1444 of Henry VI and Margaret of Anjou, a close relation of King Charles. Years of foreign domination had made the French citizenry aware of their own aspirations, however, and in 1449 a popular insurrection drove the English governor from Rouen and forced the King of France to renew military activity in the region. It is noteworthy that one of the first things that Charles did after he recovered Rouen was to order an inquiry into the matter of Joan of Arc.

Lawyers and judges at Joan's trial.

The results of that inquiry, which was based upon the transcript of the trial and the testimony of surviving witnesses, seemed to justify another, lengthier investigation, and a second inquiry—this time a full ecclesiastical one—took place in 1452. Not until three years later, after a trial authorized by Pope Calixtus III, was Joan finally cleared of the charge of heresy. On July 7, 1456, the martyred Maid was solemnly rehabilitated.

In the course of their long conflict, France and England established their reciprocal independence and achieved internal unification. By 1456, England was ready to assert her insular destiny and France was ready to undertake the development of a centralized monarchy. Elsewhere in Europe, other nations began to assert their autonomy. Each sought to establish for itself a precarious national equilibrium, one that could survive the personal ambitions of individual princes and the economic rivalries of their subjects.

At a time of such confusion and uncertainty, the career of Joan of Arc had a remarkably decisive impact upon the course of European history. In much the same spirit as the townspeople of Orleans—who once welcomed her as a heroine and a saint—historians and the general public alike acknowledge Joan of Arc's exceptional contribution to world history.

REGINE PERNOUD

The burning of Joan at Rouen.

Left Pope Calixtus III who rehabilitated Joan, thirty years after her death.

37

Henry v's young son, Henry vi, was an unhappy child who grew up amid the incessant rivalry between the Duke of Gloucester and Cardinal Beaufort. Gloucester was the leader of the party that wanted war, a popular issue, while Beaufort preferred diplomacy and favored a peaceful solution to the Hundred Years War. Henry was crowned King of England in 1429 and of France in 1431, but he had little talent for government and only wanted to withdraw from the world. His piety and love of learning found

The marriage of Henry VI to Margaret of Anjou.

their deepest expression in the foundation of his colleges for poor scholars at Eton and Cambridge.

The unpopularity of the marriage that Cardinal Beaufort had arranged between Henry vi and the high-spirited and ambitious Margaret of Anjou, coupled with military reverses in France, reflected badly on Beaufort and weakened the prestige of the crown. With the deaths of both Cardinal Beaufort and the Duke of Gloucester (who spent his last days in prison as a suspected traitor), power passed to the Duke of Suffolk, whom Parliament impeached for maladministration and corruption. The weakling King, too, turned on Suffolk who was banished in 1450 and assassinated at Calais.

Violence continued to dominate politics in England. In 1450, in what was known as Cade's rebellion, 30,000 men from Kent and Sussex marched on London to demand the head of the Lord Chancellor and the restoration of Richard, Duke of York, to the Council. Government had effectively broken down throughout the realm.

Southeast Asia

The Mongol invasion of southeast Asia in the thirteenth century had destroyed the Indian influence in states such as the Champa (covering most of the area of modern South Vietnam) and Burmese kingdoms and the Khmer Empire, but had done nothing to replace them with a strong native or Chinese-influenced civilization. It was only in the mid-fourteenth century, as the result of the decline of Mongol power, that strong native states began to develop.

In about 1350 a new kingdom was set up in Thailand with its capital at Ayudhya, and by 1400 most of Thailand was subject to the Ayudhya kings. Cambodia's position of dominance in southeast Asia, already damaged by the Mongols, was finally shattered in 1431, when a Thai army conquered the capital, Angkor Wat. War between Cambodia and Thailand had been almost continuous since the beginning of the Ayudhya kingdom, and the pressure on Cambodia had steadily increased. After the defeat of 1431, Angkor Wat was abandoned, as it was considered too difficult to defend, and in 1434 Phnom-Penh became the capital. Although warfare between Cambodia and Thailand continued into the sixteenth century and the advantage in general lay with the Thais, Cambodia's fortunes to some extent improved, and there was never any serious danger of a Thai conquest. This was largely due to the strong rule of Suryavarman (1431–59), who, without trying to recover lost territory, rebuilt and strengthened Cambodian society.

Carvings on the wall of the temple at Angkor Wat.

Laos became an independent country in the mid-fourteenth century. Taking advantage of the war between Thailand and Cambodia, a Thai prince, Fa Ngum (1310–73), set himself up as King of Lan Chang ("the land of a million elephants"). A census taken in 1376 gave the male population as 300,000. The kingdom's importance was sufficient for the Vietnamese to ask for support against China in their struggle for independence. The Laotian army, when it arrived, decided to support the Chinese against the Vietnamese—a betrayal that was to lead to hatred and warfare between Vietnam and Laos.

The struggle between independent Vietnam and Champa, which had been the main factor in the history of Vietnam for 500 years, continued. In 1418 the feeble Tran Dynasty, which had survived only with Chinese support, was replaced by the Le dynasty. The first ruler, Le Loi, started a war to expel the Chinese from Vietnam. The Chinese quickly lost control of most of the countryside, although they continued for some years to hold the larger towns. After Le Loi's capture of Hanoi in 1426, the Chinese withdrew their troops, recognizing that they could not effectively rule the country. In return, Le Loi accepted Chinese suzerainty. Le Loi's son, Le Thai Ton (1433–42), pursued a policy of peace toward his neighbors and concentrated on domestic policy.

By about 1430, southeast Asia had taken political shape. Despite the influence of European colonization from the late nineteenth century, the political map of Indochina has remained little changed for the succeeding five and a half centuries; only Champa has disappeared.

Pope Martin V

The new Pope quickly showed that he was energetic and that he had little sympathy with the conciliarist view of Church government. He was determined to restore the power and prestige of the papacy and to some extent he succeeded. His acceptance by almost all countries led the Clementine antipope, Clement VIII, to abdicate in his favor in 1429, which was the final conclusion of the Great Schism.

A monument to Pope Martin V in St. John Lateran, Rome.

Martin returned to Rome in 1420. The city had been neglected almost throughout the period of the Babylonian Captivity and the Great Schism. John XXIII had made a few efforts to rebuild damaged buildings, but had been driven out of the city in 1413 by the King of Naples. Many buildings were in dangerous condition, and Martin set about restoring them. He also tried to restore effective papal rule in the Papal States, and in this he largely succeeded, assisted by members of his family who were appointed to governorships. He was less successful in his dealings with national monarchies and churches; he failed, for example, to persuade Henry vi of England to repeal the acts of *praemunire* and provizors, and his efforts to end the Hussite difficulties were also unsuccessful. Martin was unable to ignore the letter of the conciliar decretal *Frequens* entirely, and in 1423 a council met at Pavia. The Pope showed, however, that he was able to ignore the spirit of *Frequens*—no sooner had the Council begun business than he ordered its transfer to Siena, which was friendlier toward the papacy than Pavia. Early in the following year Martin dissolved the Council. It had achieved nothing.

The Hussite Wars

The execution of John Huss in 1415 did not put an end to the Hussite problem; his followers still demanded political separation from the Empire and continued to hold their heretical ideas. King Wenceslas attempted to suppress the Hussites. At first he used peaceful means, but in 1419 a Hussite procession through the streets of Prague was started from the town hall. Rioting broke out in Prague and in many other towns and villages. The death of Wenceslas left the Queen, Sophia, who favored taking a strong line, in charge of dealing with the Hussite problem. By now Prague and several other towns were run by the Hussites, and Sophia hired a mercenary army to attack the capital. Faced with this threat, the Hussites returned Prague to the Queen, in return for guarantees of religious freedom. The more extreme Hussites refused to accept this agreement. Under the leadership of Jan Žižka, a one-eyed royal chamberlain, they set up a new township which they called Tabor. Sophia sent her mercenary army against Žižka, but the Hussites defeated it. Martin V agreed to preach a crusade to suppress the Hussites.

In most regions of Czechoslovakia the Hussites could rely on widespread popular support, particularly after they formulated their doctrines in the so-called Articles of Prague (1420). The King of the Romans led a crusading army into the country. Žižka, by now totally blind—he had lost his second eye in battle—led the Hussites into battle at Deutschbrod and decisively defeated the crusaders. He continued to defeat Sigismund's supporters, proving himself a brilliant general despite his blindness.

But military success was threatened by theological disagreement.

During Žižka's lifetime the Utraquists (advocates of communion in both kinds) and the more extreme Taborites remained allies despite their disagreements, but after his death in 1424, the quarrels became increasingly fierce. Fighting between the two groups became frequent, and it was not until 1434 after a decisive victory at Lepan that the Utraquists emerged as the dominant group. They were now able to negotiate a peace agreement with Sigismund. The Emperor was recognized as King of Bohemia, but Utraquist religious practices were allowed. The agreement did not end the Hussite troubles, which continued for most of the fifteenth century, but it did end the war between Hussites and Catholics.

The Council of Basel

The hasty translation and dissolution of the Council of Pavia had done nothing to quiet the chorus of voices demanding reform in the Church, nor had it done anything to make Martin V enthusiastic about the idea of holding another council, but he was still under an obligation to do so. In 1430, he issued a bull appointing an Italian cardinal, Giulio Cesarini (1398–1444), president of a council to be held at Basel in the following year. In a second bull Cesarini was authorized to dissolve the Council. The death of Martin before the Council opened prevented his plan for its speedy dissolution from being put into operation. His successor, Eugenius IV, was only elected Pope on condition that he reform the Church and

The reformist Council of Basel differed with the papacy on many counts.

accept conciliar decisions.

The composition of the Council of Basel was different from that of Constance: there were fewer high dignitaries and a far larger number of theologians from the universities. The only cardinal to support the Council by his continuous presence was the Archbishop of Arles, Louis d'Aleman (1390–1450). Among the lower clergy the most distinguished was Nicholas of Cusa (1400–64), who was later made a cardinal, a German who advocated far-reaching ecclesiastical reform in his *De Concordantia Catholica* (1433). Nicholas of Cusa was one of the first northern Europeans to be influenced by Humanist ideas. From the beginning, the Council, with its huge university majority, made clear its sympathy for extreme conciliarist ideas. As soon as he heard this, Eugenius dissolved it, desiring to hold a new council at Bologna, where he would be in a better position to influence it.

Eventually, in 1433, influenced by the Emperor Sigismund, by Cardinal Cesarini, and—even more important—by the Milanese invasion of the Papal States, Eugenius recognized the Council. In the meantime, free from papal constraint, it had put forward the "Compacts of Prague," which formed the basis for the settlement between Sigismund and the Hussites. Disagreements between the papacy and the Council continued, however, on many issues. Decrees restricting the papacy's freedom of action were pushed through the Council; future popes were to take an oath of obedience to the decrees of the Council of Constance; many papal taxes were to be abolished; a pope who contradicted a conciliar decree was to be declared a heretic. Further disagreement was caused by the

desire for unity with the Greek Church. Because of its distance from Constantinople, the Greeks refused to attend the Council at Basel, and wanted it moved to Italy. A minority group at the Council favored a move to Florence, where the Pope had fled to escape from the Roman Republic, and made a formal request to Eugenius for the Council to be transferred. The Pope accepted the request and announced that the Council would be moved to Ferrara. The majority, however, stayed at Basel, secure in the knowledge of the support of such princes as the King of Aragon and the dukes of Milan and Savoy, as well as the friendly neutrality of most other princes. Only the King of England actively supported Eugenius. The Pope was denounced as a heretic and was deposed. In his place the Basel Council elected the Duke of Savoy, the ambitious Amadeus, as Pope—although he was not in holy orders. Amadeus took the name Felix V. Schism had broken out again, only twenty-five years after the Council of Constance had healed the Great Schism. This time there were not only two popes but two councils too.

The birth of Gallicanism

The increasingly nationalist feeling that existed among the European kingdoms was beginning to find ecclesiastical expression. In France this was expressed through a decree, known as the Pragmatic Sanction of Bourges, issued by a church council held at Bourges in 1438. Ever since the Council of Constance and the election of Martin V as Pope, the French had felt that the papacy favored the English cause in France. As a result Charles VII followed an independent ecclesiastical policy in his possessions. The King and local church councils proclaimed the liberty of the French Church from papal interference. The hostility between the papacy and the Council of Basel provided Charles with the opportunity for an expression of nationalism. The Council at Bourges decreed that the French Church could administer its temporal property without dependence on the papacy, and that the pope could not make appointments to vacant French benefices.

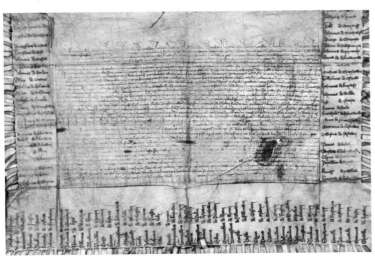

The *Protestatio Bohemorum* which condemned the burning of Huss.

A Ferment in Florence

Cosimo de' Medici—the greatest banker of his time, the most influential politician in Florence and the most lavish patron of the arts—helped ignite the cultural explosion we call the Renaissance. He encouraged Humanist scholarship and patronized such innovators as Brunelleschi in architecture and Donatello in sculpture. To do so, however, he first had to defeat the Albizzi political faction in Florence and then install Francesco Sforza on the ducal throne of Milan, bringing an end to the long and debilitating war between Milan and Florence.

A portrait of Cosimo de' Medici by Bronzino. As first citizen of Florence his power rested on popular support and subtle manipulation of the republican constitution. His descendants increasingly encroached upon the constitution and eventually became the dukes of Tuscany.

Opposite Florentine merchants: a detail from Ghirlandaio's *Miracle of the Child*. Mediterranean commerce formed the basis of the prosperity and independence of the Italian city-states.

In the later Middle Ages and Renaissance, northern Italy was different from the rest of Europe in two important respects. It had advanced industries and commerce and it had independent city-states.

Industrial products such as the steel armor of Milan or the silk of Lucca were superior to anything the rest of Europe could produce. Italian merchants also traded on a larger scale than anyone else—the galleys of Venice and Genoa carried great quantities of goods to Alexandria in Egypt in one direction and London in the other. These merchants, especially in Florence and Venice, were also the bankers of Europe, able to send money from London to Constantinople and anywhere in between.

The independent city-states had thrown off all subjection to kings and were strong enough to manage their own affairs. The most important were Milan, Venice, Genoa and Florence. They had started as isolated cities, but by 1400 they had all grown by conquering surrounding territory. Venice and Genoa, which were great ports, even had commercial empires in the eastern Mediterranean. All had come to control a large expanse of territory, including other towns.

City-states, in which the most important men were merchants or manufacturers, naturally developed appropriate political organizations quite different from those found elsewhere. Citizens had long ago joined together to form trade organizations, or guilds, which were important in politics as well and they ruled their cities through elected committees and officials. The businessmen of rising cities generally preferred republicanism to monarchy.

This is the background against which we must see the career of one outstanding individual whose life illustrates many of the characteristics of this world—Cosimo de' Medici, the greatest banker of his time, the most influential politician in Florence and the most lavish patron of the arts.

By Cosimo's time, Florence had been an independent republic and a commercial center for several hundred years. It was famous for its cloth and silk industries. Being an inland city it had not developed fleets and overseas trade to the same extent as Genoa and Venice but in compensation the Florentines had become the leading Italian bankers. The city had many big firms expert in foreign exchange with branches in other cities and provided financial services for other merchants.

The Florentines were attached to their republican constitution. The government of the city was a complicated structure of committees in which the central position was held by a body of nine men, known as the priors, who were chosen by lot from among those citizens eligible. To ensure that no individual became too powerful his term of office was limited to two months; at the end of the period every official was replaced. During their two months in office they lived in the Palace (still known today as the Palazzo Pubblico) and ruled the city. They were ordinary and often quite unimportant citizens. Important men could voice their opinions in public debates and were influential, but great care was taken to limit their power, to ensure that Florence remained a republic. The politics of the city therefore were dominated by wealthy and influential groups of men who could often command support from lesser citizens but would find it difficult to establish absolute control.

Like the other Italian states Florence was often involved in war and during the first half of the fifteenth century her great and almost constant enemy was Milan. Milan was no longer a republic. While remaining a great industrial city it had come to be ruled by a family of despots, the Visconti, who had extended their power over most of the central part of the plain of Lombardy. In the fifteenth century they were trying to expand further, into Tuscany. Florence regarded itself as seriously threatened by these moves and in combatting them was in one respect in a highly vulnerable position. As a commercial republic, Florence had no native class of fighting men, no knightly aristocracy, no royal retinue, and therefore had to fight wars with hired armies. Many Italian noblemen from the rural areas made a living by supplying and commanding these armies,

Bankers of the Tuscan town of Prato: a detail from Gerini's *Story of St. Matthew*. Despite the Church ban, usury was by now universally accepted.

condottieri as they were called. Florence was utterly dependent on these men, vulnerable to their treachery and financially strained by the heavy taxes that had to be raised to pay for their services. From 1423 to 1441 Florence was almost constantly engaged in war against Filippo Maria Visconti, and its internal politics were dominated in part by the stresses brought on by that war.

Cosimo de' Medici was born in 1389. His father, Giovanni, who died in 1429, was himself an extremely successful banker. Starting as one of many in the city, he built himself up to the leading position, in part by acquiring the largest share of the banking business connected with the court of the pope. Payments of many kinds were made from all over Europe to the papal court at Rome so that to enjoy a large share of the business of exchange and lending involved in these transactions was indeed lucrative. This formed the basis of the family's fortune. It also involved a close personal relationship with cardinals and even popes and this was to be important in Cosimo's political life.

Though not an intellectual himself, Giovanni de' Medici provided his sons with the most fashionable education that money could buy—an education in the Latin classics by the best Humanist teachers available in Florence. Cosimo became an enthusiastic and well-informed admirer of the Humanists. When his father died, he took over the business at the age of forty as one of the most accomplished and richest men in Florence. His father had advised him not to meddle in politics more than he had to, but his outstanding wealth and intelligence made it difficult for him to avoid a controversial role.

The most influential faction in Florentine politics at this time was led by Rinaldo degli Albizzi. Cosimo does not seem to have started by being hostile to Rinaldo's supporters but soon after his father's death they became associated with a disastrous political episode, the war against Lucca, to which he adopted a critical attitude leading to enmity. In 1428 there came a break in the war with Milan. In the breathing space, Florentine opinion turned violently against the nearby independent city of Lucca, which seemed to have been too well-disposed to the Visconti in the last war. Albizzi took the lead in an aggressive plan to attack Lucca and either teach it a sharp lesson or annex it. The attack was handled with extraordinary ineptitude —at one point an attempt to divert the river Serchio to flood Lucca's defenses is said to have flooded the Florentine camp instead. Though the enemy city was much weaker, the war dragged on until 1433 with no result except to load the Florentines with still heavier taxes and to invite

42

Visconti and his *condottieri* to invade Florentine territory again. Albizzi and his friends had lost face and were alarmed by the rising star of Cosimo who, after criticizing the conduct of the war, had been partly responsible for the peace by which it was ended.

In September, 1433, a new government of priors sympathetic to Albizzi and his friends took office at Florence. Cosimo, who was out of Florence at the time, was lured back by a message saying that the priors wanted to consult him. When he went to the Palace he was locked up. The government then had the problem of deciding what to do with him to destroy his influence without angering his supporters dangerously. Some would have preferred to kill him, but feared that this would turn public opinion against them. In the end, it was decided to use the classic expedient for dealing with a man who had become too powerful in a city—banishment. Cosimo was sentenced to exile in Padua for five years.

This did not turn out too badly, for Cosimo's business interests—widely spread over Italy and other parts of the world—were hardly disturbed by the events at Florence. When he went into exile, he traveled as a great man, not as a penniless refugee. Padua was controlled by Venice, one of the cities where his banks did a great deal of business, so he had money and influence there. The Venetian government suspected that the Albizzi regime might come to terms with Milan and was therefore inclined to give Cosimo political support. It was thus a safe base from which to exercise influence through his many supporters and by widespread bribery in Florence and to watch his enemies get deeper into difficulties. These difficulties multiplied as the war with Milan went badly; the Albizzi party was suspected in Florence, too, of planning to make an agreement with Milan, and this struck many people as treachery. Albizzi power declined rather than increased.

In the summer of 1434 a new factor was added to the scene in Florence: the Pope came to live there. From the beginning of his pontificate in 1431 Eugenius IV had run into crippling political difficulties, which made his reign a troubled one, but which turned out to be of great advantage to Cosimo. Eugenius' rule was disturbed by quarrels between the noble families of the Papal States, by invasions by *condottieri* and also by a council of the Church held at the German town of Basel that was trying to undermine his authority in the Church as a whole. In 1434 opposition to him in Rome itself reached the point where he had to disguise himself and flee from the city by boat. He took refuge in the friendly city of Florence, setting up his court there in the Dominican Convent of Santa Maria Novella, where he remained on and off for several years. The Pope had close ties with Cosimo, who was the Church's chief banker, and they were also personal friends.

Seeing power slipping from him, Rinaldo Albizzi decided to retrieve the situation by one decisive stroke, a coup d'état planned to take place on September 25. The plan was to have a small army seize the principal public buildings, including the Palace with the priors in it, and somehow set up a new government more favorable to him. On the appointed day the early stages of the plan were put into effect but then things began to go wrong. One severe blow was that Palla Strozzi, Albizzi's most wealthy and influential ally, decided at the last moment not to send his contingent of men. In the afternoon and evening the situation was undecided; it was unclear whether Albizzi would push through

Violence in the streets: detail from a painting of the school of Perugino. Rivalry between the Albizzi and Medici factions in Florentine politics was exacerbated by the crippling war with Milan.

his plan or not. Then he received a summons from the Pope. He went to Santa Maria Novella and remained alone with Eugenius for several hours. It is not known what was said but somehow, by playing on his political fears or on his conscience, the Pope must have persuaded him to desist. When he emerged, the plot, which was in any case disintegrating by this time, was called off.

The way was then clear for Cosimo, in response to the invitation of the government that Albizzi had unsuccessfully tried to unseat, to return to Florence the next month. Then, with the help of his political allies and his money, Cosimo set to work doing to Albizzi what Albizzi had tried to do to him. He did it much more thoroughly and ruthlessly. Not only Albizzi and Strozzi, but also a large number of their supporters were expelled from the city, and the persecution did not stop until the Medici cause was safe. And, unlike Cosimo, his enemies never came back.

From 1434 until his death thirty years later Cosimo was the most influential man in Florence. He was not a despot. His power was never remotely like that of the Visconti at Milan. Like that of Albizzi and other republican politicians before him his was a power exercised by more subtle influences, without destroying the constitutional forms, and dependent on widespread popular support. Cosimo did get the constitution changed somewhat, so that there was less election by lot and more government by committees of men chosen for their suitability. This made influence in the government by the dominant party easier. Cosimo himself rarely assumed even minor offices—he preferred to work through his friends—and most of the constitution remained unchanged. He did, however, exert a great deal of influence on the foreign policy and

finances of the city. Perhaps his greatest achievement was ending the long, crippling fight with Milan. After Filippo Maria Visconti died in 1447, Cosimo supported the claim to succeed him at Milan of a successful *condottiere*, Francesco Sforza, with whom Cosimo had long done business. Sforza successfully established a new ducal dynasty at Milan. From this diplomatic coup Cosimo was able to build a policy of general pacification, culminating in the Peace of Lodi between Milan, Florence and Venice in 1454.

Although Cosimo did not disturb republican forms very much his thirty years of personal influence were unprecedented. After his death, his supporters could see no alternative but to continue the system. And so his son Piero (1464–69), his more famous grandson, Lorenzo the Magnificent (1469–92) and his great-grandson Piero (1492–94) succeeded to his position. Under Lorenzo much larger alterations were made in the constitution, especially after he had escaped a murder attempt in 1478, but still it remained in form republican. In 1494 the Florentines turned the Medici out and tried to return to a completely republican system. Not until later, in the sixteenth century, did the Medici return, this time to become dukes of Tuscany. The events leading to this started in a sense on that decisive day in October, 1434.

One of the political climaxes of Cosimo's life occurred in 1439 when a council of the Roman and Greek Orthodox Churches took place in Florence. For a time the city of which he was the leading citizen housed both the Pope and the Byzantine Emperor, meeting in an attempt to end the schism between the two Churches. This assembly, which was attended by many learned Greek scholars, also gave a new impulse to another

The life-style of Florence's merchant-rulers rivaled that of princely courts. The earliest Italian artists were drawn from this bourgeoisie and their works produced primarily for members of their own class.

Opposite top A fifteenth-century view of Florence, intellectual and artistic capital of Italy.

Opposite bottom Cosimo de' Medici with the architect Filippo Brunelleschi, by Vasari. Cosimo's patronage of Brunelleschi enabled him to evolve the classical style of Renaissance architecture.

side of his character: his fascination with Greek philosophy.

During Cosimo's lifetime Florence was the intellectual and artistic capital of the Italian world, and the place of great innovations in those spheres. It is remarkable that Cosimo, a private citizen and not the ruler of a princely court, should have been at the heart of that aspect of Florentine life as well. Several of the students of Latin and Greek who were revolutionizing learning were among his close friends. Niccolò Niccoli the greatest book collector of his day—when book collecting involved searching out and copying manuscripts—was helped out of financial difficulties by Cosimo. Leonardo Bruni, Chancellor of Florence from 1427 to 1444 and the author of a history of the Florentine people, was his friend. This history became a model for Renaissance writers. At the end of his life Cosimo supported a young scholar named Marsilio Ficino while he began the fundamental task of translating the whole of Plato's writings from Greek into Latin, an enterprise from which Cosimo evidently expected great revelations.

These enthusiasts of the Greek and Roman world also encouraged contemporary artists to model their efforts on the works of art and writings of antiquity, to attempt more realistic figures in imitation of classical sculpture, paintings in perspective like the murals still to be seen in Roman remains, and churches modeled on Roman buildings. Here again Cosimo was a supporter. Backed by his great wealth, his taste exerted an influence on the schools of art.

Cosimo was a great builder of churches. His biggest enterprise was the rebuilding of the Convent of San Marco in Florence. He kept a cell for himself in it and also housed there the library of Niccoli after the great collector died, turning it into the first public library in Italy. But more important for the history of architecture was his support of the work of Filippo Brunelleschi, the originator of Renaissance architecture. The building which first gave him the opportunity to work out his new ideas was the Church of San Lorenzo. This was the parish church of the Medici and when it was rebuilt, starting in the 1420s, the work was done largely with their money and following their wishes. Brunelleschi rebuilt the sacristy of the church—the "Old Sacristy" as it is called now— partially as a kind of Medici chapel containing the tomb of Cosimo's father, and with arches and decorations all in classical style. The main part of San Lorenzo was the first example of a church in a specifically Renaissance style, making full use of the round arches and classical columns which were to become standard. The inspiration was of course Brunelleschi's—he was a widely admired architect and the one who solved the problem of building the dome of Florence Cathedral, which everyone had thought impossible—but Medici

46

money did much to encourage the evolution of his style.

In 1419, long before he had come to power, Cosimo became a member of a committee set up by the bankers' guild to supervise the making of a statue of St. Matthew by Lorenzo Ghiberti, for which the guild was paying. Later Cosimo established an important connection with the sculptor Donatello. Donatello was a friend of Brunelleschi and carried out a similar revolution in his own art, in part by freeing figure sculpture from its traditional subordination to religious themes and concepts. Perhaps the best example is his bronze figure of David, from which all the usual idea of David as the humble, god-fearing boy has gone, to be replaced by a sensuous figure of a handsome young man. This statue stood in the courtyard of

the Medici palace later in the fifteenth century. It may well have been made for Cosimo.

Cosimo also paid Donatello to decorate the Old Sacristy of San Lorenzo with sculptured panels that are a good illustration of the third great artistic innovation of the time: perspective. Medieval art groped slowly toward perspective—generally the backgrounds look more like cardboard scenery than real space. About 1425 Florentine artists—Brunelleschi was probably the leader—worked out a way to make drawings in perspective, using the idea of the vanishing point. The art that was most affected by this was, naturally, painting, with Masaccio and Uccello quickly producing striking examples. We do not know much about Cosimo's patronage of painting but in Donatello's work, which he did patronize, there are examples of perspective in flat-relief sculpture, among them the roundels in the Old Sacristy looking down on the tomb of Cosimo's father.

Cosimo's return in 1434 gave him thirty years of influence in Florence. Perhaps even more important than his pushing Florence a little way along the road from republicanism to despotism are his other achievements. In the political field he did more than anyone else to give a generation of stability to Italian politics, and by his patronage he contributed greatly to the advances in ideas and the arts which made Florence the unquestioned leader of Renaissance Italy.   G. A. HOLMES

Left The *David* by Donatello whose work was patronized by Cosimo de' Medici.

Below Lorenzo the Magnificent, by Giorgio Vasari. Grandson of Cosimo, he enjoyed the power and prestige of a prince, although Florence remained nominally republican.

Conquest of the "Bulging Cape"

1434

The rounding of Cape Bojador broke a psychological as well as physical barrier to the Portuguese exploration of Africa. Its conquest permitted the Portuguese to proceed by sea to the Cape of Good Hope and ultimately India. Of considerable significance in rounding the Cape was the Portuguese use of technology from Jewish and Arabic as well as Christian sources, ushering in an international cooperation in scientific affairs that would flower in the sixteenth century and beyond.

The Golden Age of Portuguese exploration covered eighty-four years, from 1415, with the conquest of Ceuta in Morocco, to 1499, when Vasco da Gama returned to report on his discovery of a sea-route to India. Portugal at the beginning of the fifteenth century had only a million inhabitants, yet by the end of the sixteenth had built an empire that stretched all the way from Brazil to the Far Eastern Spice Islands. And, by the middle of that century, Portuguese merchants had reached China and Japan and commercial colonies were maintained in Buenos Aires, Flanders and the Low Countries. Portuguese merchants and missionaries followed the Amazon and the Zambesi. For close to a century they ruled the Indian Ocean, in the vanguard of other Western nations, and their influence was such that the Indian historian, K. M. Panikkar, has named the period 1497–1945 the "Vasco da Gama epoch of Asian history."

The most successful adventurers in the period immediately preceding the Portuguese were the Italian merchants and missionary friars who trod the trans-Siberian routes to the courts of the Far East. The young Marco Polo had made this journey with his uncles, and his *Travels*, telling of the wonders of the East and all he had seen in the service (1275–92) of Kublai Khan, were widely read in Europe. However, with the rise of the Ottoman Empire in the next century and the collapse of khan rule, these trans-Asian routes were closed, and merchants, missionaries and adventurers, on the hunt for slaves, souls and spices, began to look westward. At the same time that Marco Polo was beginning the trip back to Venice, the first attempts were being made to slip through the Straits of Gibraltar into the Atlantic.

As happened nearly always in these early European explorations, religious and commercial motives were interlinked. The missionary helped the merchant as interpreter, while the merchant helped the missionary with material support—such as money for the building of churches. The crusades had brought a general restlessness to European peoples, giving them an inkling of the size of the undiscovered world.

One reason why Atlantic exploration became feasible was that there had been considerable progress in improving navigational aids. The sternpost rudder (replacing two lateral oars) was in use in the thirteenth century. This increased the amount of tonnage that could be loaded. A ship equipped with the new rudder could sail closer to the wind—necessary in all navigation. The magnetic needle for direction-finding, which had come to Europe via Chinese and Arab sources, was greatly improved upon by the fourteenth century and is mentioned by Alfonso the Wise of Castile and by Raymond Lull. Cartography, or map-making, had improved in accuracy and in 1375 the Mallorcan map-maker, Abraham Cresques, produced the Catalan Atlas, the finest of its time and one that had a profound influence on the Portuguese explorers.

Apart from the wish to renew contacts with the East and reach the sources of the spice trade, there was also in the fourteenth and fifteenth centuries a desire in Europe for a renewal of religion. It was the age of St. Francis, St. Dominic and St. Catherine of Siena, one in which a return to the purity of early Christianity was urged. It was thought that perhaps there were other Christian communities in distant lands beyond the Moslem belt, who would not only help with this reform, but who would also be useful allies in breaking the encircling grip of Islam. The Moslem threat was real. The Iberian Peninsula had been in the power of Islam since 711, and Granada was to remain a Moslem stronghold until 1492. The shores of North Africa were also ruled by Moslems and both areas were allied in spirit with the rising Turkish Empire that was knocking at the gate of Eastern Europe.

Europe felt herself confined, boxed in by hostile forces to the east and south, and bounded on the west by the mysterious and as yet uncharted ocean. Hence the discoveries undertaken by Portugal and Spain were in a real sense an attempt to break out of this encirclement, to find wealth and Christian aid beyond those countries that owed allegiance to the Prophet.

All the regions of the Iberian Peninsula played

John II of Portugal, the "perfect prince" (1481–95). He coordinated all known navigational experience in the "first scientific revolution" and established a basis for nautical science.

Opposite The adoration of St. Vincent, patron saint of navigators, showing Prince Henry the Navigator standing on the right.

their part in sea-faring. During the Moorish occupation, they had formed to an extent an economically interdependent system. The woollen interests of the center needed the help of ships on the coast for export. The coastal societies, which had flourished on maritime commerce during the Moorish occupation, continued their commercial contacts, particularly those with North Africa, after that occupation had ceased. Shipbuilding had developed in the Spanish ports of Biscay, and both Edward III and Henry VIII of England went there for ships. Seamanship was learned not only in fishing in the North Atlantic, but also in repelling Moorish attacks on the southern ports of Cadiz and Seville during the Reconquista. By the end of the fourteenth century a rivalry had grown up between the two kingdoms most concerned: Portugal with her capital and port of Lisbon, and Castile with the port of Seville.

Several factors enabled Portugal to get ahead of her rival. Portugal is an Atlantic country with a long coastline and the ocean is the key to its history far more so than is true of Spain. Situated between the Mediterranean and the Atlantic,

Portugal was a natural base for discoverers, and a meeting place for peoples of all points of the compass. Over the centuries Phoenicians, Greeks, Carthaginians, Romans, Moors, Normans had all come to this coast to plunder or to settle. Crusades went past the door. At the siege of Lisbon in 1147 Afonso Henriques, the first King of Portugal, invited a crusade made up of English, Flemish and German participants, to stop off in Lisbon and help to smite the infidel nearer home than the Holy Land—for suitable pickings.

Perhaps the most important single factor, however, that gave Portugal the edge over her neighbor, was the success in driving out the Moors as early as 1250, whereas Spain did not conquer Granada until 1492. Portugal also enjoyed relative political unity under her monarchs.

From the beginning the Portuguese crown took a commanding interest in maritime commerce and in everything to do with the sea. As early as the twelfth century, Portuguese merchants were to be seen at international trade fairs. King Diniz (1279–1325) called a navy into being, and sowed the pine forest of Leiria north of Lisbon, to provide wood for the ships. In the reign of Fernando (1367–83) special concessions were made to shipbuilders in various taxes, and in the obligation of military service.

The course Portugal would follow was determined in the fourteenth century. An economic crisis had been brought on by the Black Death

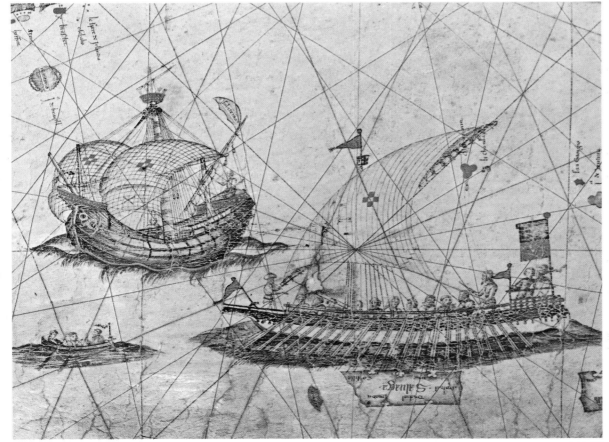

Above Portuguese carracks retained the medieval high hull and square-rigged foremast and mainmast, but allied them with the lateen-rigged aftermast adopted from the Arabs which had proved so successful on the smaller caravel. They became the standard cargo-carriers on the long haul from the East.

Left The small, light caravel and, in the foreground, a galley. The caravel design first utilized lateen-rigging and produced the most versatile vessel of the time, able to sail close to the wind and cope with the northeast trade winds which had hindered Portuguese maritime expansion.

Above A sixteenth-century woodcut showing a merchant vessel unloading at a bustling northern port.

The lure of the Orient: natives picking spices in the Indies.

(1348), which reduced manpower, with a consequent rise in wage payments. There had been discontent in the towns and revolts of apprentices and some artisans. A palace revolution had placed a new dynasty on the throne in the person of John I of the House of Aviz. The new King had come to power with the support of the rising bourgeoisie that was interested in maritime commerce. John promoted this new merchant class at the expense of the clergy and the nobility. He married a Plantagenet, Philippa of Lancaster, daughter of John of Gaunt and granddaughter of Edward III. This Anglo-Portuguese marriage (which cemented a treaty of alliance between the two countries) produced among others four remarkable sons: Duarte (1391–1438) who succeeded to the throne, Pedro (1392–1449), Henry (1394–1460) and Fernando (1402–1443).

Henry was a figure of medieval aspect. In part a visionary, he withdrew to a retreat in the south at Sagres, on the coast near St. Vincent. He never traveled—never went to sea—despite the somewhat anomalous sobriquet of "Navigator" pinned on him by English historians. The group of cosmographers and map-makers that worked with Henry at Sagres has been described by a modern historian as a "scientific congress in permanent session." This is probably an exaggeration. But if curiosity and interest in experiment be considered scientific, it seems difficult to deny completely this title to Henry. His brother Pedro, on the other hand, was a great traveler, with first-hand experience of European courts and access to the knowledge current there about overseas navigation. It was Pedro who was presented by the Signoria of Venice with a copy of Marco Polo's *Travels* in 1426, and this work was undoubtedly shown to Henry.

By the beginning of the fifteenth century, then, when Henry appeared on the scene, his country was in a strong position. The constant threat of war with Castile had been diminished by a Portuguese victory at Aljubarrota in 1385, and Portugal had been strengthened by the English alliance. Venice, Genoa, Florence and the papacy were engaged in internal rivalry. The Catalans were occupied in the eastern Mediterranean. And France was exhausted by the Hundred Years War.

From 1415 on, Portuguese policy seemed to be directed by two preoccupations, which sometimes worked in tandem, sometimes at odds. These were a drive toward Atlantic exploration, and toward expansion in Morocco. Henry, at different periods, pursued both; his brother Pedro only the former.

There were a number of reasons why Henry should be interested in maritime discovery. His first biographer, Azurara, in the *Chronicle of Guinea*, presents various motives. They seem today stereotyped and medieval, but may well have been those with which Henry wished to justify his actions to posterity. They were as follows: to find out what lay beyond Cape Bojador on the Atlantic coast of Africa; to see if there were Christians in those lands

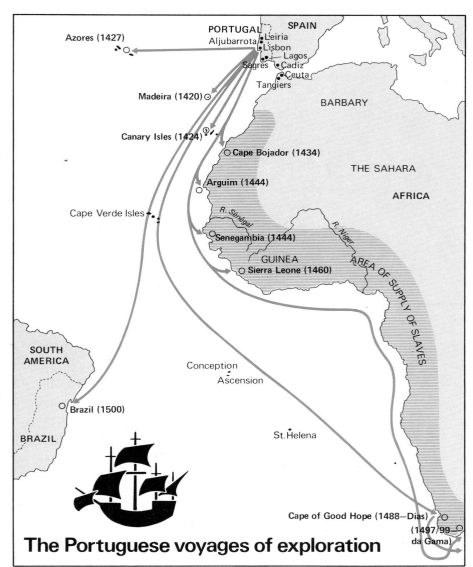

The Portuguese voyages of exploration

with whom trade could be established; to find out the extent and power of the Moors; to enlist the aid of Christian princes against the Moor (perhaps including the legendary priest-emperor Prester John, supposed to reside beyond the Moslem belt in what were loosely termed "the Indies"); to undertake the conversion of the unbeliever; and finally to fulfil his horoscope by undertaking great deeds and seeking out things hidden from other men.

There was nothing strange in this last motive. The practice of astrology was respectable and approved, a fitting interest for a royal prince. However, there were perhaps other and more practical reasons for Henry's interest. The first was undoubtedly a desire for gold. There was a shortage of this metal, as well as of silver, in Europe. Mines had been exhausted, and much had been exported against the import of luxuries from the East. Henry needed to spend—to maintain his household, to finance his voyages and to maintain the military Order of Christ of which he had become governor in 1420. Devaluation pressed hard on

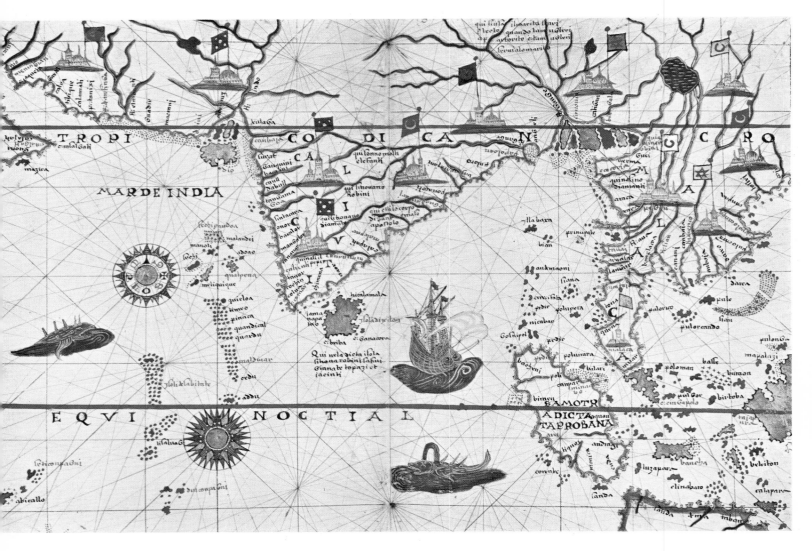

A sixteenth-century map of the Indies. At the height of its power Portugal controlled the key cities of Ormuz, Goa, Cannanore and Molacca.

fixed revenues, hence feudal lords needed more land which could only be acquired by conquest. Knights wanted a chance of a quick fortune in brigandage, and squires and the beggars and vagabonds thrown up by a decadent feudal economy were a ready source of manpower to man ships.

There was in Portugal, moreover, a lack of cereals and no money to pay for their import; hence the added need to conquer more arable land. Sugar and fishing interests, too, were not averse to new conquests. There was also a demand for slave labor. All these needs could be met either by pushing on with the exploration of the West African coast, or by colonizing the Atlantic islands, or by the conquest of Morocco; and during the fifteenth century the center of interest swung from one option to the other.

At Sagres, Jacome, son of Abraham Cresques the Mallorcan cartographer, was working with Prince Henry in 1420. The father's Catalan Atlas showed clearly the routes followed across the Sahara by the gold caravans. The notes written in Catalan leave no doubt as to the abundance of gold in the area of the Niger and Sénégal rivers. What could be a more attractive operation than to divert these routes away from the Mediterranean ports to the Atlantic ports of West Africa?

The policy, with its double aim of expansion in Morocco and exploration down the west coast of Africa, was begun with the conquest of Ceuta in 1415. The probes into the Atlantic were started between 1419 and 1425. After 1420 Madeira was rediscovered and Henry began its settlement and colonization. An expedition to the Canary Islands in 1424 failed, but the finding of the Azores in 1427 was important, since they formed a base for further voyages which could sweep a much larger area of the ocean. It may have been from here that ships gathered the first information about Brazil.

Henry's great achievement in exploration came in 1434 when one of his squires, Gil Eanes, rounded Cape Bojador, the "Bulging Cape." Legend, and difficulties with winds and currents, had combined to make this point a psychological as well as a physical barrier that had defied all efforts to get beyond it for fifteen years. It was believed that beyond the cape was a sea of darkness, or that the sea boiled, or that it was so hot that you turned black or that the Devil was lurking in wait for the foolhardy mariner who ventured so far.

54

About this time came an important development relating to the movement of winds in the Atlantic. A major obstacle to successful navigation had been the contrary northeast trade winds, which prevented a return to Portugal from the West African coast. With the adoption by the Portuguese of a new ship design, the caravel (copied from the Arabs), there came into use the most versatile vessel of the time. Long, lean, three-masted and lateen-rigged it could tack out into the Atlantic, sailing close to the wind, until in the region of Madeira and the Azores. Then a course would be set for Lisbon, running before the westerlies that prevailed in that latitude.

The voyages continued. Nuño Tristão and Antão Gonçalves, both of Henry's household, had reached Arguim island (the first trading station) and Senegambia by 1444. These years also marked the beginning of the slave trade with the first "black ivory" being brought home to the market in Lagos in the Algarve. Azurara, Henry's chronicler, tells of the first sale of slaves in harrowing detail.

In the meantime Henry's attention had shifted from exploration to conquest in Morocco, and he had urged his brother, King Duarte, to attack Tangiers in 1437. The reasons given were that Ceuta could not survive without support from a neighboring fortress. Portuguese military strength in this area would, moreover, effectively bar any attempt on the part of Castile to move into Africa. This was also a region rich in corn and cloth, commodities in demand on the Guinea coast and therefore coveted by Portuguese traders. The proposal to attack Tangiers met strong opposition from Henry's brothers Pedro and João. They doubted the ethics of the attack, and both pointed to the enormous expense that would be involved and to the difficulties of occupation should the attack be successful. The attack was launched but turned into disaster owing to faulty planning. The Portuguese force escaped with difficulty and then only at the price of hostages, which included Henry's younger brother Fernando who died in a Moroccan jail. This calamity had the effect of swinging popular support behind Pedro, who became regent on the death of Duarte in 1438. The voyages received strong support from Pedro, and more traders and adventurers were willing to risk wealth and health after the first slaves and gold dust were brought back in 1442.

During the regency of Pedro there were many voyages of exploration and no attempt to conquer Morocco. It would seem fair, therefore, to extend the association of the royal House of Aviz with these voyages and recognize the part played in them by Pedro. After his death in civil war (1449), the claims of the nobility were again heard, and his successor King Afonso v, "the African" (1438–81), once more pursued expansion in Morocco, giving exploration over to private enterprise.

In 1460, the year of Henry's death, one of his household, Pedro de Sintra, reached Sierra Leone. In the last twenty years of the century the move-

Vasco da Gama. Second to round the southern cape, he opened up the sea-route to the East: an early portrait from a seventeenth-century book.

ment of discovery quickened in rhythm. Interest veered toward the search for a sea-route to the spice markets, and further probes were made into the Atlantic. Under the energetic guidance and initiative of John II (1481–95), the "perfect prince" as history has called him, navigational aids handed down from Arab and Jewish mathematicians and astronomers, including new tables for calculating a bearing taken on the sun, were brought to a new level of accuracy. This coordination of known experience has been termed the "first scientific revolution" and on it was based all subsequent development in nautical science. The culmination of the century-long effort was first the rounding of the southern cape by Bartholomew Dias in 1488, named "Good Hope" by John II because it pointed the way to India. Second was the epoch-making voyage of Vasco da Gama in 1497–9, with the opening up of a sea-route to the East. This resulted in the diversion of the spice cargoes from the overland route via Alexandria (in Moslem hands) to Lisbon. And then in May, 1500, came the Portuguese landfall in Brazil.

Thus was begun a new age of knowledge by experience, international in aspect, with experts in technology sharing their know-how with ordinary seamen. It was to usher in the beginnings of European science a century later. And it is not too extravagant to claim Copernicus, Galileo and Newton, among others, as the inheritors of this fifteenth-century Portuguese experience.

DENIS BRASS

Medicean Florence becomes the first home

Florence was not the only Italian city to be troubled by war in the early fifteenth century. Milan, under Duke Filippo Maria Visconti, was still briskly expanding its territory. In 1421 he annexed Genoa, and in the following year Francesco Carmagnola, working for the Visconti, defeated the Swiss in battle at Arbedo, bringing more territory under Milan's rule. Milan and Florence were almost continuously at war from 1423 to 1454. Between 1425 and 1428 Milan was completely isolated militarily and faced an alliance of Florence, Venice, the Papal States and Naples. As a result of the pressure which this alliance was able to bring to bear, Milan was forced to grant Bergamo and Brescia to Venice by the Treaty of Ferrara in 1428. During the 1430s under the leadership of the mercenary general Niccolò Piccinino, Milanese armies were more successful. But the use of mercenaries—as so often in the fifteenth and sixteenth centuries—proved unreliable: Francesco Sforza (1401–66), who led the Venetian army, and Piccinino both quarreled with their employers and changed sides. The death of Filippo Maria Visconti in 1447 was the excuse for a vigorous war of succession. A republican government was set up in the city while the Venetians made an invasion attempt. The King of Naples laid claim to the throne, as did Charles, Duke of Orleans. But the successful candidate was Sforza. By 1450 he had established his claim to most of the duchy by conquest, and after he besieged Milan, the citizens suppressed the three-year-old Republic of Sant' Ambrogio and "invited" him to become Duke.

The Neapolitan succession

The history of the Kingdom of Naples—Sicily was no longer part of the kingdom as it had been annexed by Aragon in 1409—had been troubled throughout the fourteenth century. The first half of the fifteenth century was to be little more peaceful. The century had opened with civil war, which ended in 1411 when the Angevin claimant returned to France. Under Queen Joanna II (1414–35) the kingdom's troubles multiplied; dissolute and inept, Joanna was unable to control the barons, her lovers or her heirs. Civil war and

Francesco Sforza and *condottieri*.

invasion, the characteristics of her reign, continued after her death. The Angevin Louis III struggled hard to gain the kingdom from Alfonso of Aragon, but the close proximity of Sicily gave Alfonso an enormous advantage. In 1443, when Louis admitted defeat, Alfonso became undisputed King and peace became possible. Alfonso's reign marked the beginning of Spanish interference in Italian politics, which was to be the main feature of Italian history in the sixteenth and early seventeenth centuries. Spain was not alone in expanding its interests abroad in the fifteenth century. Portugal too was looking overseas, but its gaze was into the Atlantic.

Joanna II, the amorous Queen of Naples.

The Papacy

Until the twentieth century, the histroy of the papacy cannot be divided from that of the Papal States. The problems of the Avignon papacy were largely caused by financial difficulties and the spiritual pronouncements and claims of popes were often based on material considerations. With the return of Martin V to Rome the papacy was once again caught up in the wars and politics of Italy. Martin had been able to re-establish papal power, but only by pushing members of his own family, whom he could trust, into positions of responsibility. When Eugenius IV was elected he found himself surrounded by members of Martin's family, the Colonna, and at once attempted to diminish their influence. The methods he chose, under the influence of their rivals the Orsini, were sometimes violent, and the Colonna rebelled, with the support of other discontented nobles. The rebellion failed, but Eugenius' vicious punishment of all concerned, even if they had only played a minor role, made him many new enemies.

Influenced by the Duke of Milan, the Colonna rose again in 1433, which resulted in Eugenius' recognition of the Council of Basel. But recognition did not end the rebellion, and the people of Rome, so far quiet, now rose against Eugenius, whom they regarded as an arrogant tyrant. In May, 1434, they proclaimed Rome a republic. The Pope escaped by boat from a castle outside Rome, pursued by boatloads of Romans, and moved to Florence, where he knew he could rely for support on the enemies of Milan. Although the Republic of Rome soon dissolved, Eugenius

was afraid to return until Rome had been subdued by his legate, Cardinal John Vitteleschi, whose ruthlessness was only matched by his ambition. It was not until 1443 that Eugenius felt secure enough to leave Florence, and it was not until the end of his pontificate that the Papal States were entirely pacified.

Pope Eugenius IV bestowing the baton of command upon his general.

The end of the Council of Basel

The election of Felix V was not intended to cause a full-scale schism; Felix did not appoint his supporters to offices in the Curia. After his election, support for both the Council and its Pope withered away. The gradual entry of the German Empire into Eugenius' camp was the most severe blow to the Council, which had depended on the Empire's continued neutrality. The new Emperor, Frederick III, needed help against the electors, who had supported the Council, so it was natural for him to turn to the Pope for recognition. The new Pope, Nicholas V, was happy to oblige. Little less serious for the Council was a financial dispute with Felix, who had been elected mainly because it was thought that his wealth would enable him to support himself; Felix expected to be supported financially.

In 1448 the Emperor wrote to the city of Basel forbidding it to continue as the seat of the Council. The members of the Council moved to Lausanne. The Council was now anxious to save itself from total defeat. Felix had grown bored with being a powerless pope and offered his abdication to the Council in 1449. The Council

# of Humanism

accepted it and elected Nicholas V as Pope and then dissolved itself. For his part, Nicholas made Felix a cardinal and allowed him the outward honors of the papal rank. He also recognized several of the cardinals whom Felix had appointed.

The schism was over, but it had had its effect. The failure of the Council of Basel meant that in the future any reform must come from within the Curia, but the fifteenth-century Curia soon showed itself incapable of offering the necessary reforming leadership. The attitudes of the fifteenth-century papacy also influenced the development of national states. Claims based on the papal plenitude of power were treated with growing suspicion by kings and princes, who saw them as contrary to their own rights.

The Orthodox Church and the Council of Ferrara-Florence

The capture of Salonika by the Turks in 1430 had reminded the Byzantine Empire of its dangerous situation. Without support from the West, Constantinople itself was threatened. The Emperor, John VIII Palaeologus, sent ambassadors to Pope Eugenius to ask him to preach a crusade, which the Pope refused to do unless the Greek Church acknowledged the primacy of Rome and gave up its "heretical" views about the Holy Spirit. The Greeks agreed to discuss this at a general council, but refused to go to Basel because of the difficulty of communications with Constantinople. This provided Eugenius with his excuse for transferring the Council of Basel to Ferrara. The Emperor, with a large group of nobles and bishops, arrived at Ferrara early

The Emperor Frederick III giving the future Pius II the poets' crown.

in March, 1438, three months after the official opening of the Council. It soon became clear that many of the Greeks did not favor union on Rome's terms. The leader of the opposition, Mark Eugenikos, the Metropolitan of Ephesus, could rely for support on the Emperor's son, Demetrius. The Emperor was, however, determined to push the union through quickly, and the arguments of the leader of the unionist party, John Bessarion, Archbishop of Nicaea, swayed many of the Greeks. The opponents of union were eventually ignored by the Emperor who wanted to return to Constantinople quickly. The Pope was little less anxious to get rid of the Greeks for expenses were enormous, particularly as he had undertaken to pay all their costs. Furthermore, Ferrara was in danger of attack by mercenaries of the Duke of Milan. Cosimo de' Medici offered to pay 12,000 crowns if the Council was moved to Florence, an offer that Eugenius immediately accepted. The Council moved to Florence in February, 1439, and five months later the decree of union was signed.

The union was, however, short-lived. The Orthodox synods in Constantinople refused to ratify the decree, and popular feeling favored the opponents of union. The failure of the Latins to provide effective military support for the threatened Empire proved the last straw.

Humanism

The birth of Humanism presented an alternative culture to that of the Christian Middle Ages. A few ancient authors apart from Aristotle were known throughout the Middle Ages. Although Aristotle was regarded as "The Philosopher" and was the main philosophical influence on medieval thought, some works of Plato were always known, Latin translations of the *Meno* and *Phaedo* and large parts of the *Timaeus* existed, as well as smaller quotations from other books in patristic works.

There was, however, little real interest in the classics which were not thought to be worthy of systematic study as they did not help forward an understanding of Christian theology. The idea of seeing Plato or Virgil as "Chris-

tians before Christ" led to the birth of a new attitude from the early fourteenth century onward, but it was a long time before this could grow to fruition, mainly because of the lack of knowledge of the classics. Francesco Petrarch (1304–74) had laid the foundations for a new attitude; he had copied out thousands of classical manuscripts from libraries in Italy, France, Switzerland and southern Germany, and his collection of ancient writings was probably larger and better organized than any other of his time.

As early as the fourteenth century a revival of Greek studies in the West began. A chair of Greek studies was set up at Florence University in the 1360s, and a Greek exile, Leontius Pilatus, was appointed the first professor. During the earlier Middle Ages there had probably always been a few Westerners who had understood Greek, but their chief interest had been in diplomacy or trade, and it was only in the fifteenth century that the study of Greek became at all usual among even the most erudite of scholars. But it was the knowledge of Greek that opened up to Humanists a vision of a new different world.

Around 1400, Poggio Bracciolini (1380–1459), influenced by the Florentine Greek professor Emanuel Chrysoloras, began translating the works of Plato and Aristotle from manuscripts brought from Constantinople. The other main sources of Greek were the libraries of a few great monasteries, and Spain where Christian and Moslem cultures were at this time coexisting.

The Council of Florence, unsuccessful though it was in permanently healing the schism between East and West, encouraged scholarly communication between Constantinople and the West. Cosimo de' Medici encouraged Greeks to come to his city, and Florence became the first home of Humanism. The study of "humane letters" came to be identified particularly with the study of Plato, just as medieval Western thought was based particularly on the study of Aristotle. John Bessarion, whose support for the union between the Latin and Greek Churches was rewarded with a cardinal's hat, upheld the view that Plato was a greater philosopher than Aristotle in *In Calumniatorem*

Title page of a work by Flavio Biondo printed in Basel.

Platonis. More influential as a publicist, if less profound as a thinker, was Marsilio Ficino (1433–99), who translated the complete known works of Plato into Latin.

The effects of the new Humanism were felt in most cultural fields. A new critical approach in scholarship became possible. In 1440 Lorenzo Valla (1406–57) published *De Falso Credita et Ementita Constantini Donatione*, which was probably the first serious work of historical and textual criticism of the Renaissance. It was a scathing attack on one of the foundations of the papal claims to temporal sovereignty, the so-called Donation of Constantine. Valla proved that the Donation could not have been written in the fourth century both because the style of the Latin was of a later period, and because some of the towns mentioned in the Donation had not existed in the fourth century. In fact, the Donation was written in the ninth century. A measure of the wide acceptance of Humanist ideas was that despite this energetic attack on papal claims Valla was given a senior job in the papal secretariat a few years later by the Humanist-influenced Pope Nicholas V. Others soon followed Valla's lead, and one of them Flavio Biondo (1392–1463), revolutionized historical thinking by introducing the concept of the Middle Ages. Biondo's studies of Roman history were also important.

Humanism provided a new secular way of understanding the world, which influenced all aspects of life. This was particularly important in art and sculpture.

TEMPLA DOMVM EXPOSITIS·VICOS·FORA·MOENIA PONTES·
VIRGINEAM TRIVII QVOD REPARARIS AQVAM·
PRISCA LICET NAVTIS STATVAS DARE COMMODA PORTVS·
ET VATICANVM CINGERE SIXTE IVGVM·
PLVS TAMEN VRBS DEBET·NAM QVAE SQVALORE LATEBAT·
CERNITVR IN CELEBRI BIBLIOTHECA LOCO·

A Service to Men of Learning

The need for a central library was not of pressing concern to the early Church, but by the fifteenth century that need was becoming real. In part it was the rise of Humanism that inspired the foundation of the Vatican Library, which was begun by Pope Nicholas V. From modest beginnings—and with a few setbacks—the Library was built into one of the great collections of the world, and even today it remains an important source for scholars.

Christianity is preeminently a religion of the Book. The very word *Bible* is simply the Greek for "books." Throughout the fourteen centuries between the crucifixion and the invention of printing, Christians had spared neither time nor labor in preserving, transcribing, translating and explaining the sacred books. The early Christians may not have invented the *codex*, or folded and sewn form, which is more likely a legal innovation, but they recognized its convenience and approved its lack of association with the older roll forms associated with pagan literature. Indeed, the survival of literature and the art of writing in the West is largely due to Christianity. For centuries monastic *scriptoria* were almost the only source of books, and cathedral and monastic libraries their chief place of preservation until the rise of the universities in the twelfth century brought increasing demand for books and a flourishing book trade.

Inevitably books would tend to accumulate around the central institution of Christendom, which makes the date 1450 seem very late for the foundation of the Vatican Library. Obviously the papacy needed archives and there is evidence of a papal library as early as the pontificate of Damasus I (366–84). But that was a personal library, not the repository of learning that the Vatican Library was intended to be.

The pope who established the Vatican Library was Nicholas V, born Tommaso Parentucelli at Sarzana in Liguria in 1397. The son of a physician, he was forced to leave his studies at the University of Bologna for lack of funds upon his father's untimely death. For two years thereafter he acted as tutor to rich families in Florence, then the center of intellectual ferment and Humanist studies. By the second decade of the fifteenth century, the revival of learning was well under way and book hunting had become something of a national sport with Florence its base. During his stay there, Tommaso made the acquaintance of the leading Humanist scholars and their patrons, including Cosimo de' Medici, for whom he drew up

his *canon*, or list of books necessary for the ideal library—a list that was the basis for several Italian collections.

In 1419 Tommaso was able to resume his studies at Bologna and when, three years later, he took his Master's degree he was given a post on the staff of the Bishop, the saintly Niccolò Albergati, whom he served for twenty years. At the same time he was able to pursue his own predilections for scholarship and for the seeking out of manuscripts. Albergati died in 1443 and Tommaso was appointed to succeed him the following year. Two years later he became a cardinal and in 1447 was elected Pope.

Nicholas V had lofty ambitions. Primarily he sought peace and unity in the Western Church and here his generosity of spirit brought much success. He also hoped to reconcile East and West by carrying forward the work of the Council of Florence, but it was probably already too late. He wished to rebuild Rome and made notable progress in that direction, and he wished to enlist the resources of the new Humanist learning in the service of the Church. Humanism is now loosely used as a synonym for agnosticism and even atheism, but in the fifteenth century it meant primarily the study of the classical literature of Greece and Rome and the attempt to cultivate something of the classical style in literature and art. Thus Erasmus and Thomas More were Humanists and even today classical studies at Oxford are known as *Literae Humaniores* and professors of Latin in the older Scottish universities are known as professors of Humanity.

Nicholas declared 1450 a Holy Year of Jubilee. The first Holy Year had been held by Boniface VIII in 1300, with the intention that one should be held each century. Later the interval was reduced to fifty, thirty-three and, finally twenty-five years, but even so it was an event not likely to occur more than twice in an active lifetime. Pilgrims were attracted to Rome by the promise of plenary indulgences and special ceremonies, including the canonization of the popular preacher Bernardino of Siena, who was but five years dead. Although the rejoicings

Pope Nicholas V, Humanist scholar and founder of the Vatican Library. He sponsored the collection of manuscripts and the translation and copying of the major works in Greek: a miniature from Lorenzo Valla's translation of Thucydides.

Opposite Pope Sixtus IV appointing Bartolomeo Platina librarian. Sixtus officially inaugurated the library and set it up in its present building. Platina made good the damage done to Nicholas' collection, and produced a comprehensive catalog. The fresco by Melozzo da Forlì is in the Vatican.

A fresco by Fra Angelico showing Pope Nicholas V giving alms to the poor: from the Chapel of Nicholas V in the Vatican.

the same amount for Thucydides, while double the amount was paid for Strabo. The enormous sum of 5,000 ducats—the Vatican librarian under Pope Sixtus IV was paid ten ducats a month—was offered for the Aramaic text of St. Matthew's Gospel, but was never earned. As a result of such feverish activity, by the end of Nicholas' short reign the original nucleus of about three hundred and forty manuscripts, which he had inherited from his predecessor Eugenius IV, had grown to some fifteen hundred volumes.

On March 24, 1455, Nicholas died. His last years had been saddened by the fall of Constantinople, which he had tried ineffectively to prevent, and by a Roman republican conspiracy. But he had performed great services to learning, among which was the foundation bull of the University of Glasgow in 1451. In 1849, the historian Thomas Babington Macaulay delivered the customary address as Rector of the University, paying notable tribute to the scholarly Pope.

He was "the greatest of the restorers of learning . . . the centre of an illustrious group composed partly of the last great scholars of Greece and partly of the first great scholars of Italy, Theodore Gaza and George of Trebizond, Bessarion and Filelfo, Marsilo Ficino and Poggio Bracciolini . . . .

"No department of literature owes so much to him as history. By him were introduced to the knowledge of Western Europe two great and unrivalled models of historical composition, the work of Herodotus and the work of Thucydides. By him, too, our ancestors were first made acquainted with the graceful and lucid simplicity of Xenophon and the manly good sense of Polybius."

Nicholas had envisioned a great library and had amassed a notable collection, but he did not live long enough to establish it on a secure basis. His successors had other preoccupations. The octogenarian Calixtus III (1455–58) is said to have exclaimed on being shown the library, "Just see what the property of God's Church has been wasted on!" Pius II (1458–64) had himself been a distinguished Humanist and poet, and had a fine personal library, but his energies as Pope were concentrated on fighting the Turks. Paul II (1464–71) disliked the Humanists. Consequently it was not until the reign of Sixtus IV (1471–84) that the library was put on a permanent footing.

Francesco della Rovere, who was invested as Sixtus IV on August 25, 1471, at the age of fifty-seven, has evoked a mixed response. A Franciscan and a distinguished theologian, his private life was free from blame. But he was perhaps unduly complacent in the face of growing irreligion and the clamant need for Church reform. His chief vice was nepotism and he had many nephews. Nonetheless we owe to him the construction of the Sistine Chapel, and in the matter of the Vatican Library he can scarcely be faulted.

There had been a false start in the first year of his pontificate when a proposal to erect a new building came to nothing. But activity began

were marred by an outbreak of plague and by a disaster on the bridge of St. Angelo in which two hundred died, pilgrims in their thousands came from all over Europe. Many were poor and a charge on papal hospitality but a goodly number were rich and their lavish offerings were deployed to further the project that Nicholas had nearest to his heart—assembling a large library that would include a copy of every known Greek and Latin work, and that would be at the service of all men of learning.

In hunting for manuscripts for the library no expense was spared. Papal agents were dispatched not only throughout Europe but as far away as Turkey and an army of copyists, artists and binders was set to work producing worthy copies. (The potentialities of printing had yet to be realized.) The manuscripts produced were often works of art in their own right. Beautifully written on parchment, they were copiously illustrated with illuminations that frequently retain their freshness even after the lapse of five centuries. The bindings, too, were richly ornamented with gold, silver and jewels. The expense of producing copies of such high standards helps explain why Renaissance libraries had so few volumes compared with the collections of today or even those of antiquity.

A vast program of translation of all the standard Greek works was also sponsored. A sum of 500 ducats was paid for the translation of Polybius and in 1475. On February 4, the papal librarian, Bishop Bussi, died and was succeeded later in the same month by the distinguished Humanist Bartolomeo Platina. Platina, who was born near Cremona, was by this time fifty-four and had enjoyed a varied career as soldier, student, teacher and author. In 1464 he had been taken into the papal service by Pius II but the accession of Paul II cost him his job and when he protested too vigorously he was imprisoned. He came back into favor under Sixtus, to whom he had dedicated and presented, in 1474, his chief work: *Liber de vita Christi ac omnium pontificum*, covering the lives of all the popes from St. Peter to Paul II (who comes off badly). Despite its prejudices the work, the manuscript of which is in the Vatican Library, has considerable historical value.

The Vatican Library proper began with a papal bull of June 21, 1475, in which Sixtus declared that he was setting up a public library in a single suitable place, with Platina in charge, and made financial provision for its continuance. The place chosen was, appropriately enough, the ground floor of a building erected by Nicholas V and close to the Sistine Chapel.

The floor was divided by party-walls into four rooms of unequal size. The first and largest formed the Latin Library; the second, about half the size, the Greek Library. Taken together, these formed the Common or Public Library. The third and smallest room was the Secret or Reserved Library, where the more precious volumes were kept, as well as works in Hebrew and Arabic, while the fourth, the Pontifical Library, housed the papal archives and the rarest volumes. These two rooms were not open to the public. Two rooms adjoining the Latin Library accommodated the librarian and his three assistants.

Platina seems to have had a free hand in organizing, furnishing and decorating the library and, as he kept meticulous accounts, it is possible to follow his progress step by step, almost day by day. He went vigorously to work. New windows were inserted to improve the lighting, notable artists—including the Ghirlandaio brothers and Melozzo da Forlì—were commissioned to decorate the

Sixtus IV and Platina in one of the reading rooms. There were no shelves, the books being laid flat on the desks: painting of the school of Melozzo.

HAEC · SVNT · NOMINA

filior̄ isr̄l qui ingressi sunt in egyptū cum Iacob
singuli cū domib; suis introierunt. Ruben: Symē
on: Leui: Iudas: ysachar: zabulon et Beniamin
Dan: et Neptalim. Gad: et Aser: Erant igitur
omes anime eor̄ q egressi sūt de femore Iacob
septuagita. Ioseph aūt in egypto erat. Quo
mortuo et uniuersis frib; eius: omni q cognatio
ne sua: filii isr̄l creuerūt et quasi germinantes
multiplicati st̄: ac roborati nimis impleuerūt
terrā Surrexit interea rex nouus super egyptū
qui ignorabat Ioseph. Et ait ad pplm suum. Ec
ce populus filior̄ israel multus et fortior nobis.
Venite sapienter opprimamus eū: ne forte mul
tiplicetur: et si ingruerit contra nos bellū: ad
datur n̄ris inimicis: expugnatisq; nobis egredi
atur de terra. Preposuit itaq; magistros operū
ut affligerēt eos oneribz: edificaueruntq; urbes
tabernaculor̄ Pharaoni Phiton: et Ramesses.
quātoq; opprimebant eos: tanto magis multi
plicabantur: et crescebat. Oderantq; filios isr̄l
egyptii: et affligebāt illudentes eis: atq; ad a
maritudinē perducebant uitā eor̄ operibus
duris luti: et lateris: omniq; famulatu quo in
terre opibus premebatur. Dixit aūt rex e
gypti obstetricibus hebreor̄: quar̄ una uoca
batur Sephora: altera Phua: precipiēs eis. Qn

obstetricabitis hebreas: et partus tēpus aduene
rit: si masculus fuerit interficite eū: si femina
reseruate. Timuerunt obstetrices deum: et nō
fecerunt iuxta preceptū regis egypti: sed con
seruabāt mares. Quibz ad se accersitis rex ait.
Quid nā est hoc quod facere uoluistis ut pueōs
seruaretis? Que r̄nderūt. Non sūt hebree si
cut egyptie mulieres. Ipse enim obstetricādi
hēnt scientiā: et priusq̄ ueniamus ad eas pa
riūt. Bene ergo fecit deus obstetricibz. Et cre
uit pplus cōfortatusq; est nimis. Et qa timue
rūt obstetrices deū: edificauit illis domos. Pre
cepit aūt Pharao omni pplo suo dicēs. Qcqd
masculini sexus natū fuerit: in flumē proicite:
quicqd femini reseruate. C II
Gressus est post hec uir de domo leui accepta
uxore stirpis sue: q cōcepit et peperit filium.
Et uidēs eum elegantē: abscōdit mensibz tribz.
cūq; iam celare non posset: sumpsit fiscelam
scirpeā: et liniuit eā bitumie ac pice: posu
it q intus infantulū: et exposuit eū in carep
to fluminis stāte procul sorore eius: et cōsi
derate euentū rei: Ecce aūt descēdebat fi
lia Pharaonis ut lauaretur in flumine: et pu
elle eius gradiebātur p crepidinē aluei. Que
cū uidisset fiscellā in papirione: misit una de

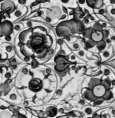

walls. One of Melozzo's frescoes for the Latin Library was transferred to canvas in the early nineteenth century and can still be seen in the Vatican. It depicts newly appointed Platina kneeling before Sixtus and two of his cardinal nephews.

The furniture was especially made. In the public rooms were twenty-four long desks, sixteen in the Latin and eight in the Greek Library. They were approximately twenty-eight feet long, had two, or sometimes three, shelves and could hold between forty and fifty volumes. The list for the Latin Library gives some idea of the scope and order of the collection. The nine desks on the left held respectively: Bibles and Commentaries; Jerome and Augustine; Augustine, Ambrose and Gregory; John Chrysostom; Thomas Aquinas; Theology and Liturgy; Canon Law (desks seven and eight); Civil Law. The seven desks on the right held in their turn: Philosophy; Astrology and Medicine; Poetry; Oratory; History; Church History; Grammar. The books, their bindings protected by metal bosses, were chained to the desks, but they could be borrowed and removed from the library.

The Secret Library had six desks, five cupboards and a settle, while the Pontifical Library had twelve desks and a settle. Both these rooms had special chests attached to the desks. The library also contained a map of the world and globes.

Above The interior of the Vatican Library. Platina was chiefly responsible for its organization and commissioned eminent artists to decorate the walls.

Opposite A page from the Urbino Bible. Painstakingly transcribed and lavishly illustrated, this is a fair example of the quality of the library's manuscripts.

Left A letter from the Byzantine Emperor, housed in the library archives. These are the repository of many documents of historical value.

Above Queen Dido of
Carthage offering a sacrifice
to the gods: an illustration in
the fifth-century *Codex
Vaticanus*.

Right A detail from Raphael's
portrait of a pope, showing a
clasped tome and reading
glass.

The manuscript shows an illuminated page with the word "SILENTIVM" at the top and Latin text.

A session of the Sacra Rota, the supreme ecclesiastical court: from a manuscript in the library archives.

In winter, heating was provided by a brazier on wheels that could be moved where it was most needed. Juniper was used for fumigation; brooms were bought for cleaning the floors and fox-tails for dusting the books.

The collection amassed by Nicholas v had suffered by depredation and neglect and under Platina's leadership energetic efforts were made to recover the missing volumes and rebind and refurbish those remaining. A catalog drawn up on Platina's original appointment lists 2,527 volumes; 770 in Greek and 1,757 in Latin. This represents a considerable increase over the original collection of Nicholas v and probably the great bulk of it came from Sixtus' own collection. Platina produced a catalog of the new library by subject and author. There is a melancholy note at the end which says that it was completed "by Platina, librarian, and Demetrius of Lucca his pupil . . . on the 14th day of September, 1481, only eight days before his death." This catalog records 3,499 items, an increase of nearly a thousand in the six years of Platina's librarianship. Sixtus survived his librarian by three years; the Library has survived them both by nearly five centuries.

It is difficult to overestimate the significance of the founding of the Vatican Library, which came just when the invention of printing was about to transform the world. The wisdom of the past, formerly the preserve of scholars and the rich, could now become the common inheritance of mankind. But this wisdom had to be sought out, transcribed and edited before it could be diffused and here the papal initiative provided an inspiration and example for all Christendom.

The Vatican Library has long outgrown its original home. Through five centuries it has had its vicissitudes, its periods of stagnation and spectacular growth. The fifteen hundred manuscripts of Nicholas v have grown to more than sixty thousand while the printed books are approaching the one million mark. At one time the greatest library in the world, it has long been surpassed in size by the great national and university collections. But for the sheer quality and importance of its holdings, it remains one of the world's great libraries and although all roads may no longer lead to Rome many scholars must still make the Roman pilgrimage, grateful for the vision of Nicholas v, the generosity of Sixtus iv and the energy of Bartolomeo Platina.

R. K. BROWNE

65

The English assumed that the "spell" cast by Joan of Arc, the "sorceress of Orleans," had been lifted when she was executed, and they anticipated that the English conquest of France would soon follow. As an essential preliminary to recovering and expanding England's continental holdings—and in order to discredit the coronation of Charles VII at Reims—Cardinal Beaufort crowned the ten-year-old Henry VI in Paris in December, 1431. But, within a year the strained alliance between England and Burgundy began to founder.

At the same time the intrigues initiated by the Duke of Gloucester were undermining the authority at home of the Duke of Bedford who was forced to return to England. France rallied in his absence. English influence in northern France was soon confined to Normandy and Paris. Despite Bedford's energetic leadership, a second campaign was a failure. The Duke of Burgundy decided to abandon the English alliance and summoned a general peace congress at Arras. He also agreed to recognize Charles VII as King of France but the terms of the *entente* humiliated Charles who soon broke the spirit of the treaty. Philip had expected to become Charles' principal counsellor and greatest feudatory, but the French King never lost his deep suspicion of him.

The Congress of Arras offered England the whole of Normandy and extensions to the Duchy of Gascony if the English would agree to a treaty recognizing Charles as

Humphrey, Duke of Gloucester, who forced Bedford to return to England.

King of an attenuated France. Bedford, ever hopeful that the fortunes of war would shift in his favor, refused the terms. If Bedford had lived, time might have proved him right, but he died a year later. English authority in France, deprived of his leadership, crumbled, and Charles entered Paris. Almost at once he faced a rebellion of some of his greatest nobles—Brittany, Alençon and Bourbon, who supported the Dauphin, the future Louis XI. The English were able to take advantage of French dissension to reconquer Harfleur, but the Duke of York, the English regent in Normandy, failed to exploit his success, and French troops reconquered most of Gascony. By 1444 both sides were too exhausted to pursue the fighting and a truce was signed at Tours. The truce led to a marriage between Henry VI and Margaret, daughter of the Duke of Anjou.

France captures Bordeaux

Five years after the Truce of Tours, England was on the verge of civil war, and France had broken the truce and seized the whole of Normandy. As fighting resumed, Charles VII's military reforms soon began to tell. The French soldiers proved better disciplined and more effectively led than their opponents and they were determined to rid their homeland of foreign troops. Bordeaux fell in June, 1451, but the town's inhabitants—who had been privileged subjects of the kings of England for generations—had little love for French taxes and military obligations, and in the following year invited the English army back. Margaret of Anjou instructed John Talbot, Earl of Shrewsbury, to bring the whole province under English rule. A massive French army counterattacked in the spring of 1453, and in July of that year besieged the English at Castillon near Bordeaux. Chanting their war cry "Talbot, Talbot, St. George," the English garrison marched out to attack the French, but after a day of heavy fighting were overwhelmed. Talbot himself was slain and his men fled.

Charles VII was able to enter Bordeaux in triumph on October 19, 1453—an event that marked the effective end of the Hundred Years War. It had taken a century of almost constant warfare to

Bordeaux surrenders to the forces of Charles VII.

convince England's kings that it was not feasible for them to administer domains in France without the willing consent of the French monarchy. The English were, however, permitted to retain Calais and a few neighboring places. Charles VII, "le bien servi," had indeed fulfilled the prophecies of the peasant girl from Domremy.

Frederick III

Albert of Austria, who succeeded Sigismund as Emperor in 1437, showed in his brief reign that he was no more able than his predecessor. In 1440 Frederick III, Archduke of Austria, was elected King of the Romans. From the beginning of his reign he was troubled by the ambitions of the imperial electors. At first he favored the Council of Basel against the Pope, but Eugenius' legate, Aeneas Sylvius Piccolomini, later Pope Pius II, persuaded him to change his mind. After his formal recognition of Nicholas V (1448) he was crowned Emperor (1451).

Frederick attempted to impose his imperial authority on the

The Emperor Frederick III with Eleanor of Portugal.

Swiss, who refused to acknowledge his rights. Although French mercenaries fighting for Frederick beat the Swiss in battle at Saint Jakob, the Emperor failed to press home his advantage. The Treaty of Zeffingen in 1444 was a diplomatic victory for the Swiss.

Although popular at the beginning of his reign, Frederick lost much support because of his idleness. His failure to extract better terms in return for his recognition of the papacy, his unwillingness to oppose the Turks effectively and his refusal to attend diets made him many enemies. Most of the electors opposed him, but they were unable to agree on a suitable replacement.

Like earlier emperors, Frederick looked to the eastern provinces as an area where he could strengthen his power base. He was not successful. In 1457, Ladislas, King of Hungary and Bohemia, died. Frederick tried to gain the crowns of both countries, but only managed to obtain lower Austria, a tiny part of Ladislas' possessions. Even here Frederick was ultimately unsuccessful. His brother Albert, who had succeeded him as Archduke of Austria, drove his men out.

Russian independence

Moscow's leadership of the Russian peoples had begun to develop as early as the thirteenth century, but the victory of Duke Dimitri III of Moscow over the Golden Horde at Kulikova Pole in 1380 was the beginning of its real supremacy. The defeats by Timur and constant pressure from the rulers of Poland–Lithuania left the Golden Horde in a weak position at the beginning of the fifteenth century. Moscow was given an opportunity to expand its influence into real power at the expense of the Mongols.

The dukes of Moscow, although nominally viceroys of the Mongols, were in practice largely independent. In 1400, the Golden Horde unsuccessfully besieged Moscow in an attempt to restore their authority over the dukes. The difficulties of the Mongols were intensified by succession disputes, which led to rebellion and civil war. Under Dimitri's successors in the duchy, Vasili I (1389–1425) and Vasili II (1425–62), Muscovite pretensions to power over the surrounding regions grew, al-

Church of the Vestments, in the Kremlin.

though the pretensions were not always matched by reality. The efforts of the brother of Vasili I, Juri of Galich, to seize power from Vasili II set back Muscovite hopes and caused the defeat and capture of Vasili in 1445 by the Khan of the Golden Horde, Ulug-Mahmed. This proved to be no more than a temporary setback, as Ulug-Mahmed's son, Mabumdek, murdered his father and released the Duke the same year. More serious was a rebellion in Moscow in 1446, when supporters of Juri seized and blinded the Duke. Loyal boyars, however, drove the rebels from the city. By 1452, despite his blindness, Vasili was firmly established. He now felt strong enough to start setting up tributary Mongol states to support him against the Golden Horde. The Christian states of Russia, too, were increasingly accepting his authority, and in 1453 Novgorod itself accepted Muscovite sovereignty.

In ecclesiastical matters, also, Russian independence was coming to be recognized. The Metropolitan of Russia had moved his see from Kiev to Moscow in 1328. Most of the Russian bishops refused to acknowledge the Union of the Churches arranged by the Council of Florence, and the Greek Church was regarded with suspicion because it had accepted the Union. The fall of Constantinople to the Turks made the Russians even less willing to accept the authority of the Patriarch of Constantinople, and in 1461 St. Jonas, the Metropolitan of Moscow, refused to acknowledge the primacy of Constantinople. Some of the Russians continued to be loyal to the patriarchs, and the bishops of Kiev began a schism, but the majority decided to follow Moscow's lead.

The recovery of Islam

After the death in captivity of Bayazid in 1403, three of his sons set up independent empires in the remains of the old Ottoman Empire: Isa was based at Brusa, Mehmet farther north and east at Amasia, while Suleiman took the old capital at Adrianople in Europe as his base. Isa was soon beaten by Mehmet, and by 1413 most of the supporters of Suleiman, who had been killed in 1411, were quiet. But Bayazid's heritage continued to be troubled by his large family, and Mehmet was forced to fight two more of his brothers, Musa and Mustafa. Even after Mehmet's death in 1421 the fighting continued. His successor, Murad II, finally beat Mustafa in 1423. Secure on the throne and with the backing of all the former Ottoman lands, both in Europe and Asia, Murad attempted to extend his power in the Balkans. Salonika was captured in 1430, and Serbia invaded in 1439, although it had already paid Murad tribute. In 1440 Murad besieged Belgrade. The rulers of the Balkan states uncharacteristically joined together in an alliance and drove the enemy back, the despot of Serbia, who had fled to Hungary when his land was attacked, returning with an army he had raised with Hungarian support. In 1444 he defeated the Turks at Kunovitsa, and by the Treaty of Adrianople Murad restored Serbia to him. In the previous year the Hungarians had beaten Murad at the Battle of Zlatica.

In 1444 Murad abdicated. He had reunified the Ottoman Empire and had expanded its territory both in Greece and Anatolia, and although he had not achieved his ambitions of Balkan conquest, the situation in the Balkans seemed stable and there appeared to be little danger either from the now-tiny Byzantine Empire or from the West. The Holy Roman Emperor Albert, however, saw the situation rather differently. Believing that the tide of Moslem conquest had turned and that Murad's abdication was a sign of weakness, he lead a crusading army to the Bulgarian port of Varna. Murad quickly emerged from retirement and beat the Christian Emperor decisively, killing many nobles from Hungary, Bohemia and Poland. Although the Battle of Varna did not result in the immediate conquest of the Balkans by the Turks, it made Christian princes chary of resisting them.

Fighting went on in the Balkans. The Albanian leader Skanderbeg beat the Turks in 1447, but was himself defeated the following year, although not decisively. In the same year, Murad beat the Hungarians at Kossovo. After the victory at Varna, Murad did not abdicate again, but remained Sultan until his death in 1451. Murad's son, Mehmet II, was then restored to the throne. His second reign was to prove more interesting than his first brief reign in 1444. Murad had restored the Ottoman Empire to a position stronger than it had before Timur's invasion. Mehmet was to crown this achievement by the conquest of Constantinople.

Sultan Murad II receives a dignitary.

Le siege du grant turc auec ij deses principaulx conseilles
Le siege du capiteine general de la turquie

The Fall of Constantinople   1453

The Eastern Roman Empire had endured for eleven centuries, but now it was reduced to little more than the city of Constantinople itself. Another Constantine—the last to sit on the Byzantine throne—ruled the decaying city and nervously watched the Ottoman Turks inexorably advancing from the east. Eastern and Western Christendom were split over doctrinal disputes— and there would be no help coming from Europe. Overtures to the Turkish Sultan were dramatically rebuffed; Constantine's ambassadors of peace were beheaded as they arrived. On Easter Monday, 1453, the Sultan's advance guard was sighted and the gates to the city were closed. The Greeks heroically resisted the Turkish siege, but it could have only one outcome. As the Turkish victors streamed into the fallen city, they were witnessing the end of one long and brilliant chapter in man's history—and the beginning of another.

The traveler from the West, seeing Constantinople for the first time during the early decades of the fifteenth century, would have been saddened—even possibly horrified—by what lay before him. Brought up on tales of this golden metropolis—second only to Rome itself in splendor, and seat of an Empire that had lasted more than a thousand years and could boast the longest chain of unbroken monarchy in the history of Christendom—the traveler would have found instead a crumbling ruin of a city, half-deserted and shot through with despair. "Its inhabitants are few," wrote Pedro Tafur, a young Spaniard who arrived in 1437. "They are not well-clad, but miserable and poor, showing the hardship of their lot . . . The Emperor's palace must have been very magnificent, but now is in such a state that both it and the city reveal the evils which the people have suffered and still endure . . . Inside, the building is badly maintained, except for those parts where the Emperor, the Empress and their attendants live, and even these are cramped for space. The Emperor's state is as splendid as ever, for nothing is omitted from the ancient ceremonies; but, properly regarded, he is like a Bishop without a See."

Tafur's description was accurate; the once-glorious Empire of the East, which had formerly stretched from Italy to the borders of Mesopotamia, now extended little farther than the walls of Constantinople itself. For centuries the Empire had stood as a bulwark against the tide of Islam, allowing Christianity time to put down deep roots in Eastern Europe—and even after the loss of the Anatolian heartland to the Seljuk Turks in the eleventh century, the Empire had remained rich, powerful and—ostensibly—prosperous. The quays of Constantinople were crowded with the shipping of three continents, and merchants from every land and clime thronged its bazaars. City wharves and warehouses overflowed with silks and spices, ivory and gold, while beneath the mosiac-encrusted cupolas of its thousand churches lay some of the holiest relics of Christianity.

Constantinople's prosperity aroused increasing envy and cupidity among Western crusaders throughout the twelfth century, and it was perhaps inevitable that they should make their own bid for control of the Greek metropolis. The seizure of the city, on Good Friday, 1204, by that exercise in unmitigated piracy still ludicrously known as the Fourth Crusade, stripped Constantinople of its treasures and condemned it to fifty-five years of misrule by Frankish thugs occupying the throne of the Byzantine emperors. The city was left weak, desperately impoverished and well-nigh naked to its enemies.

Not long after Michael VIII Palaeologus rode back into his shattered capital in 1259, a new dynasty sprang up in the Turkish-held lands across the Bosphorus: the House of Osman—or, as we now prefer to call them, the Ottomans.

Under Osman and his successors, Turkish conquests came swiftly. By 1340 virtually all of Asia Minor was in their hands; in the next twenty-five years they crossed the Dardanelles, set up their capital at Adrianople (modern Edirne) and made themselves masters of western Thrace. Their victory at Kossovo in southern Yugoslavia in 1389 won them Serbia and the Balkans. By that time the Byzantine Emperor, surrounded by enemies, plagued by palace revolutions, his morale further shaken by the Black Death, had been forced to acknowledge the Turkish Sultan as his overlord. Only one hope now remained: a grand Christian alliance to deliver the Empire and save Europe—while there was still time—from the Moslem invader.

The possibility of such an alliance was dim. The Eastern and Western Churches had long been in schism, and it seemed unlikely that the Pope would declare a crusade for the rescue of schismatics who did not even recognize his primacy. The Catholic princes of the West, blind as ever to political realities, tended to look on the Turkish conquests as divine retribution for those who had rejected the Christian

A janissary by Giovanni Bellini: the janissaries were a corps of highly trained troops from Christian families who formed an elite corps in the Sultan's army.

Opposite The siege of Constantinople by the Turks, showing Turkish boats being dragged across land behind the suburb of Pera: from the *Voyage d'outremer de Bertandon de la Bronuiere.*

69

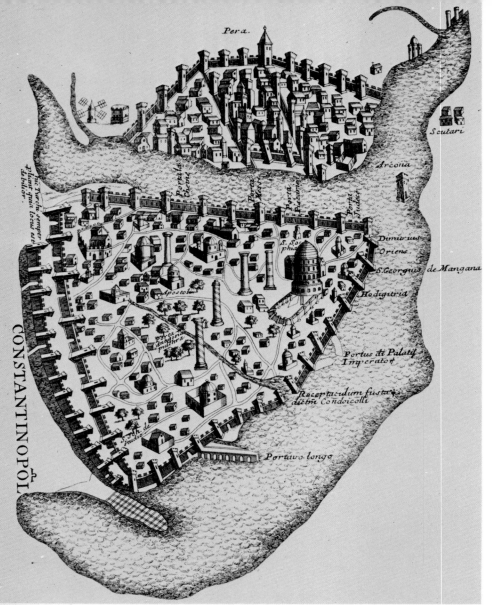

The city of Constantinople.

II had given proof of a character to be respected and feared. An intellectual who spoke six languages —including excellent Latin and Greek—he was by nature introverted and morose, almost pathologically secretive and possessed of a streak of cruelty that terrified his subordinates. From childhood Mehmet had hated all Christians, and as he grew older this hatred had been transformed into a single, burning idea: to capture Constantinople. Now that he was Emperor, he intended to lose no time in realizing that ambition.

When the Greek ambassadors came to congratulate him on his accession, however, the young Sultan affirmed his peaceable intentions and blandly promised to respect Byzantine territory. But within a matter of months he had summoned architects and masons from all over his dominions, and on April 15, 1452, the first stones were laid in the construction of a great castle on the European side of the Bosphorus, a few miles north of Constantinople, where the straits are at their narrowest. Neighboring churches and monasteries were razed to provide building materials, and just four and a half months later, on the last day of August, the fortress—now known as Rumeli Hisar—was completed. Constantine sent ambassadors to ask Mehmet his intentions, although he must have known them only too well. Mehmet's answer was clear: as each ambassador arrived, he was immediately beheaded.

And still Europe would not understand. The Pope was genuinely concerned, but could stir no enthusiasm for a relief expedition; the Western Empire was a broken reed. In November a Venetian ship that refused to stop when hailed from Rumeli Hisar was sunk by Turkish cannon, its crew was decapitated and its captain publicly impaled—but the Most Serene Republic, which was doing good business in Ottoman ports and had no wish to become involved in an expensive war, chose to ignore the incident. Genoa took a similar line. The whole district of Pera to the east of the Golden Horn was a Genoese colony whose best hope of preservation seemed to lie in coming to an agreement with the Turks rather than in taking up arms against them. France and England were still exhausted after the Hundred Years War, and England was further handicapped by a King, Henry VI, whose apparent saintliness was insufficient to conceal his undoubted imbecility. From all the other monarchies of Europe the response was equally unpromising. By March of 1453, when the immense Ottoman army—well over a hundred thousand strong—began to move from Adrianople toward the Bosphorus, it was clear that the city's survival was going to depend on its inhabitants alone.

The Emperor now ordered a hasty census of all able-bodied men—including monks—who were capable of bearing arms. The results were even worse than he had feared: after nine successive visitations of the Black Death in less than a century, Constantinople had lost some 40 per cent of its already dwindling population. There were, however, more than a thousand foreign residents of the city, including almost the entire Venetian community, who pledged

Truth. Was Constantinople worth a Mass? Its Emperor thought so; and in 1439, at Florence, the emissaries of John VIII Palaeologus accepted papal authority. In theory the Churches were now reunited, but in practice the schism survived. "Better the Sultan's turban than the Cardinal's hat," declared the Byzantine minister Lucas Notaras—and the majority of his compatriots agreed with him. When John died in 1448, he left his brother Constantine an embittered and divided city.

We know very little about this last and most tragic of all the Byzantine emperors. At the time of his accession he was forty-four. Although no reliable portraits have come down to us, he seems to have been tall and rather swarthy—a little unimaginative, perhaps, but straightforward and absolutely honest, an able administrator and, above all, a brave soldier. It was just as well. Before Constantine had been three years on the throne, the Turkish Sultan, Murad II, died of apoplexy at Adrianople. By the standards of his time, Murad had been a peaceable ruler, prepared to live on friendly terms with his Christian subjects. His successor was a young man of a very different stamp.

Though still only twenty-one, already Mehmet

their support—and these had recently been joined by a Genoese contingent led by a famous soldier of fortune, Giovanni Giustiniani Longo. Disgusted by the apathy of his government, Giustiniani raised a private army of seven hundred on his own. Constantine gave them an enthusiastic welcome, but even with foreign reinforcements he had less than seven thousand men to defend fourteen miles of walls.

Those walls were for the most part in excellent repair. The ramparts that ran along the Golden Horn needed little defending, since the harbor could be closed by stretching a chain across its mouth from Acropolis Point, the southern tip of the Horn, to the shores of Pera on the north. The Marmara walls, south of the city, rose straight out of the sea and were protected by treacherous shoals—making them equally inaccessible. The weight of the Turkish attack therefore was expected to come from the landward side. Here a great three-fold rampart ran for some four miles in an unbroken line across the neck of the peninsula on which the city stood, joining the imperial palace at Blachernae in the north with the Marmara walls at Studion in the south. It was, and still is, a magnificent fortification—and it had never been breached since its construction by the Emperor Theodosius, one thousand and six years before.

On Easter Monday, 1453, the advance guard of Mehmet's army was sighted by the Byzantine lookouts. At once the Emperor ordered all the gates to the city closed, the bridges across the moats destroyed and the boom laid across the Golden Horn. Within three days, the Turkish army was drawn up along the whole length of the land walls. At the center was the red and gold tent of the Sultan himself, surrounded by his picked corps of Janissaries. The defenders saw for the first time what they would have to face—and on the following day they felt it. Mehmet

prided himself on his cannon—a comparatively new weapon, which he planned to use on an unprecedented scale. Three had already been employed to considerable effect from Rumeli Hisar, but the Sultan had brought several others from Adrianople. These had been specially made for him by a renegade Hungarian engineer, and included one twenty-seven-foot-long monster, capable of hurling cannonballs weighing half a ton for a mile or more. But the walls held against the bombardment.

The walls of Constantinople.

Rumeli Hisar, which controls the Bosphorus. Built by Mehmet in 1452, this was the first sign that he intended to capture the city.

At sea, too, the long battle had begun. The Ottoman navy had sailed up through the Dardanelles and the Sea of Marmara, and now lay at the entrance to the Bosphorus, about a mile away from the mouth of the Horn. Mehmet's navy was not doing well. Repeated efforts to force the boom had been beaten back by an effective combination of arrows and "Greek fire," an incendiary invented by the Byzantines that burned on the surface of the water. And on April 20, three Genoese galleys and an imperial transport had actually managed to smash their way through the enemy and, under cover of darkness, had slipped into the harbor.

This reverse infuriated Mehmet. He immediately ordered the speeding-up of a plan he had formulated during the first days of the siege: the construction of a huge causeway up the valley that led from the Bosphorus shore, over the hill of Pera, behind the Genoese colony and down again to the waters of the Horn. On Saturday, April 22, Constantinople witnessed what was possibly the most extraordinary scene in all its history, as countless teams of oxen dragged some seventy ships on wheeled cradles over

a two-hundred foot ridge and then slowly lowered them down the other side into the harbor. The Greeks' amazement must have been darkened by despair—they could no longer rely on a safe anchorage for their fleet. Yet, more important, they now had another ten miles of wall to defend. The Genoese colony of Pera, whose benevolent neutrality had hitherto been an invaluable source of information on Turkish movements, was surrounded.

Another month went by, during which food supplies began to run short. The defenders struggled valiantly on, but the walls were beginning to crumble under the incessant pounding of the cannon, and Constantine was finding it increasingly difficult to maintain his subjects' morale. Then, on May 23, came a last, shattering blow to Christian hopes. During the preceding winters, the Venetians in the city had sent an urgent appeal to their republic, begging Venice to intervene on Constantine's behalf. At last in early May, they had secretly dispatched their fastest brigantine to look for the relief expedition. The ship had searched the Aegean, but found no trace of an Italian fleet. The crew, knowing that their return to Constantinople meant almost certain death, had nevertheless insisted on doing so. The Emperor wept as he thanked them. Only Christ, he murmured, could save the city now.

To many, however, it seemed that Christ too had deserted Constantinople. On May 24 the moon went into eclipse, and while the city's holiest icon was being carried in procession through the streets it suddenly slipped from its platform. Hardly had it been replaced when a hailstorm burst over the capital—a storm of such fury that the whole procession had to be abandoned. And the next day men awoke to find Constantinople shrouded in a dense fog—a phenomenon unheard of at the end of May.

Five months earlier, a service of reunion with Rome had been held in Hagia Sophia, and since that time the church had been avoided by the Orthodox faithful. But now, in this final hour of trial, doctrinal differences were forgotten. On the evening of May 28, when it was plain that Mehmet was preparing for his final assault on the land walls, the Emperor joined his people in the great church where, with Orthodox and Roman priests officiating side by side, the Christian liturgy was celebrated for the last time in Constantinople.

At half-past one in the morning the Sultan gave his order to attack. The sudden noise, bursting out of the stillness, was immediately answered by all the bells of the city, rallying every able-bodied defender to the walls. Though each man must have known that the cause was lost, all still fought magnificently; two successive Turkish charges, the first by the irregular *bashi-bazouks*, the next by a wave of fanatical Anatolians, were driven back—and a third, by Mehmet's own regiment of Janissaries, fought hand-to-hand for an hour or more without making any appreciable headway. Suddenly Giustiniani fell, mortally wounded. Seeing their leader carried from the walls, the Genoese soldiers panicked and fled, leaving the Greeks to face the enemy alone.

John VIII Palaeologus, the penultimate Byzantine Emperor: from the *Journey of the Magi* by Benozzo Gozzoli.

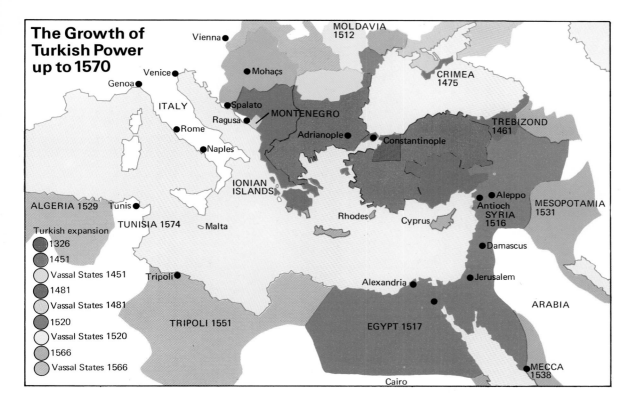

The Growth of Turkish Power up to 1570

MOLDAVIA 1512
Vienna
Venice
Genoa
Mohács
ITALY
Spalato
Ragusa
MONTENEGRO
Rome
Adrianople
Naples
Constantinople
CRIMEA 1475
TREBIZOND 1461
IONIAN ISLANDS
ALGERIA 1529
Tunis
Rhodes
Cyprus
Aleppo
Antioch
SYRIA 1516
MESOPOTAMIA 1531
TUNISIA 1574
Malta
Damascus
Tripoli
Alexandria
Jerusalem
ARABIA
TRIPOLI 1551
EGYPT 1517
MECCA 1538
Cairo

Turkish expansion
- 1326
- 1451
- Vassal States 1451
- 1481
- Vassal States 1481
- 1520
- Vassal States 1520
- 1566
- Vassal States 1566

Almost simultaneously came another, even greater catastrophe. At the northern end of the walls, where they joined the imperial palace, was a tiny postern gate, through which the defenders had been making occasional sorties to harry the Ottoman flank. By some mischance the gate had been left unbarred; the Turks fell upon it and burst through.

The Byzantine Empire was finished. The Emperor, seeing that all hope was gone, seized his sword and ran to where the fighting was thickest. He was never seen alive again. Much later, his body was identified among the piles of corpses. It had no head, but on its feet were purple buskins, embroidered with the imperial eagles of Byzantium.

As the victorious Turks streamed across the walls and through the streets, the massacre and carnage became appalling. Moslem tradition permitted three days of rapine and looting after the storming of a city, but the Sultan restricted his soldiers to one. He himself seems to have been strangely calm and subdued in the hours of his supreme triumph. Not till late afternoon did he enter Constantinople. He rode slowly to Hagia Sophia where, before the high altar, he touched his turban to the ground in thanksgiving.

Thus the Byzantine Empire gave place to the Ottoman. The news of its fall was received with horror among the peoples of the West, who suddenly felt profoundly guilty—as well they might. For it was Western Europe, with its Fourth Crusade, that had inflicted the first mortal wound upon the Eastern Empire; the Turks had merely administered the *coup de grâce*. Even at the end, the Christian princes, by firm and concerted action, might have delayed the inevitable; but they did not choose to do so. Instead, they argued and prevaricated—and while Europe dithered, Byzantium died. The Empire's life had been long, brilliant and glorious.

Taken as an isolated event, Constantinople's

fall was not a matter of as much direct political significance to Europe in general as was at one time believed. Many of the great developments for which the city has been wholly or partly credited—events that mark the end of the Middle Ages—were already under way. Explorers and navigators had long since begun seeking out and mapping new trade routes to the Indies. In Italy the Renaissance had run half its course, and Byzantine scholars there had been revealing the mysteries of Greek culture for fifty years and more. Nor can it be argued that Mehmet's victory opened up Europe to Turkish invasion, for the Turks had already gained a European foothold.

For the Greeks and Turks, however, the events of May 29, 1453, are still annually commemorated— by the former as their greatest tragedy, by the latter as their most shining triumph. And it is right and proper that they should, for on that day the histories of both peoples were radically changed. The Greeks entered upon nearly four centuries of subjugation, during which their Church provided their only national focus. The Turks saw the defeat of their archenemy as the confirmation of their European Empire.

After five centuries, the rest of us can afford to take a dispassionate view. We can applaud the way the new capital soared, phoenix-like, from the ashes of the old, and we can accept the events here related as just another proof that the dominions of this world, even that of God's vice-regent on earth, cannot last forever. But we too owe a debt to Byzantium— which preserved and cherished the Greek spirit for a thousand years while Western Europe was groping its way through the Dark Ages, and which somehow combined that spirit with a new religious awareness, to form a technique of expressing spiritual values in visual terms that is without parallel in Christian art. When Constantinople fell, the world was diminished.

JOHN JULIUS NORWICH

Sultan Mehmet II, conqueror of Constantinople, by Giovanni Bellini.

Burgundian power grew dramatically in the reign of Philip the Good. Philip's successful change of side in 1453 left him with complete freedom of action. He was not required to pay homage to Charles VII, and the King formally apologized for the murder of John the Fearless, Philip's father. Burgundian territory was expanded by the gift of four counties—Mâcon, Auxerre, Bar-sur-Seine and Ponthieu—and also several towns along the Somme River. Philip also laid claim successfully to the Duchy of Brabant, thus expanding his possessions in the Low Countries. He had already inherited Flanders and Artois, and now forced one of his cousins to surrender her lands in Holland, Zeeland, Hainault and Friesland.

Philip effectively consolidated Burgundy as a powerful "middle kingdom," between France and Germany. He achieved his design of centralizing the government of this collection of provinces by compelling the vigorous municipalities in each region to submit to his rule. He was strongly opposed by many of the towns and faced frequent rebellion in the Low Countries. Ghent, for example, opposed him for years, but he finally crushed its independence in 1453. He was much less successful in his attempts to dominate the King of France, and during his later years he quarreled with both Charles VII and his successor, Louis XI.

The Burgundian court during Philip's reign set new standards in ceremony and etiquette—much of which was later adopted by kings of France and England. In 1454

Philip the Good, Duke of Burgundy.

he and many of his courtiers swore to take part in a crusade. The promise was not kept, but the Feast of the Pheasant, at which it was made, came to be regarded as the ideal of a solemn feast.

England after the Hundred Years War

The defeat of the English army at Castillon and the death of the English commander John Talbot, Earl of Shrewsbury, in 1453 ended the fighting in the Hundred Years War. Little besides Calais remained to England from the inheritance of Eleanor of Aquitaine. The

Edward IV, by an unknown artist.

Continental conflict was finally settled, but fighting soon resumed—this time in England itself. Richard, Duke of York and heir apparent to the weakling Henry VI, raised a private army. In 1453, when Henry became temporarily insane, York was appointed protector and sent Edmund Beaufort, Duke of Somerset, who favored the Queen, to the Tower of London. Henry recovered, Margaret produced an heir and Somerset was released and restored to the royal council, but York was determined to fight for the throne.

The Wars of the Roses

York's supporters under the Earl of Warwick defeated those of Queen Margaret and Somerset at St. Albans in 1455 and captured the King. The Wars of the Roses—a long series of short campaigns between the houses of Lancaster and York (represented by red and white roses)—had begun. Lack of "governance" and the utter breakdown of feudal society had made civil war inevitable, and the numerous soldiers of fortune who were returning from France (where they had been accustomed to the spoils of warfare as much as

The execution of the Duke of Somerset after the Battle of Tewkesbury.

to the prowess of arms) took readily to the only profession that they knew. There was extensive civil disorder and the government's inability to rule effectively encouraged the French to attack the southern coastal town of Sandwich in 1457. Fundamentally, Richard of York stood for the restoration of law and order—and against the incapacity of the crown. He received more support from the Commons than did his opponents, but most of the population remained indifferent to the strife.

In 1459, with the Yorkist general, Warwick, out of the country—he was fighting in France—Queen Margaret suddenly seized Ludlow Castle, a Yorkist stronghold in the west of England. She secured the castle by bribing the garrison, and prominent Yorkists in the region were forced to flee to Ireland. However, it was one thing for the Queen to capture a castle and another for her to govern the country effectively. The population was increasingly sympathetic to the Yorkists.

In 1460, York openly claimed

the throne. An army under the Earl of Warwick landed in Kent, which rallied to the Yorkist cause. At Northampton the royal forces were routed and the King captured again. With the King in his hands, York withdrew his claim to the throne, and Parliament accepted him as Henry's heir. Meanwhile the Queen gathered an army in Wales, and at the Battle of Wakefield, York was killed. At the second Battle of St. Albans, the King was recaptured by his wife. The wheel seemed to have come a full circle.

York's son, Edward, Earl of March, then rallied the Yorkists at Mortimer's Cross, marched south to join the Earl of Warwick and took the capital. At the age of nineteen, March became King Edward IV. He defended his title at Towton in Yorkshire, and Henry and Margaret fled to Scotland. Relations between Edward and Warwick soon broke down because Warwick wanted to control policymaking, while the King preferred to be his own master. Edward was briefly captured by Warwick, but the

government makes civil war inevitable

Earl found that he was unable to govern, and was forced to release the King. The next months were anarchic.

Henry was able to make a return to nominal kingship in October, 1470, after Warwick (who came to be known as "the Kingmaker") had shifted his support to the Lancastrian camp. His restoration was shortlived. On Easter Day, 1471, Edward IV won a decisive victory in the mist at Barnet—and with the subsequent defeat of Margaret's Welsh army at Tewkesbury and the brutal murder of Henry VI, Edward was at last secure on the throne.

The Teutonic Knights and Poland

As a result of the Battle of Tannenberg the power of the Teutonic Knights waned seriously during the first half of the fifteenth century. During the Council of Constance, attempts were even made to suppress the Order. Some of its members were accused of being infected with Hussite ideas, although the real reason was jealousy of its power, just as it had been when the Templars were accused of witchcraft a century before. The Order was also seriously affected by an outbreak of plague in 1427 in which many of the Knights and tens of thousands of their subjects were killed.

Meanwhile the Poles looked on. During the reign of Ladislas III they were unable to take advantage of any opportunity, and after his death there was an interregnum (1444–47), because it was not certain whether he had been killed at the Battle of Varna. Only after the election of Casimir IV of Lithuania was it possible to deal effectively with the Knights. Casimir's opportunity came in 1454, when there was a rebellion against the high taxation imposed by the Order. The rebels—aided by Casimir—were militarily successful, and were able to lay siege to Marienburg, although much of the countryside remained loyal to the Knights. The rebellion was mainly an urban one—Thorn, Danzig and Königsberg were among the towns that rose. Polish support for the rebels, formerly secret, was now open, and Casimir declared all Prussia to be part of Poland and invaded it.

The Teutonic Knights could find no allies to assist them, but the Grand Master, Louis d'Erlichshausen, was able to hire a mercenary force of 8,000 men, which defeated the levy of the Polish gentry at Chojnice. But the price of the Knights' victory was little less than that of defeat. In order to pay the mercenaries, the Knights had to give them much of Prussia, including Marienburg, and the capital of the Order was moved to Königsberg. Casimir bought much of the Knights' former territory including Marienburg from the new owners. The war continued, and in 1466 the capture by the Poles of Chojnice made it clear to the Knights that continued warfare would lead to the Order's complete defeat. They agreed to make peace, and by the Treaty of Thorn, signed in the same year, were allowed to retain parts of East Prussia, but had to pay tribute for it and to allow Poles to join the Order. Danzig became a free city, but Casimir obtained most of the rest of the lands of the Teutonic Knights in Germany. The weakness of the position of the Order encouraged others to attack it. They held land in Sicily, but the papacy and Aragon joined together to deprive them of it.

For the rest of his long reign—it lasted until 1492—Casimir concentrated more on internal matters than on war. He seems to have tried to avoid war with Russia, and he preferred to try to extend his influence through a policy of dynastic marriage. Despite the difficulties that were to engulf Poland after Casimir's death, his reign was a golden age for Poland.

India

The invasion of India by Timur destroyed the power and prestige of the Sultanate of Delhi. The last of the Tughluk dynasty, Mahmud II (1393–1413), returned to his shattered capital, but was unable to recover much of his territory. After his death the notables of the city attempted to set up one of their number as Sultan, but in 1414 the Punjabi ruler, Khize Khan, conquered the city in Timur's name, and established a new dynasty, the Sayyid. The power of this Mongol dynasty was, however, confined to the city and its immediate surroundings.

In 1451, Alam Shah, the last of the Sayyids, was deposed, or rather forced to abdicate "cheerfully" by Bahlul Lodi, one of the Afghan rulers who were attacking northern India at this time. The Lodi managed to establish their rule for the next seventy-five years, but they found Delhi difficult to defend and moved their capital to Agra, 120 miles southeast. The move symbolized the almost total collapse of Delhi's power. The Lodi sultans, although nominal overlords of all the Afghan invaders, were unable to exercise effective rule.

In the southern part of India the regions still Hindu were falling gradually under the sway of a new empire, that of Vijayanagar, which emerged in the middle of the fourteenth century. It claimed sovereignty over much of the south, although it was often unable to realize its claims. It did, however, prevent further penetration by the Moslem rulers of the Deccan.

The unity of the Bahmanni Kingdom of the Deccan, which had successfully revolted against Mohammad II in 1347, was destroyed in the fifteenth century. The danger of collapse was foreseen by the rulers, who, in 1432, moved their capital from Kulburga, within striking distance of the border with Vijayanagar, to Bidar, farther north, where it was hoped that the ruler's presence would prevent rebellion. Rulers such as Humayan (1457–61) did nothing to enhance the prestige of the dynasty. He was deposed by his subjects because of his cruelty, and his brother Hassan was put on the throne. But Humayan had his brother blinded, seized the throne again and embarked on a second lap of his bloodthirsty rule. He was eventually assassinated by his own slaves. The early part of the reign of Mohammad (1463–1515) seemed to promise a better future, but this was largely due to an able minister, Mohammad Gowan. After Gowan's execution for treason, Mohammad showed his complete inability to rule. Rebellions broke out, and his kingdom broke up into five independent states in around 1490. Even the tiny kingdom that was left to Mohammad was effectively ruled by a slave. The weakness of the five kingdoms of the Deccan helped to preserve Hindu civilization in the south and also probably facilitated the rise of the Mogul dynasty in the north.

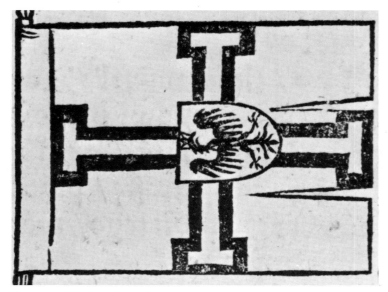

The banner of the Teutonic grand masters.

The tomb of the Afghan conqueror, Bahlul Lodi.

Incipit epla sci Jeronimi pbri ad paulinū presbiterū de omnibus diuine historie libris. Capitulum primū :

Frater ambrosius tua michi munuscula perferens detulit simul et suauissimas litteras: que a principio amiciciarum fide probate iam fidei et veteris amicicie preferebant. Vera enim illa necessitudo est et xpi glutino copulata: quam non utilitas rei familiaris non presentia tantum corporum non subdola et palpans adulatio: sed dei timor et diuinarum scripturarum studia conciliant. Legimus in veteribus historijs quosdam lustrasse prouincias nouos adijsse populos maria transisse: ut eos quos ex libris nouerant coram quoque viderent. Sic pitagoras memphiticos vates sic plato egiptum et architam tarentinum eamque oram ytalie que quondam magna grecia dicebatur laboriosissime peragrauit: et ut qui athenis mgr erat et potens cuiusque doctrinas achademie gignasia personabant fieret peregrinus atque discipulus: malens aliena verecunde discere quam sua impudenter ingerere. Denique cum litteras quasi toto orbe fugientes persequitur captus a piratis et venundatus tyranno crudelissimo paruit ductus captiuus vinctus et seruus: tamen quia philosophus maior emente se fuit ad tytumliuium lacteo eloquentie fonte manantem de ultimis hispanie galliarumque finibus quosdam venisse nobiles legimus: et quos ad contemplationem sui roma non traxerat unius hominis fama perduxit. Habuit illa etas inauditum omnibus seculis celebrandumque miraculum: ut urbem tantam

ingressi : aliud extra urbem quererent. Apollonius siue ille magus ut vulgus loquitur siue phus ut pitagorici tradunt intrauit persas ptransiuit caucasum albanos scithas massagetas opulentissima indie regna penetrauit : et ad extremum latissimo phison amne transmisso peruenit ad bragmanas : ut hyarcam in throno sedentem aureo et de tantali fonte potantem inter paucos discipulos de natura de moribus ac de cursu dierum et siderum audiret docentem. Inde per elamitas babilonios chaldeos medos assirios parthos syros phenices arabes palestinos reuersus ad alexandriam perrexit ad ethiopiam: ut gignosophistas et famosissimam solis mensam videret in sabulo. Inuenit ille vir ubique quod disceret: et semper proficiens semper se melior fieret. Scripsit super hoc plenissime octo voluminibus phylostratus.

Quid loquar de seculi hominibus: cum apostolus paulus vas electionis et magister gentium qui de consciencia tanti in se hospitis loquebatur dicens. An experimentum queritis eius qui in me loquitur cristus post damascum arabiamque lustratam ascenderit ierosolimam ut videret petrum et manserit apud eum diebus quindeci. Hoc enim misterio ebdomadis et ogdoadis: futurus gentium predicator instruendus erat. Rursumque post annos quatuordecim assumpto barnaba et tyto exposuit cum apostolis euangelium: ne forte in vacuum curreret aut cucurrisset. Habet nescio quid latentis energie viue vocis actus: et in aures discipuli de auctoris ore transfusa fortius sonat. Unde et eschines cum rodi exularet et legeret illa demostenis

Gutenberg's "Right Worthy Art"

Printing in the Western World was first embodied in the magnificent Bible produced by Johann Gutenberg of Mainz. Its invention was a remarkable achievement. It was made possible by a synthesis of several skills—the metallurgist's craft for casting the type, the adaptation of the screw press to printing, the production of paper suitable for use in the press and the making of an appropriate ink. By putting all these elements together in the making of his masterpiece, Gutenberg also made the written word available to men of all walks of life.

On August 24, 1456, Heinrich Cremer, Vicar of St. Stephans-Stift in Mainz, noted that he had completed the binding and the rubrication (writing lines in red) of a large bible in two volumes. It was not unusual for a scribe to record the thankful completion of a long task in this way, but this Bible was not an ordinary manuscript; it has been estimated that there were as many as one hundred and sixty other copies in existence at that time. The copies that survive are the most treasured possessions of the world's greatest libraries, for this is the "forty-two-line Bible," the world's first book printed from single type.

The forty-two-line Bible consists of nearly thirteen hundred pages, each about sixteen by eleven inches. The text, as was usual in large volumes, appears in two columns in the narrow "black letter" gothic type that followed the form of the writing used for important, formal work all over northern Europe at that time. In most of the copies, each of these columns contains forty-two lines of type, which gives it its name and helps to distinguish it from the many other printed bibles that were to appear during the next few years, for many of them, like this one, give no indication when the book was printed or by whom. It is a beautiful book. Page after page of crisp well-cut type is impressed on thick paper, and some copies, perhaps as many as thirty of the original one hundred and sixty, are brilliantly printed on vellum, the prepared calf-skin that was used for the finest books. By any standard, whether that of the scribes who had produced books until this date, or that of the printers who were to follow, the forty-two-line Bible is one of the most magnificent books ever made.

From this we can infer something of the skill and labor that went into it. Setting the type and printing the sheets must have begun in or soon after 1450 for the bible to have been completed in time for Heinrich Cremer to do his work of rubrication and binding. This gives us an approximate date of 1455. But who did the printing? What exactly was the "invention of printing," and why did it happen when and where it did? These are questions that have been discussed for centuries, and the arguments used have sometimes shown more ill-natured chauvinism than dispassionate examination of the evidence. The more that evidence is sifted, the more it looks as if we can still place some trust in those who set down the facts they knew when the invention of printing was still within living memory.

The fullest and most debated of these statements is by Johann Koelhoff, a printer of Cologne. In his *Chronicle* (or universal history) of 1499, he singles out the year 1440 as worthy of special mention. Under the heading "Of printing, and by whom this useful art was invented," he writes:

. . . This right worthy art was invented first of all in Germany at Mainz, on the Rhine. And that is a great honor to the German nation that such ingenious men are found there. This happened in the year of Our Lord 1440, and from that time until 1450 the art and all that pertains to it was investigated, and in 1450, which was a Golden Year, men began to print, and the first book printed was the Bible in Latin, and this was printed with a letter as large as that now used in missals.

Although this art was invented at Mainz, as far as regards the manner in which it is now commonly used, yet the first prefiguration was invented in Holland from the Donatuses which were printed there before that time. And from and out of these the aforesaid art took its beginning, and was invented in a manner much more masterly and subtler than this, and the longer it lasted the more full of art it became.

A certain Omnibonus wrote in the preface to a Quintilian, and also in other books, that a Walloon from France, called Nicolas Jenson, was the first inventor of this masterly art. But the first inventor of printing was a burgher at Mainz, and was born at Strasbourg, and called Junker Johann Gutenberg.

What Koelhoff meant by the "prefiguration" of printing in Holland has been the cause of much of

A printing press from the title-page of an early sixteenth-century printed book.

Opposite The first page of the forty-two-line Bible. The illumination was added by hand.

the argument over the invention of printing, but it is hardly disputed that Johann Gutenberg, citizen of Mainz, deserves the credit for developing a process that required a mastery of several kinds of technology to the point where it could challenge the most lucrative and ambitious products of the medieval scribe.

Gutenberg can best be understood not so much in relation to the brilliant minds of the Renaissance, whose intellectual curiosity led them to try to understand the world about them, such as Leonardo da Vinci, but to the great practical engineers of the nineteenth century, men like Isambard Kingdom Brunel and Henry Bessemer, to whom were due the cheap rapid travel and the cheap reliable steel that laid the foundations for modern society. But even Gutenberg could hardly have foreseen the part his invention would play in changing the medieval world.

Johann Gutenberg was born into the family of Gensfleisch, one of the patrician families of Mainz, somewhere between 1394 and 1399. During the struggles for power between the leading families of Mainz, Gutenberg moved to Strasbourg, 140 miles up the Rhine. The records of a lawsuit brought against him in 1439 show that his life had already taken on a pattern that is familiar enough in the biography of inventors. The action was brought by the heirs of Andreas Dritzehn, an official of Strasbourg, with whom Gutenberg had been in partnership until Dritzehn's death in 1438. The proceedings talk at length, but with tantalizing imprecision, about the work for which the partnership was responsible, yet a few facts emerge.

Gutenberg had supplied the practical technical ability in an enterprise that had been at first concerned with the polishing of stones and later with the making of hand-mirrors for sale to pilgrims on their way to Aachen. Gutenberg's family connections were no doubt responsible for his training in this field, for several relations, including his father, were connected with the archiepiscopal mint at Mainz, an imperial city which was a major center for workers in metals of all kinds.

The immediate cause of the lawsuit was an error over the date of the pilgrimage to Aachen, which led Dritzehn to draw up a new contract stipulating that Gutenberg should instruct him in other secret techniques on which he was working. The lawsuit was brought when Gutenberg declined to share the secret with Dritzehn's heirs.

It is far from clear whether the secret was in any way related to the experimental work on which Gutenberg must long have been engaged for the forty-two-line Bible to appear with such technical perfection in 1455. A heavy investment by Dritzehn was at stake, and the work involved the purchase of lead and other metals. A "press" had been constructed by one Conrad Sahspach, and Hans Dünne, a goldsmith, testified that three years previously (in 1436) Gutenberg had paid him 100 florins "solely on account of material belonging to printing." The argument turns on words like "printing" and "press" which were in common use in many trades, and which were only later to acquire special significance.

In the aftermath of the lawsuit, Gutenberg may have left Strasbourg, and his movements are uncertain until 1448, when there is a record of a loan contracted by him in Mainz. Shortly after this, Gutenberg contracted a further partnership. This time there is little room for doubt that the purpose was the development of printing from movable type.

In about midsummer of 1450, Gutenberg negotiated the first of several large loans from Johann Fust, a lawyer and citizen of Mainz. When the partnership was dissolved in 1455, Fust's own deposition referred to recurrent advances of money for the purchase of parchment, paper and ink. Fust then declined to advance further money without being taken into partnership in "the work of the books." The terms allowed Fust to sue for the repayment of the loan, and, in default, to seize the equipment and stock. That he chose to do this on November 6, 1455, has been seen as an unscrupulous means of depriving Gutenberg of the rewards of his ingenuity, for, whether or not it is the work specifically referred to in the document, the forty-two-line Bible must have been virtually complete at precisely this time.

At this point, it will be as well to enquire what Gutenberg's "invention" consisted of. Invention is not quite the right word, for it was essentially a work of synthesis, in which several different skills were allied in one new process.

Printing began in China. *The Diamond Sutra*, the oldest extant printed book, dates from 868, and between the tenth and the fourteenth centuries all the major Chinese classics appeared in print. Chinese printing was a logical development of the custom of incising prayers on stone tablets, from which pilgrims could take rubbings that reproduced the wording and the calligraphic quality of the text with perfect fidelity. The text was written in reverse on a block of wood and the unwanted surface cut away so that an impression could be taken by hand from the inked surface on a sheet of paper. The development of the process by making each character separately offered no great advantages in Chinese with its huge vocabulary, and there is no apparent connection between the use of cast copper types in Korea in the fourteenth century and Western printing.

The use of paper, however, which was in common use in China by the third century AD, can clearly be traced across the great silk route. By the ninth century it was being made in Samarkand, and Damascus became the center of supply for Europe. Mills were set up in Europe in the twelfth century, first in Moorish Spain, and then in France. In 1390 the first German paper mill was working in Nuremberg. But European paper was changed to suit a different manner of writing. While the soft Chinese paper was ideally suited to writing with a brush, the Latin scripts were made with a sharply-

cut pen on smooth, hard vellum. Adding animal size, made from bones, to the pulp gave Western paper a relatively hard, impervious surface. It was necessary to soften the size by dampening the paper before an impression could be taken.

The next requirement was ink that would work with metal type. "Oil paints," made by adding pigment to a varnish produced by boiling linseed or walnut oil, had been in use sporadically since the early Middle Ages. Their use as a medium for painters dates from the brilliant colors used by the Flemish painter, Jan van Eyck, at the beginning of the fifteenth century. Printers' ink, as it was made for centuries, was varnish to which lamp black had been added.

The screw press had also existed for centuries. It was certainly used by the Romans for extracting oil from olives and for pressing the juice from grapes and it is possible that its use was continuous in the German vineyards from the days of the Roman Empire. It was certainly used in early paper mills for squeezing excess water from the sheets. An

An early sixteenth-century woodcut of the printer at work.

Opposite above Fifteenth-century printer's type — letters cast in relief on the end of rectangular metal bodies. The essence of Gutenberg's invention lay in the casting of type.

Opposite below A reconstruction of Gutenberg's workshop in Mainz.

Right The first example of two-color printing. The initial was produced from a metal block made in two parts which were inked separately and printed together.

Gutenberg holding his forty-two-line Bible. By 1522 there was a printed bible in every European language.

uncle of Gutenberg's had connections with a nearby paper mill.

The printing press, as it was known for centuries in Europe, was essentially the paper or wine press with a steeper pitch to the screw (to make for quicker working) and a folding frame—the tympan—for holding the paper in the correct position in relation to the type, which was set in pages on a flat stone drawn under the press on runners by means of a windlass. Apart from the screw, there was nothing about it that could not be made quickly and cheaply by a carpenter and a blacksmith.

The making of type called for skills of quite a different order, and this process must be considered the essence of Gutenberg's invention. Printer's type consists of a letter cast in relief on the end of a rectangular metal body. The matrix from which each letter is cast is made by striking a steel punch into a block of copper. None of this would have been outside the experience of a medieval goldsmith, but the casting of type called for the making of thousands of parts quickly, cheaply, and with an accuracy that would permit their assembly in a solid page. Something like the traditional typefounders' mold must have been available to cast the types of the forty-two-line Bible: two L-shaped pieces, sliding together, which adapt themselves readily to the different widths of the matrixes for i and o and m.

One last refinement lay in the choice of alloy in which to cast the type. A mixture of tin and lead with bismuth or antimony gives an alloy that flows freely at relatively low temperatures, gives a crisp face to the type and neither shrinks nor expands as it comes from the mold. Whether or not Gutenberg had discovered the exact formula by which later types were made, no city was so well provided as Mainz with the practical knowledge of metallurgy that made possible the accurate casting of type. So soundly was every aspect of Gutenberg's invention based that it is only in the last decade with the development of litho and gravure printing that a new technology has brought major changes to an industry that has consisted of the nineteenth-century mechanization of the fifteenth-century process.

Wood blocks cut in the Chinese manner were used before Gutenberg's invention, but only for pictures with a line or two of text. The few surviving European examples of complete books printed from wood blocks are thought to date from long after the introduction of movable type. The small number of characters in the Latin alphabet gave a decisive advantage to the West in mechanizing the making of books. The early types were encumbered with characters that reproduced the many combined letters of the medieval scribe, and a few of these, like fi, survive today; but a complete set or font of characters could be laid out in a single tray that brought each letter within one man's reach. In the Western system, corrections could be

An illustration from the 1483 Nuremberg Bible—an example of how early printing copied the style of manuscripts.

made rapidly to single words and lines, and the setting of many pages together could increase the output of a press that was already more rapid than the Chinese method of printing.

Contemporary reaction to the introduction of printing seems to have been gratitude for a means that made books more accessible rather than a recognition of the profound changes that printing might bring. There was already a highly organized book trade, with booksellers combining the role that was later divided between the publisher, who commissions books, and the retailer, who sells them. At one end of the scale were booksellers, like Vespasiano da Bisticci, dealing in the elaborately illuminated manuscripts that printers showed less and less inclination to compete with in the later fifteenth century. At the other end were the great *scriptoria* (or writing houses) that supplied the quantities of law books that were required by a university such as Bologna. The printed book fitted easily into this system, but so well organized was the production of manuscripts that there is evidence that for a time printed and manuscript editions were available on competitive terms, and there are examples of manuscript books copied word for word from printed ones—even to the name of the printer.

Eventually, the economics of quantity production began to tell on the side of the printers. Johannes Andreae, Bishop of Aleria, in the preface to the *Letters* of St. Jerome, which Conrad Sweynheym and Arnold Pannartz printed in Rome in 1468, remarked that the most desirable books could now be bought for what the blank paper and unused vellum had once cost.

The cost of paper dropped steadily during the late fifteenth and early sixteenth centuries. Another economy was effected by reducing the size of books, and this in turn was made possible by the improved technology of type casting. As books ceased to be the expensive, static possessions of institutional libraries, smaller formats were devised to suit buyers who wanted to carry books about with them. The size of the pocket edition of the classics for which Aldus Manutius of Venice was famous is close to the format internationally used today for paperbacks.

Printing spread throughout Europe with astonishing rapidity, to commercial centers rather than intellectual ones. It survived a series of crises that resulted from overproduction during the 1470s, and recovered strongly during the last years of the century. About forty thousand separate items—books and broadsides—were printed during the fifteenth century. If we estimate the number of each item at a conservative two hundred and fifty copies, that is a total of ten million pieces.

There is little evidence that printing changed the kind of book that was available at first. The religious books and grammars and legal works that the early printers produced were those for which a steady sale was guaranteed. But the sheer quantity of output began to have its effect. While the international community of Humanist scholars provided a market for the editions of the Latin classics, the cheapening of books created a wholly new readership of books in the vernacular, and by 1522 there was a printed bible in every European language.

Only belatedly was it realized that printing, with its ability to multiply copies of a text at an unprecedented rate, was a threat to religious and political orthodoxy. By that time, it was too late to bring it under more than partial control. In all subsequent centuries, there have been cities such as Lyons and Geneva, Venice and Frankfurt, Amsterdam and London, rich and independent enough to ensure the survival of the freedom that was implicit in the process that produced the forty-two-line Bible of Johann Gutenberg. JAMES MOSLEY

Nicholas v's successor, the Spanish Cardinal Alfonso de Borgia, had no sympathy for his predecessor's ideas. He was not a Humanist, and did not believe that the papacy should patronize the arts. Profoundly affected by the fall of Constantinople, he directed all his efforts toward persuading the kings of Europe that the Turks constituted a serious threat to Western Europe, and that only by uniting in a crusade could they avert the threat. His appeals met with little success. Uninterested in the complexities of Italian politics—except for the nepotistic advancement of his family that characterized all the popes of the fifteenth century—Calixtus III was in part responsible for the Sicilian succession dispute that broke out after the death of Alfonso v in 1458.

Pope Pius II

Like his two immediate predecessors, Pius II owed his rise in the Church to his diplomatic successes during the conciliar epoch. Aeneas Sylvius Piccolomini was born near Siena in 1405. His family, although noble, was poor. He was educated in Siena and Florence, and for a long time put off the decision whether to take Holy Orders. Although his interests were chiefly literary, his career was that of a diplomat. He was secretary to Domenico Capranica, whom Martin v had appointed as a cardinal. Eugenius IV tried to demote him, so Capranica appealed to the Council of Basel. Aeneas persuaded the Council to withdraw the demotion, but Capranica could not afford to pay his secretary as the Pope still refused to accept him. Aeneas went instead to become secretary to Cardinal Niccolò Albergati (c. 1380–1443), who was sent by Eugenius to attempt to arrange peace between France and England in 1435. Although the mission ended in failure, it enabled Pius to travel in northern Europe. After the mission's failure he did not return to Rome but to Basel, where he acted as secretary to several of the leading figures at the Council and sometimes acted as secretary to the Council itself. When Amadeus of Savoy was elected Pope, Aeneas became his secretary. He was at this period an ardent conciliarist and in 1440

The Madonna appears to Pope Calixtus III.

wrote a treatise on conciliar authority.

But his real interests during these years remained poetic, and his love story *Euryalus and Lucretia* —an unexpected work to come from the pen of a future pope— was a great deal more popular than his conciliar tract. His poetic interest led to his coronation as Poet Laureate by Frederick III in 1442, and he also became Frederick's secretary. Frederick sent him as ambassador to Eugenius, and when he reached Rome he changed sides and became an opponent of the Council. After his mission was completed he returned to Germany, where he persuaded Frederick to support Eugenius against the Council.

Because of his change of sides Pius was rapidly promoted. He gave up poetry and took Holy Orders. Nicholas v made him Bishop of Trieste in 1447, and of Siena in 1450. He went on several diplomatic missions, including one to Bohemia, and after the fall of

Constantinople was prominent for his support for a crusade. As a result he was made a cardinal by Calixtus in 1456.

Aeneas was elected Pope in 1458, despite the energetic opposition of the archbishops of Rouen and Bologna. Pius was as enthusiastic about the idea of a crusade as was his predecessor. He summoned a congress at Mantua in 1459 in an attempt to persuade the princes of Europe of the need for concerted action, but all that the congress showed was that the princes were more interested in their own affairs than in the idea of Christendom. Undaunted, Pius pushed ahead with his plans and decided to organize a crusade without their help.

Unlike Calixtus, Pius was able to see the importance of other matters. He persuaded Louis XI to withdraw the Pragmatic Sanction of Bourges, a great moral victory for the papacy—although it did not succeed in crushing Gallicanism. Pius' bull *Execrabilis*

(1460), which attacked appeals from papal decisions to a council, shows how far he had moved from the conciliarism of his youth. In a bull of 1463, Pius wrote "Reject Aeneas, accept Pius," a reference to his disapproval of the views he had formerly held.

But Pius did not abandon his Humanist ideas or his belief that the Church needed reform. One of his first acts was to appoint the German Humanist, Cardinal Nicholas of Cusa, to reform the government of the Holy See. But it soon became apparent that opposition within the Curia would make any substantial reform impossible, and Pius—unable to fall back on the conciliarism that he had deserted—was forced to abandon his reformist plans. In his choice of cardinals, Pius favored Humanists of undistinguished family background over members of great families. Pius commissioned many works of art, including jewelry, and also spent substantial sums on improvements to St. Peter's and to the Vatican Palace. He could not afford the extravagance of Nicholas v as this would have clashed with his desire for a crusade. His greatest monument was built after his death; this is the Piccolomini Library in the Siena Cathedral, where the brilliant frescoes by Pinturicchio (c. 1450–1513) portray incidents from his life. The village of Corsignano (Pienza), Pius' birthplace was adorned by him with a cathedral and many secular buildings. Pius' last years were dominated by his crusade. He gathered an army at Ancona, hoping to lead it over the Adriatic to Ragusa, but the transport promised by the Venetians never arrived, and the army faded away. Pius died at Ancona, still dreaming of his crusade. Despite the failure of his main ambition, Pius increased the authority of the papacy, and his obvious desire for reform gave the Church a breathing space. His successors did not take advantage of Pius' legacy.

Sicily and Naples

The interest of the Aragonese Prince Alfonso v in Naples and Sicily, which he much preferred to his native Spain, resulted in his devoting the bulk of his attention to Italy. From the capture of

Spanish master

Alfonso the Magnanimous, King of Naples and Sicily.

Naples in 1442, he showed that he was also interested in the welfare of his Italian subjects, an interest that earned him the nickname "the Magnanimous." During his later years he lived in Italy the whole time, and took on many of the characteristics of an Italian Renaissance prince. He became a patron of the arts and took a full part in the complex diplomacy of the time. He proved himself so successful as a diplomat that Filippo Maria Visconti, Duke of Milan, bequeathed him the bulk of his possessions—although Alfonso foresaw enormous difficulties if he tried to claim his

inheritance, and took no interest in Milan. Later Spanish rulers were to be less moderate in their Italian ambitions.

Alfonso took advantage of the summons of Calixtus III to a crusade to gather together a fleet— paid for out of Church tithes— which he used to destroy the Genoese hold on the island of Sardinia. By 1458, when Alfonso died, Aragon was the dominant power in the Italian peninsula. He had seen that by balancing the power of the different Italian states against each other, he could increase his own influence at little cost. Alfonso followed the normal Aragonese practice of dividing his territory among his family: Aragon and Sicily went to his younger brother John, while Naples was left to the capricious Ferrante (Ferdinand), Alfonso's bastard son. Ferrante was almost immediately threatened by a rebellion inspired by John of Anjou, but the Angevin was beaten by 1462. The papacy, however, continued to support the Angevins and refused to recognize Ferrante. Under Paul II (1464–71), successor to Pius II, relations between Naples and the papacy broke down completely, and there was fighting in 1469. In 1478 Ferrante invaded Florence. It

Lorenzo de' Medici returns to Florence, by Botticelli.

soon became clear that the Florentine army would be beaten, and Lorenzo de' Medici went to Naples and put himself at the King's mercy, despite Ferrante's reputation for cruelty. For once the King's actions belied his reputation. He made peace with Lorenzo and allowed him to return to Florence, an event triumphantly recorded by Botticelli.

In 1481 Ferrante had to defend himself against a Turkish fleet which captured Otranto. Even the shock of Turkish invasion could not keep Italy at peace for long. Within six months, Venice and the papacy were at war with Naples, Florence and Milan, and it was five years before peace was concluded.

Ferrante and his son, Alfonso of Calabria, an effective general but as cruel as his father, were glad of the peace when it came, as it brought a baronial insurrection to an end. Ferrante promised a general amnesty to the rebels, and to seal the bargain arranged a marriage between his great-niece and the son of one of the rebel leaders, the Count of Sarno. At a huge feast to celebrate the marriage, Ferrante seized Sarno and most of the other prominent rebels and had them murdered— although food was sent to the dungeons daily to make it look as though they were still alive. For the last few years of Ferrante's reign, Alfonso was the effective ruler of the kingdom. He lacked his father's ability, however, and his maneuvers helped to bring about the French invasion of 1494.

Spain

The death of Alfonso the Magnanimous left Aragon in the hands of his younger brother John, who had in any case been governing the country because of Alfonso's absence in Italy. John attempted to extend Aragonese authority within Spain. He was King of Navarre, but had great difficulty in holding the kingdom against his eldest son, Charles. Catalonia rebelled in 1461 and attempted to set up an independent republic. In order to put down the revolt John needed the help of French troops, and had to offer Louis XI the County of Roussillon and Cerdagne to get it. This pledge was later to be a source of trouble between France and Spain.

Portugal

Despite the expansion of its overseas interests, Portugal was beset by internal difficulties during the fifteenth century. The nobility were able to press successfully for increased power and privilege. During the minority of Afonso V (1438–47), the leader of the aristocratic party, the Duke of Braganza, was able to secure the dismissal of Pedro, Duke of Coimbra from the regency: Pedro of Coimbra, who favored an increase in royal power, decided to fight to retain his position, but was killed in battle in 1449. The King was forced to give enormous grants to the nobility, and within a few years the Duchy of Braganza alone controlled nearly one third of the land of the kingdom.

But an even more serious threat was posed by Spain. Afonso married the daughter of Henry IV of Castile and claimed the crown, but Henry's half-sister, Isabella, also laid claim to the throne, and she could rely on her husband, Ferdinand, for support.

John II, King of Aragon and Navarre.

Ferdinand Marries Isabella

The marriage of the heirs to two minor, hopelessly disorganized and insolvent principalities in Spain resulted in the transformation of the world. From this dynastic conjugation came the unification of Spain, the expulsion of the Jews—followed shortly by the Moors—the Spanish Inquisition, the discovery of the New World, centuries of enmity with England and the beginning of the long Hapsburg hegemony over much of Europe.

On October 19, 1469, in the city of Valladolid, Isabella, heir to the throne of Castile, married Ferdinand, King of Sicily and heir to the throne of Aragon. The couple, and those who had engineered the marriage, hoped it would help solve certain personal, political and social problems, but no one foresaw—or could have foreseen—its consequences to the history of Spain or to the world.

Ferdinand was the seventeen-year-old heir apparent to a kingdom that was essentially a federation of three autonomous states, Catalonia, Valencia and Aragon, each with its own parliament, constitutional structure, law and economy. The powerful Louis XI of France, coveting Catalonia for its extensive commercial Mediterranean empire, had laid a claim based on the fact that the kings of Aragon were no longer of the ancient lineage of the counts of Barcelona. John II, Ferdinand's father, was the reigning monarch of the three states only because he had been accepted by their three parliaments, as his father, the Castilian Prince Ferdinand, had been before him. To Catalonia John was an inefficient as well as a foreign prince, and the region was in open revolt. The revolt could be crushed, but in the longer term Ferdinand's best hope for inheriting the whole of his father's kingdom, and for keeping Catalonia out of French hands, was to acquire the resources of Castile through marriage with Isabella. Therefore, when Isabella's envoys arrived in Aragon with the news that Ferdinand's suit had been preferred to others, Ferdinand and his father were overwhelmed with joy.

So was John's second wife, Joan Enriquez, the daughter of the Lord High Admiral of Castile, but of royal blood only through illegitimate connections (John's first wife had been Queen of Navarre in her own right). Joan was popularly credited with the murder of her stepson, Charles, Prince of Viana, and heir to the thrones of Aragon and Navarre. She certainly had a hand in the events preceding his death, and for years had plotted on behalf of her own son, Ferdinand, now heir to Aragon. This marriage could make him King of Castile as well.

There was in the court of Aragon a group of

Humanists headed by the Chancellor, Cardinal John Margarit i Pau, who advocated, for the good of the common people of Spain, the restoration to the Iberian Peninsula of the political unity "Hispania," which had existed under the later Visigothic kings. The ideal had its adherents, but not among the men with the power to effect it—the sovereigns and feudal lords of the four Christian kingdoms of the peninsula, Castile, Aragon, Navarre and Portugal, who were more interested in the retention of their local lordships and the aggrandizement of their personal wealth than in the common good. The history of the Reconquista, the struggle to recover the peninsula from Islam, had been one in which brief moments of united action by kings and nobles had been followed by long periods of war among these same kings and nobles. By the middle of the thirteenth century, sustained joint action by the four kingdoms (or even by Castile on its own but with king, dukes and lords united) could have led quickly to reunification, yet for two hundred years the frontier between the remaining Islamic Kingdom of Granada and Christian Spain had been more or less static. Castile, Aragon, Navarre and Portugal had from time to time intervened in the Hundred Years War between France and England or, in the case of Aragon, in Mediterranean adventures but Granada had been left, generation after generation, the bridgehead of Islam in Western Europe.

Isabella, half-sister of King Henry IV of Castile, had been schooled in the doctrine that it was the duty of the ruler of Castile to complete the Reconquista, but before that could be thought remotely feasible, the kingdom would have to be set in order. Henry's personal habits, practices and outlook on life were an offence to decency. His wife, Joan of Portugal, had a daughter, but no one in the kingdom believed her to be his: her reputed father was Henry's favorite, Beltran de la Cueva, whence her nickname, "La Beltraneja." Henry's rule over vast regions of Castile was purely nominal; dukes and counts did as they pleased within a wide radius of their strongly fortified castles and the kingdom was infested with bandits. The scandals of the court, and the fear that the chaos

Ferdinand and Isabella. The union of the heirs to two Spanish principalities transformed Spain and the world.

Opposite Ferdinand and Isabella sitting in state. A tapestry from Lérida Cathedral.

The fall of Granada, marking the end of the seven-hundred-year struggle against Islam in Spain.

A crusader's tomb from Sigüenza Cathedral. Castile's soldiers were known for their endurance, temperance and stoicism.

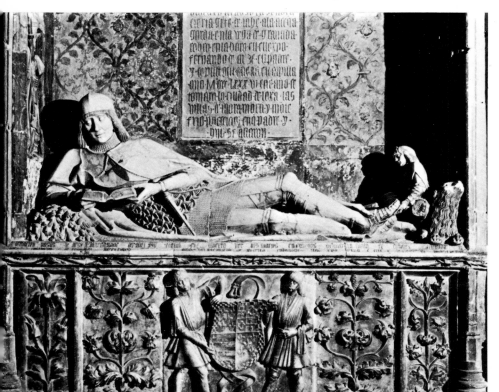

would be perpetuated if La Beltraneja were to succeed to the throne, had led to a rising in 1465 headed by the militarily powerful Primate of Spain, Cardinal Carrillo, Archbishop of Toledo, and including some nobles. In deeply religious Avila the rebels had deposed Henry in effigy, and declared Isabella's eleven-year-old brother Alfonso, King. Avila and the cities thereabouts, however, were not the whole country. Other nobles had come to the aid of Henry, lest a victorious Carrillo, even better as a military commander than as arch-

bishop, should force on them obedience to the sovereign once Henry was out of the way. Skirmish and battle had brought Henry almost to his knees when, in 1468, young Alfonso died. Carrillo thereupon offered Isabella the crown, but she declined it with a reply to which Carrillo had no answer: "If I should gain the throne by disobedience to the King, how could I blame anyone who might rise in disobedience to me?"

Carrillo had therefore come to terms with Henry. On a field near Avila, where he could well have destroyed Henry and his army, he obtained from the King his acknowledgment of Isabella as his heir, a promise to summon the Cortes (or parliament of Castile) to ratify the acknowledgment and an agreement to allow Isabella to choose her husband herself on condition that she did not proceed to marry without Henry's consent.

This last was a major concession. As a child at his court Isabella had endured innumerable improper suggestions from courtiers, and more recently had been pressured by the King to marry either the brother of one of his more repulsive favorites, or King Afonso V of Portugal—a man more than twice her age—or the French prince, Charles of Valois. France was anxious to have the Castilian navy at her disposal again, whereas Afonso V also wanted that navy as well as Castile's considerable manpower to back his expansion into Africa. France and Portugal both offered money for Isabella's hand and hinted at war if they did not get it.

Carrillo considered neither marriage desirable. Castile had need of a strong resident ruler. Marriage with either the King of Portugal or a potential King of France would entail the absence of Isabella from Castile, which would become simply an adjunct of a foreign power. He advised her therefore to marry the heir to Aragon, a prince a year younger than herself, healthy, presentable, brave in battle and prepared to accept, as he did in March, 1469, the priority of her rights as Queen of Castile over his as King of Aragon. He would reside in Castile and not leave his wife's side without her consent; he would acknowledge that all the rights of the King of Castile would be vested exclusively in the Queen and that his title of King of Castile would be purely honorary; he would fight for his wife's cause in Castile and in the completion of the Reconquista. Ferdinand however was not acceptable to Henry: Aragon had no money. In fact, John II was as bankrupt as Henry.

After the treaty with Carrillo Henry duly summoned the Cortes to the town of Ocaña. Isabella went to hear herself acclaimed by them as heir to the throne; but Henry dissolved the Cortes before they had had a chance to ratify the treaty, and again tried to persuade Isabella to accept the hand of the King of Portugal. Under the circumstances Isabella considered herself absolved from her part of the bargain and sent Ferdinand word to come at once and marry her.

Spies communicated the news to the King who

ordered her arrest, but the people of Ocaña armed themselves, surrounded her house and helped her escape. Henry, not yet beaten, arranged ambushes along the route that Ferdinand could be assumed to take to reach Isabella. She was now in Valladolid protected by a regiment of Carrillo's cavalry, men-at-arms belonging to the Admiral of Castile, Ferdinand's grandfather, and the people of a city that had no love for Henry. Ferdinand, disguised as muleteer to a group of merchants, reached Isabella's territory. Ironically it was then that he came closest to being killed, when a sentinel at a castle held by one of Isabella's supporters took him to be an emissary from Henry and let fly from the battlements a boulder that grazed Ferdinand's head as it fell.

Ferdinand and Isabella met for the first time on October 15, 1469. They approved of each other but one impediment to the ceremony remained. Bride and groom as second cousins were within the forbidden degrees of kinship, and a papal bull of dispensation was required. The Admiral of Castile produced one on the spot. Only later did Isabella discover that it was a forgery, and had the marriage regularized with a genuine bull. This was a wise precaution, for by then Ferdinand had begun to show those traits of character that earned him the admiration of Machiavelli. If politically expedient, he would have had little compunction in repudiating his wife.

Louis XI of France, thwarted by Isabella's marriage from renewing the Franco-Castilian alliance, prevailed on Henry to proclaim La Beltraneja as his daughter after all, and so heir to Castile. Half the country accepted his word, half did not. When, on December 11, 1474, Henry died, Isabella proclaimed herself Queen of Castile. The anti-Isabella barons offered the hand of La Beltraneja to Afonso of Portugal who invaded Castile on their behalf, but was soundly beaten. The barons thereupon took refuge in their castles, and what was essentially civil war continued until 1479. Each castle had to be taken separately. Isabella ordered their destruction as they fell, and her successes made even her supporters realize that their days as military rivals to the monarch were over. She took control of the military orders that had outlived their medieval usefulness as protectors of the kingdom against Islamic invasions—and also took their vast revenues. She overhauled taxation and tax collecting, local and central government and the whole judicial system. She traveled the length and breadth of Castile, appointing to office men versed in law or administration, "discreet and capable officials though socially only of middle rank, in preference to important figures of high lineage," as a contemporary remarked. In her new council of Castile, both the central governing body of the kingdom and its supreme court of justice, the key men were jurists. Grandees could be heard, but had no vote. She allowed local judicial systems and "liberties" to survive, but she insisted that local lords or town councils maintain high standards of

Baptism of the Moors. After their conquest of Granada the Pope awarded the royal couple the title "Reyes Católicos"— Catholic Kings.

justice. She established a nationwide rural police force to deal with the bandits.

Thus the aristocracy lost its political power to Isabella, though not its social or economic power. That had to survive, for she required the help of all noblemen who could fight as well as muster—and pay for—men-at-arms for the enterprise closest to her heart, the completion of the Reconquista. The difficulty of this task cannot be overestimated. The terrain favored defense, and throughout the Kingdom of Granada were scores of forts, castles and fortified towns built to withstand weeks of pounding by artillery. The conquest of Granada seemed certain to take years but Ferdinand's Machiavellian skill in setting one Islamic lord against another speeded the process. Nonetheless the campaigns demanded courage and determination and took a full ten years. The attack began in 1482; the city of Granada capitulated on January 2, 1492.

With the collapse of Granada, the seven-hundred-year struggle against Islam in Spain was over. Ferdinand had proved himself an able strategist and an even more able schemer, but something else had come to light. The men of Castile had shown a remarkable resistance to disease, extraordinary endurance, temperance in eating and drinking and an acceptance of victory or defeat. To these men discipline and even accepting arrears of pay were a point of honor. Moreover, among the Castilian captains one, Gonzalo Fernandez de Cordoba, had proved to be an out-

Toledo: the Church of St. John, built by the Catholic Kings, the first of the long line of Spanish heads of state to insist upon supremacy over the Church.

standing leader. Given such a commander and such men, Ferdinand had the means to defend the territories of Aragon in Italy—Sicily and Naples—against the imperialist French King Charles VIII. Gonzalo arrived too late to prevent the fall of Naples in 1495, but for the next seven years held his own against the French, though heavily outnumbered. The French recognized his genius in defense and called him "The Great Captain." He was that and more. In fact, he was the most original military thinker in a millennium. His reorganized army, first at Cerignola in 1503 and then at Garigliano, proved to the French that the day of the medieval cavalry with infantry in support was over, that the future lay with well-disciplined, multi-weaponed infantry battalions and that Spain's infantry could take on a force double its size and win. This infantry was to dominate the battlefields of Europe for the next hundred and forty years.

Isabella accepted Ferdinand's defense of the dependencies of Aragon in Europe, but once Naples was back in Spanish hands she would have had Ferdinand use his forces to expel Islam from the north coast of Africa, for she believed that Spain would not be safe from further invasion unless that were done. But there was another factor in the priority she gave Africa. The religious fervor behind the popular support given to Carrillo's rising against Henry IV had increased with his death, and

had given impetus to the Reconquista. The success of this "Holy War" had persuaded Castilians that the destruction of Islam, from Morocco to Turkey, was their God-given destiny. And the Italian wars could not be presented as holy—especially after Ferdinand had ordered the papal nuncio to Naples hanged to show the Pope who was master there.

Ferdinand and Isabella were, in effect, the first of the long line of Spanish heads of state to insist upon supremacy over the Church. As part of their process of establishing this supremacy, rebel prelates as well as laymen had been deprived of castles and fortresses. But the political power of the Church rested on more than military bases. According to custom, an heir to a lay title had to have his heritage confirmed by the Queen, and Isabella had made the transfer of cities and places to the crown a condition of this confirmation—the dukes of Medina-Sidonia, for example, had thus been forced to give up Gibraltar. In this way the authority of the crown over secular noblemen had been reinforced, but so long as prelates were appointed by the Pope instead of the crown, similar control of the Church was impossible. Isabella resolved to break the Church's hold and this Ferdinand succeeded in doing piecemeal, using all the artifices for which Renaissance princes are renowned, including the spoliation of Church property, the threat of war and even of schism. Though the Pope retained some control into the next reign, the crown of Castile had by 1492 a hold over the Church as firm as Ferdinand's son-in-law Henry VIII of England was to acquire.

After the conquest of Granada the Pope gave the Spanish royal pair the title "Reyes Católicos" (Catholic Kings). The long history of the Church's relations with Ferdinand since his marriage with a forged bull, and even the words in which the award was couched, however, made it clear that the object was to inhibit Ferdinand and Isabella from taking the next logical step, the establishment of a schismatic, national church. Such a church would have been schismatic, but otherwise doctrinally orthodox. Orthodoxy in all things, was one of Isabella's ideals—the enforcement of law, the language of the realm, artistic expression, not only religious doctrine. But doctrinal orthodoxy became such a popular obsession that the creation of the special royal council—the Inquisition—to root out false converts to Christianity must be attributed to the people as much as to the crown. Its use for political ends under the veil of religion was probably not originally intended. Another act, seemingly religious in inspiration, was, however, certainly intended and was economic in purpose from its inception—the edict of 1492 to expel the Jews. This is clear, for the severity with which the edict was imposed varied in proportion to the victim's wealth. The poor Jew might be overlooked but the financiers, the entrepreneurs, were mercilessly expelled, many to take refuge in the Papal States.

In the long term the expulsion seriously damaged the economic wellbeing of Castile, but in the short term it benefited the royal treasury, then much in need of money. Financially, the war in Granada had not helped. "All the grandees and noblemen, and *hijos de algo* who served in it," a contemporary recorded, "received favors each according to his rank, namely houses, lands and vassals." The crown could keep little money if it was to retain the loyalty of the nobles. When Christopher Columbus came to see Ferdinand and Isabella in 1486 with his plans to reconnoiter a westward route to the East, their plea that they had no money to finance him was true. When he came again five years later it was the enormously rich Duke of Medinaceli who first offered him the men, ships and supplies and the possibility that the voyage might result in the discovery of new lands that would then belong to the Duke, made the royal pair resolve to find the money themselves. How they did it is not clear, but it is probable that a part came from men who were to be expelled from Spain penniless a year later.

The discovery of America did not change Isabella's view that Africa should have priority for Spanish military activity and she insisted upon it in the will she dictated as she lay dying in 1504, but Ferdinand was in no position to follow her instructions. In order to save Aragon's Italian territories from the French, he had married his daughters to the Hapsburgs, to Portugal and to England, and consequently Spain could no longer escape embroilment in Europe.

From the marriage with Henry VIII of England came nothing but personal tragedy to the Princess Catherine, and ultimately centuries of wars between Britain and Spain. The marriage with Portugal united the Iberian Peninsula for a brief sixty years (Ferdinand had annexed Navarre in 1512), but not without war before and wars two hundred years thereafter. The marriage of the sad, demented Joan, Isabella and Ferdinand's oldest daughter and heir, after the death of their one son, to Philip, Archduke of Austria, first brought a period of military glory under the Emperor Charles V, their son, followed by a century and a half of wars in the Netherlands and Italy. These wars ruined Spain, not only depriving her of the many killed in battle but drawing from her to other parts of Europe by far the greater share of all the gold and silver and other treasures which Spanish galleons brought from the New World. However, all was not tragedy and loss. But for Ferdinand, Isabella would never have been Queen of Castile; but for the Queen of Castile the foundations would not have been laid for the development in Spain of the schools of philosophers and lawyers which followed, nor of a golden century of painters, poets, prose writers, dramatists, composers and architects. The reign that began with the marriage in 1469 brought about results that were crucial to the entire world.

GEORGE HILLS

Ferdinand and Isabella entering Granada Cathedral.

Burgundy—the cradle of northern

In 1387, Norway, Sweden and Denmark had been united into one kingdom under the rule of Margaret of Denmark, but the kingdom proved to have little stability. Margaret's grand-nephew, Eric VII, succeeded her and was at first able to rule effectively because of her suppression of the opposition. Eric defeated the Hanseatic League in 1427, in a war over Denmark's right to impose taxes on ships passing through the straits between Copenhagen and the mainland, then tried to encourage Dutch merchants to become the commercial rivals of the League in Scandinavia. His troubles started soon afterward. Eric had laid claim to Schleswig, a part of the Duchy of Holstein which the Danes called South Jutland, in 1404 and in 1424 his claim had been accepted by Sigismund, King of the Romans. The claim was contested, however, by the counts of Holstein, and there was fighting over the Duchy from 1404 to 1433. Holstein was able to rely on support from the Hanseatic League, and in 1432 Schleswig was united with Holstein.

Eric's problems within his huge kingdom were even more serious. Queen Margaret had succeeded in holding back the power of the aristocracy, but under Eric it grew again, and was reinforced by political separatism. In 1435 rebellion broke out in Sweden. A popular leader, Englebrecht, led a Swedish uprising and at an assembly held by the rebels Englebrecht was elected regent. His murder the following year did not quell the rebellion, and the Norwegians, seeing Eric's inability to suppress the rising, rebelled also. The King was forced to make concessions to restore order.

In 1438 rebellion broke out

again. In Sweden, a nobleman, Charles Knutson, was elected regent. The Danish nobility also rose, forcing Eric to leave Copenhagen. His inability to unite Scandinavia was clear to all, and in 1439 he was deposed. His successor, Christopher III (1439–1448), proved no more able and it was only under Christian I (1448–81) that a measure of order was restored, although even Christian was troubled by rebellions in favor of Charles Knutson in Sweden and Norway. In 1460 he succeeded in becoming Duke of Schleswig and Holstein, but the "perpetual union" between the two was to be the cause of difficulties as late as the twentieth century.

Burgundian civilization

Alone among the courts of northern Europe the Duchy of Burgundy had created a climate of artistic patronage that formed the basis for artistic achievement in the fifteenth century. The van Eycks, who were both helped by ducal patronage, created a unique Flemish school of painting, rich both in detail and in color. Much of their work reflected the magnificence of the court of Philip the Bold, but the intensity of their religious painting demonstrated a depth of feeling that forms a counterpart to the writings of Thomas à Kempis. Jan van Eyck was court painter to Philip the Good from 1425 to his death in 1440. The van Eycks' finest achievement, on which each in turn lavished his genius, was the large and complex polyptych of the *Adoration of the Lamb* in the Church of St. Bavon in Ghent, painted about 1425. Jan, the younger brother, developed a

Detail from van Eyck's polyptych of the *Adoration of the Lamb.*

novel technique of painting in oils with varnish that helped preserve his brilliant colors for posterity.

Although there was no individual of the ability of the van Eycks in the following generation, the standard of artistic achievement at the court of Charles the Bold was high. The outstanding artist of the mid-fifteenth century was Rogier van der Weyden (1400–64). Although he did not succeed Jan van Eyck as court painter—he was city painter of Brussels from 1436—he carried out many commissions for the Burgundian royal family and their courtiers. Among van der Weyden's pupils Hans Memling (d. 1494) and Dieric Bouts (c. 1415–75) were the most distinguished, but there were many other artists whose works have survived although their names are often unknown. These are mostly known for particular pictures as, for example, "the Master of *Mary of Burgundy*."

Music

Court influence extended to music. From about 1300, music had increasingly freed itself from the narrow restraints imposed upon it by poetry and religion. This was the main characteristic of the fourteenth-century musical style, which a contemporary composer, Bishop Philippe de Vitry (1291–1361), described as *ars nova* (new art)—a name that is still used. Music was the only art in which the leadership was not Italian in the later Middle Ages. During the

fourteenth century French musicians led the way, although a few Italians, of whom the blind Florentine organist Francesco Landino (c. 1325–98) was the most distinguished, had a considerable impact. The *ars nova* was distrusted by the papacy, and in his bull *Docta Sanctorum* (1325) Pope John XXII attacked the tendency to hang words onto the music rather than writing music around the words of the Bible, but this attitude merely encouraged composers to write secular instead of religious music, as the restraints were fewer. The increasing use of instruments in music of all types made further developments possible and helped to break down the rigidity of the *ars nova*.

In the fifteenth century innovation was more widespread. In England John Dunstable (c. 1370–1453) had great impact because of his developed use of harmony. Dunstable was helped by Henry V and held a post in the Chapel Royal. But Burgundy was a more important center musically than England. The outstanding composer of the fifteenth century was Guillaume Dufay (c. 1400–74) whose reputation spread throughout Western and even Eastern Europe. Dufay, even more than Dunstable, was helped by royal patronage. He traveled widely and was commissioned to compose works not merely for northern princes, but for notables in Italy and even for the Byzantine Emperor. He had been a choirboy at Cambrai Cathedral, from which Bishop Pierre d'Ailly had en-

Danish flag from the time of Eric VII with Scandinavian and Pomeranian emblems.

Europe's Renaissance

couraged him to travel to Rome, where he sang in the papal choir, and to Paris, where he studied theology at the Sorbonne. He became a canon of Cambrai, in addition to holding other ecclesiastical offices. His musical versatility was matched by his talent. He developed the use of counterpoint—several independent parts—and tried to get away from the rigidity that the *ars nova* imposed. The influence of Dufay can be seen from the number of composers and singers from the Burgundian Netherlands who emigrated to the Italian courts during the second half of the fifteenth century. Where Italy thought itself deficient in the arts it simply bought the best foreign talent available. As a result, the achievements of the Burgundian school were quickly transferred to a wider stage.

Louis XI of France

While England's nobility slaughtered each other during the Wars of the Roses, France's history was slightly more peaceful. In 1461 Charles VII died, and his son—or rather his wife's son; his paternity was doubtful—became King as Louis XI. Even during Charles' lifetime Louis had shown his strength of will, and demonstrated that he was willing to incur his father's displeasure to follow his own wishes. He had an opportunity to practice the arts of government while still young through

his rule over the Dauphiné in southeastern France. In this backward province Louis abolished feudal rights and established central administrative control, while his cunning diplomacy earned him the title "the spider."

In 1456, his father, angry at the Dauphin's independence, invaded the Dauphiné and Louis fled to Brussels, where he received the protection of the Duke of Burgundy. Until Charles died, Louis was forced to stay as Philip's guest. As soon as news of his father's death arrived, Louis went to Paris. He immediately showed himself an energetic king with no nonsense about him. At first it seemed that the quarrel between France and Burgundy would be ended and the court at Paris seemed little more than an extension of that of Burgundy. But the Duke wanted to influence the King's policymaking, while Louis wanted to be completely independent; France and Burgundy were soon at war.

In part the quarrel was about style of government: the Burgundian court believed in making their power felt through outward impression of magnificence, state and show. Louis traveled with a small retinue. During his coronation dinner, Louis amazed his courtiers by removing his crown because he found it uncomfortable, but they soon grew accustomed to his ungainly figure, his coarse language and his penchant for ambling about the realm in shabby

Louis XI of France, "the spider."

clothes and an old felt hat. Here was a Renaissance tyrant ruling by decree who was very different from the princes of Italy. He frowned on the wearing of silk, considered gilding a luxury and lacked money to patronize artists. As he felt that it was provident to keep in the Church's good graces, he showed himself to be a man of religion.

The real differences between

France and Burgundy went much deeper. Louis XI was determined that only the King should govern France. The Duke of Burgundy and many other great nobles were not willing to give up their rights and privileges. It was Louis' great achievement to destroy finally the power of France's greatest feudal lord, and to isolate the dukes of Brittany, little less independent than those of Burgundy. He established a government that was firmly under royal control, and made sure that its edicts could not be ignored with impunity anywhere in France. In addition, the administration was overhauled and talented men of humble origin replaced the great lords in many government posts. His achievement was similar to those of Ferdinand and Isabella in Spain, the Emperor Maximilian and Henry VII of England. The key to this policy was the conquest of Burgundy (or at least that part of it that lay in France). It was years before his opportunity came, but he waited patiently for it.

Lady musicians, from a fifteenth-century manuscript.

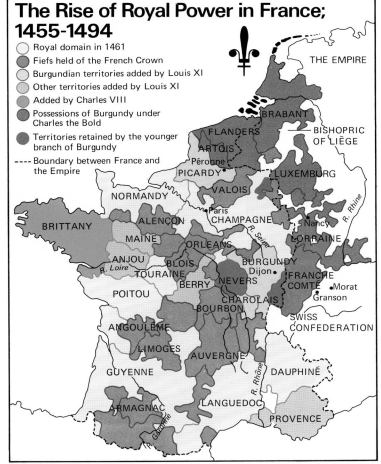

The Rise of Royal Power in France; 1455-1494

- ○ Royal domain in 1461
- Fiefs held of the French Crown
- Burgundian territories added by Louis XI
- Other territories added by Louis XI
- Added by Charles VIII
- Possessions of Burgundy under Charles the Bold
- Territories retained by the younger branch of Burgundy
- ---- Boundary between France and the Empire

THE EMPIRE
BRABANT
FLANDERS
BISHOPRIC OF LIÈGE
ARTOIS
Péronne
PICARDY
LUXEMBURG
NORMANDY
VALOIS
Paris
CHAMPAGNE
Nancy
R. Rhine
BRITTANY
ALENÇON
LORRAINE
MAINE
ORLEANS
R. Seine
ANJOU
BLOIS
BURGUNDY
R. Loire
TOURAINE
Dijon
FRANCHE COMTÉ
BERRY
NEVERS
Morat
POITOU
CHAROLAIS
Granson
BOURBON
ANGOULÊME
SWISS CONFEDERATION
LIMOGES
AUVERGNE
R. Rhône
DAUPHINÉ
GUYENNE
R. Garonne
ARMAGNAC
LANGUEDOC
PROVENCE

Louis XI Overthrows Burgundy

Devious, calculating and utterly unscrupulous, Louis XI of France alternated bribery and threats with patience and diplomacy in order to destroy his powerful rival Charles the Bold, Duke of Burgundy. By isolating him from his allies and friends, Louis led the headstrong Duke to his death. He then assimilated those portions of Burgundy that were French, greatly strengthening the power of the monarchy. However, the marriage of Charles' daughter to Maximilian of Hapsburg thwarted Louis' plans in part and set the stage for a power struggle that would plague Europe for more than two hundred years.

A council of war between the dukes of Burgundy, Berry and Bourbon. During the reign of Charles VII these and the other great dukes had revolted three times.

Opposite The prosperity of the many towns of the Low Countries, which were the economic heart of the Burgundian State, is well shown in *The St. Elizabeth's Flood*, an anonymous fifteenth-century painting of the Dutch School.

On January 5, 1477, Charles the Bold, Duke of Burgundy, fell in battle at Nancy in Lorraine, leaving his nineteen-year-old daughter as his heiress. On hearing the news, his arch-enemy, Louis XI of France, plunged quickly to the task of seizing as much of Burgundy as he could, for the powerful and independent duchy was the French monarch's greatest threat. It was not only a symbol of resistance to the rapidly spreading royal power, but a potential leader of other great independent feudatories against their sovereign and a tempting ally for any English king who might want to intervene again in French affairs. Although not successful in all his aims, by the end of his reign Louis was able to dispose of Burgundy and leave the monarchy in almost undisputed control of a united France.

When Louis had succeeded to the throne in 1461, France had made remarkable strides toward making good the devastation caused by the Hundred Years War. Accounts from 1453 tell of vast areas of territory laid waste by the march and countermarch of armies, of fields untended, villages in ruins and a large part of the population living in desperate poverty. But France, like Germany in 1945, was such a naturally rich country that she amazed Europe by the speed of her recovery.

For the monarchy, the war had provided an opportunity for establishing a strong centralized government, which Louis' father, Charles VII, and his advisers had taken advantage of. First as Dauphin and then as King, Charles had made himself the symbol of resistance to the invader and as his armies were successful and the English driven out, his prestige was greatly increased and with it the prestige of the monarchy. Support for the King was widespread among the middle and lower classes who longed for peace, and who were prepared to allow him to acquire far greater powers than they would in more settled times.

At first, the King had been obliged to call various "estates" (provincial assemblies) to obtain grants of taxation in their areas, but as the frequency of royal demands for money with which to fight the war increased, the estates agreed that certain taxes—including the *taille* (land tax)—should be levied in perpetuity without consulting them. From 1435 the royal council was able to decide the rate at which these taxes were levied, and developed a financial organization to collect them. The monarchy thereby had acquired an independent, centralized source of revenue.

During the war the King also acquired the other essential for independent government—a standing army. The military disasters of the war had shown up the weakness of depending on royal vassals to raise troops, and the monarchy began to raise and maintain a permanent force paid for by taxation and led by professional commanders whose loyalty was to the crown.

These developments meant that Louis inherited a potentially strong, centralized government, which was breaking clear of the restrictions that had hampered French kings in the past. But one major problem still remained, one that had actually been increased by the long years of disorder. Although Charles VII had enjoyed considerable success in winning over the lesser nobility, who had been impoverished by the war, the great lords who controlled more than half France had steadily increased their powers and with it their independence of the King. The royal domains, which centered around Paris, were surrounded by the lands of such great dukes as Anjou, Bourbon, Brittany, Berry, Orleans and—greatest of all—Burgundy. Three times during Charles' reign these great vassals had revolted against the spread of royal power and he had been forced to buy them off with grants of privileges. On the last occasion he had even seen his son Louis take their side. Toward the end of the reign, Louis had taken refuge at the court of Burgundy, but Charles refused to

disinherit him, and contented himself with the shrewd prophecy: "My cousin of Burgundy is nourishing the fox that will eat his chickens."

On his succession Louis at first allied himself with the great nobles, ignoring his father's middle-class advisers, but the danger of allowing himself to fall into their hands was too obvious—and was tactlessly emphasized at his coronation when the Duke of Burgundy arrived with a larger, more lavish entourage than that of the King. Louis resolved to break their power but made his intentions too plain, and in 1465 was faced by another great feudal league led by Charles, Duke of Charolais, soon to become Duke of Burgundy. This league claimed to be acting for "the Common Good" of the population against the King's arbitrary rule. Louis was forced to cede parts of the royal domain to the various nobles, but he was soon able to start breaking up this alliance by detaching the smaller and weaker members with a combination of bribery and threats.

Nevertheless, there remained the one opponent that could neither be bribed nor threatened—Burgundy. On his succession in 1467, Charles the Bold had inherited wealthy and powerful territories which had been built up by his three predecessors. Starting with the Duchy and County of Burgundy, a series of advantageous marriages had added Flanders, Luxemburg, Brabant, Picardy, Limburg and a number of smaller territories, so that a great belt of land across France's northern and eastern borders, including almost all the Low Countries, was now held by Charles. Moreover, most of the northern territories were held from the Holy Roman Emperor rather than the King of France, so the dukes had considerable extra independence from him which was increased by their great wealth.

The prosperity of the towns of the Low Countries and their freedom from the invasions that had ravaged the rest of France had enabled the dukes of Burgundy to build up a court that was one of the most splendid in Europe and the greatest center of art north of the Alps. Every sort of patronage that might enhance the prestige of the dukes was considered to be worth lavish expenditure. Guests were entertained at banquets and tournaments of great splendor; the court acquired a reputation for rich ceremonial which far overshadowed that of Paris; and the Order of the Golden Fleece, instituted by Philip the Good to commemorate the golden hair of one of his mistresses, swiftly became one of the most sought-after awards of chivalry. Among the artists who worked for the dukes were Jan van Eyck, Rogier van der Weyden and the sculptor Claes Sluter, while the ducal library, tapestries and other treasures were renowned throughout Europe.

Yet, despite its magnificence, Charles' inheritance had two ultimately fatal weaknesses: his possessions in the Low Countries were completely separated from Burgundy, and because it had grown up through dynastic marriage and piece-

:neal acquisition his domain lacked coherence. There was no common language or tradition and little to hold the territories together except the personality of the dukes.

Under Philip the Good, Burgundy had been able to play the role of a third force in French politics, standing between the English and the French monarchy and playing one against the other. The Duke had never lost an opportunity to show that he considered himself to be more than equal to any king, and on occasions showed that he would have liked to turn the duchy into a kingdom and resurrect the ninth-century "Middle Kingdom," which had stretched from Holland to the Alps. Indeed he liked to recall the barbarian Kingdom of Burgundy which had been "usurped by the Franks." Contemporaries referred to the Burgundian leaders as the "Great Dukes of the West." But for Philip there was one great restraining factor—he and his predecessors had liked to think of themselves as good Frenchmen. They might dream of a kingdom and fight against the French monarchy, but they were reluctant to be seen as enemies of France itself.

It was only with the accession of Charles the Bold that specifically anti-French rather than anti-monarchic feelings began to be voiced in Burgundy as Charles showed that he would not hesitate to break down France in order to achieve his ambition to weld his lands into a coherent whole which could withstand outside assault. Such a scheme would require time to develop a common identity and to undertake the dedicated, painstaking work of building a centralized government, but this sort of leadership was just what Charles was temperamentally unable and unwilling to provide. For Charles had all the flamboyance and faults of his age. He was a romantic: impatient, quick-tempered and ambitious, eager to put into action any scheme for expanding his domains and increasing his power, and reckless of making enemies. Perhaps his greatest misfortune was that he had as an enemy a man whose character was the exact opposite of his, who was ideally suited to take advantage of all Charles' weaknesses and use them to his advantage.

Louis XI was cold, calculating, consumed with a desire for power and utterly unscrupulous in how he achieved it. He believed that any man could be bought provided the bribe was big enough, and he lied and cheated shamelessly. The "Universal Spider," as he became known to his contemporaries, was also intelligent, patient and persevering. At times his deviousness and love of intrigue created unnecessary difficulties for himself, but Louis' adviser Philip of Comines—whom he had bought over from the Burgundian court—called him "the cleverest man I have known at extricating himself from an adverse situation" and "the one who worked hardest to win over a man who could do him harm or who could serve him." These characteristics made Louis a formidable opponent for the headstrong Duke of Burgundy.

The personal struggle between the two men had begun when Charles had been a leader of the League of the Common Good. Shortly after his accession as Duke, he found himself in a position from which it seemed he might have ended the contest almost before it got under way, for Louis had overreached himself. He had been pressing for a meeting with the new Duke, and in 1468 traveled to see him at Péronne, on Burgundian territory. But he had also just completed secret negotiations to have Liège, one of Charles' subject cities, revolt, and while Louis was at Péronne, the revolt took place. When the news and a report

Haymaking in June and July from *Les Très Riches Heures du Duc de Berry* by Pol de Limbourg.

Opposite above The Marriage of Arnolfini by Jan van Eyck.

Opposite below The tomb of Philip the Bold of Burgundy, carved by Claes Sluter and Claes de Werve.

Louis XI presiding over the first meeting of the Order of St. Michael, which he founded in 1469.

Above right Charles the Bold of Burgundy. With his accession, specifically anti-French rather than anti-monarchic feelings began to be voiced in Burgundy.

of the King's implication reached Charles he was livid, and for three days held Louis prisoner. Comines, then still with the Duke, describes how "the third night, the Duke never took off his clothes. He only lay down on his bed two or three times and then started to pace up and down as was his way when he was worried. I slept in his room that night and sometimes I walked up and down with him. In the morning he was in a greater rage than ever, making threats and vowing that he was ready to carry out a great deed."

However, Charles soon realized that he could not hold the King prisoner indefinitely, nor could he hope to make too extreme demands which might antagonize the other great nobles. Louis gained his freedom by promising to help Charles put down the revolt at Liège and making some territorial concessions. The King had been humbled by his great vassal, and his determination to destroy Charles was strengthened. Even the concessions that Charles had gained were of little help, for a short while later an assembly of nobles freed Louis from his promises on the grounds that they had been extorted under pressure.

A year later Charles achieved a major success in bridging the corridor dividing his territories when he persuaded the Emperor to cede him Alsace as a security against a loan that Charles had given to raise an army against the Swiss Confederation. But Charles' intentions were now beginning to cause alarm to the rulers of neighboring territories and Louis began working secretly to incite the Rhineland princes and the Swiss, who felt particularly threatened.

At this stage, both rulers became embroiled in the affairs of England where the Wars of the Roses provided an opportunity for putting a friendly king on the throne. Louis hesitated between the rival houses of York and Lancaster, but when Charles the Bold married Edward of York's sister and allied himself with the Yorkists he was forced to seek an effective answer. His opportunity came when the powerful Earl of Warwick, the "King-maker" who had been instrumental in putting Edward on the throne in place of King Henry VI, deserted the Yorkists and fled to France. With Louis' aid a Lancastrian restoration was engineered in 1470—Edward IV fled to the Low Countries and Henry was released from imprisonment and returned to the throne. Louis now proposed a joint attack on Burgundy, with the duchy being divided up and England receiving the Low Countries.

This plan swiftly collapsed within a year, when Edward, with the support of Burgundy, invaded England and murdered Henry, thereby putting an end to the Lancastrian monarchy. It was now Charles' turn to plan an attack on France. In 1474 he and Edward signed the amazing Treaty of London by which France was to be split between them. Edward would be King but hold little territory in the north and east of the country while Charles would receive the territories he needed to unite the scattered parts of his duchy.

Charles must have felt that his goal of destroying Louis was in sight, but in reality the patient diplomacy of the King of France was beginning to have an effect and his own carelessness in making enemies was about to rebound on him. Through

impatience and tactlessness Charles had offended the Holy Roman Emperor, Frederick III, from whom he held most of the Low Countries and leased Alsace. He had also antagonized the Duke of Lorraine (whose lands lay between his) by forcing him to grant Burgundian troops rights of passage. He had gained the enmity of the Rhineland princes and the Swiss Confederation, while at home his demands for massive taxation to support his armies led his subjects to detest him. The Flanders Estate refused him any further money, and several of his advisers deserted to Louis.

Charles' downfall was now rapid. Before the end of 1474, Alsace had revolted, with Louis giving aid to the rebels. Then the Emperor, again with money supplied by Louis, was able to repay his debt and demand Alsace back. By the end of the year Louis had formed alliances with the Swiss and Emperor Frederick III so that Charles was surrounded by enemies.

Apparently unable to understand how dangerous

Fighting between the Swiss (on the left) and the Burgundians. Below, old, impoverished Switzerland converses with new, rich Switzerland. Louis XI incited the Swiss against Burgundy.

The Burgundian court. The dukes had established one of the most splendid courts in Europe and the greatest center of art north of the Alps.

his situation was, Charles went off campaigning in the Rhineland in the spring of 1475, thereby missing the rendezvous with Edward IV and his English army specified by the Treaty of London. Louis seized his opportunity and by the Treaty of Picquigny bought Edward's neutrality, pledging to pay 75,000 crowns immediately and give an annual pension of 60,000 more. Charles, showing up belatedly, was unable to reenlist his former ally.

As Louis was unwilling to risk in battle what he had gained by diplomacy, he then arranged a truce with Charles but subsidized the Swiss and the Duke of Lorraine to continue fighting him. Charles now turned on them and was defeated at Granson on Lake Neuchâtel in March, 1476. Three months

later he lost even more heavily at Morat near Berne. Finally, without money or allies, he attacked Lorraine and was overwhelmed and killed at the Battle of Nancy.

Louis' task of assimilating Burgundy was complicated because half the duchy was held from the Holy Roman Emperor making it difficult to find a good excuse for wholesale annexation. He first attempted to settle the problem by marrying his oldest son to Charles' daughter Mary, but this was frustrated when she married Maximilian of Hapsburg, the son of Emperor Frederick III. Louis then declared as many Burgundian fiefs as possible forfeit to the French crown under the Salic Law, which barred female succession, and forcibly annexed them. The Hapsburgs objected and

en mille chose de ce monde ne se pourroit trouuer / mais chascun de nous le cognoist tard / et apres ce que en auions eu besoing. Toutesfois vault encores myeulx tard que jamais ▨▨▨

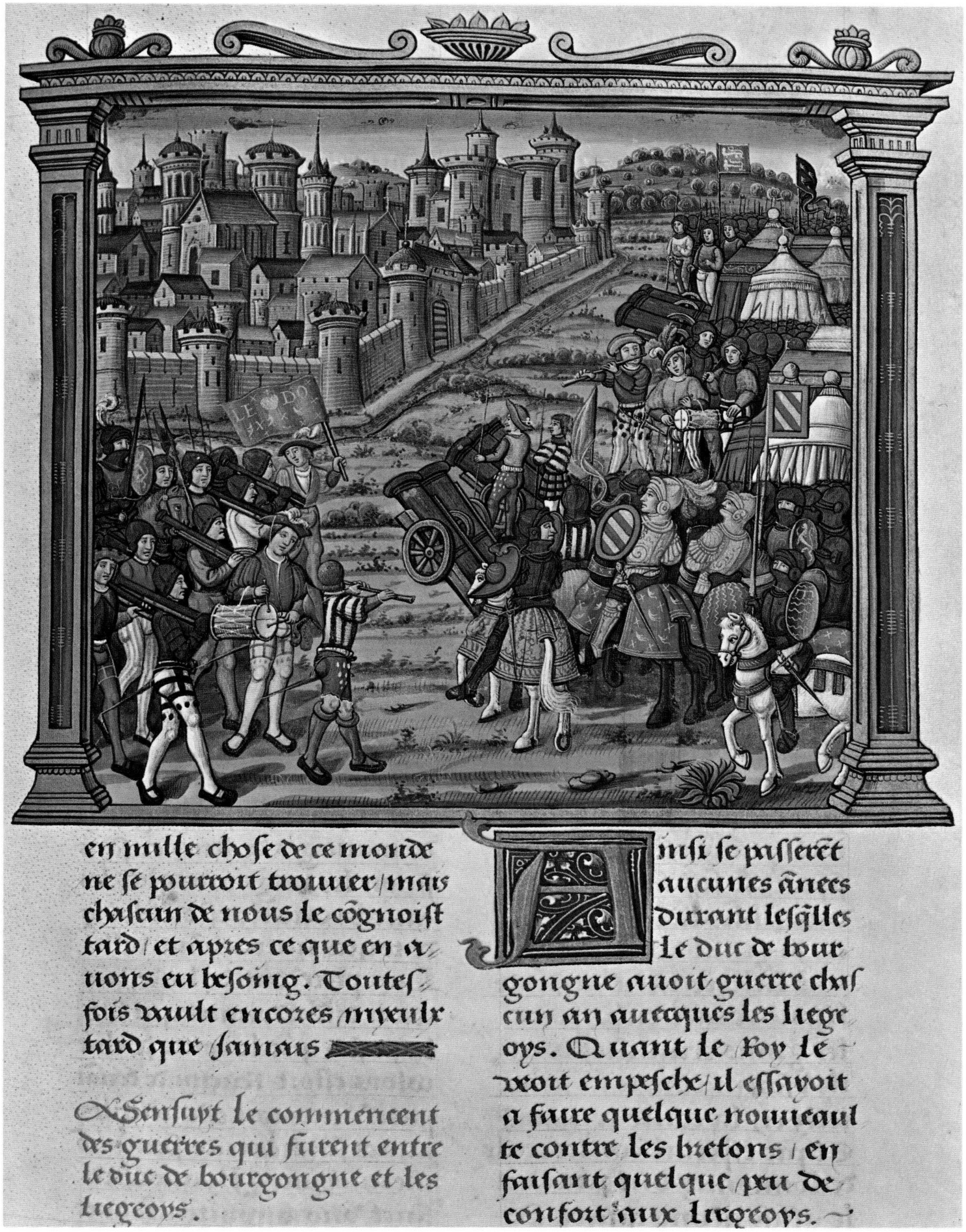

Sensuyt le commencent des guerres qui furent entre le duc de bourgongne et les liegeoys.

Ainsi se passeret aucunes ânees durant lesqlles le duc de bourgongne auoit guerre chascun an auecques les liegeoys. Quant le roy le vroit empesche / il essayoit a faire quelque nouueaulte contre les bretons / en faisant quelque peu de confort aux liegeoys.

fighting broke out, with peace finally arranged in 1482 by the Treaty of Arras. Louis received the original Duchy and County of Burgundy together with Artois and Picardy in northern France, while Flanders and the other Burgundian provinces in the Low Countries remained Hapsburg.

Louis had brought down the mighty House of Burgundy by patience and diplomacy, but he failed to win all that he wanted. For the marriage of Mary of Burgundy to a Hapsburg was crucial to the history of Europe. It began the real extension of Hapsburg power into the Netherlands which was to make that dynasty the most powerful in Europe in the next century and a constant threat to France for more than two hundred years.

JONATHAN MARTIN

99

Scotland's royal dynasty, the Stewarts or Stuarts, had battled since 1371 against the anarchy and feudal problems that had characterized Scotland's history since the death of Robert the Bruce in 1329. James I (1424–37) and James II (1437–60) had enjoyed some success. Southern Scotland had been recovered from English hands, and the power of the Douglases, Scotland's mightiest feudal house, although not broken, had been humbled. James III (1460–88) was less successful, despite the considerable achievement of bringing the lordship of the Isles under the crown. For the first few years of James' reign, his guardian, James Kennedy, Bishop of St. Andrew's, was able to hold the country in his firm grasp, and even after Kennedy's death in 1464, when James was only twelve, the country remained quiet. This was largely due to the ambitious Earl of Arran, who arranged a marriage between James and Margaret, daughter of Christian I of Norway. This brought the royal family control of the Shetland and Orkney islands as the agreed dowry was

The Silver Pavilion, Yoshimasa's aesthetic retreat outside Kyōtō.

not paid, and the islands had been pledged as surety. In 1469 Arran overreached himself and was overthrown.

James' rule makes an interesting contrast with that of Louis XI of France. Both men sought to strengthen their governments by similar methods—the promotion of men of undistinguished family background, whose only loyalty would be to the king; energetic traveling throughout the kingdom in order to make the royal power felt; and attempting to suppress the power of the nobility. But James lacked Louis' forceful character, and the power of the Scottish nobility—at least in the highland areas, which virtually formed a separate kingdom—was even more deep-rooted than that of the French feudal lords, largely because of the clan system, which ensured loyalty to the family rather than to the state.

James had continual problems with his cousins, the earls of Mar and Albany, and also with the Douglases; he managed to overcome the threats that they posed, but his hold on the throne was weak, and his attempts to secure peace with England made him unpopular. He died in 1488, fleeing from rebels, and Scotland was left in a dangerous state.

Japan

Japan's government in the second half of the fifteenth century, during the shogunate (or office) of Yoshimasa (1449–90), went from weakness to weakness. Great lords and monasteries were continually at war with each other. From 1467 there was a civil war over the issue of control over the shogunate, which, however, soon widened into an attempt to overthrow the established feudal families. Although the war nominally ended in 1477, it had demonstrated the decline in the government's authority, and as a result the peace was not observed. For the next century war became the normal state of affairs in Japan. The structure of government remained unaltered, but powerful families rose and fell with great rapidity. Yet despite—or because of—the civil strife, the rule of Yoshimasa was one of the greatest periods of Japanese art and culture. In the Silver Pavilion on the outskirts of Kyōtō, Yoshimasa organ-

ized a community of artists. The central government, forced to cancel debts owed by the nobility, and too weak to raise armies itself, was unable to influence events, and was driven steadily deeper into its artistic seclusion.

Vietnam

The Le dynasty of Vietnam reached the height of its power in the second half of the fifteenth century. This was largely achieved during the rule of Le Than Thou (1460–97). The weakness of the state of Champa to the south throughout the first half of the fifteenth century had excited the greed of Vietnam. Several invasion attempts had been made, but although sometimes successful in taking the Champa capital, the Vietnamese were unable to make their conquest permanent. But in 1471 Le Than Thou managed to secure the whole country as far south as Cape Varella.

After securing Champa, Le Than Thou went on to attack Laos. The hostility between Laos and Vietnam was largely due to the betrayal of the Vietnamese by the Laotians during the war with China during the 1420s. In 1479 the Vietnamese captured Luang Prabang and, although they did not continue to occupy it, forced the Laotian royal family to recognize Vietnamese overlordship.

Skanderbeg

The danger of the Turkish conquest of the whole of Europe in the years after the fall of Constantinople was seen clearly by the papacy. Other states such as Venice and Hungary only noticed the threat when they were actually under attack. But Turkish advances in the Balkans were hindered largely because of one man, Giorgio Castriota (1403–67), an Albanian prince. Castriota had been a hostage at the court of Murad II from 1423 to 1443, had become a Moslem and had risen to become the governor of a province. Taking advantage of John Hunyadi's victory at Nis in 1443, he seized his independence and set up a principality in the almost impregnable Albanian mountains. Using this as his base, and with the assistance of a small force of peasants, he terrorized the Turks. They soon came to hold him in superstitious awe, and called him Skanderbeg (Iskander Bey)—Prince Alexander—as they believed that he was a reincarnation of Alexander of Macedon.

The Turks recognized the independence of the Principality of Albania in 1461. But Skanderbeg's son, who succeeded him as Prince, had little taste for the constant warfare necessitated by living on the Turkish borders. He sold his inheritance to the Venetians in 1474 and retired on the proceeds

James III of Scotland and his son.

of the sale. The Venetians soon saw that protecting a barren principality of valueless mountains against the Turks was a waste of time and in 1478, threatened by Turkish invasion, they sold the principality to the Turks—at a profit.

Bohemia and Hungary

The death of Emperor Sigismund in 1437 had created a succession problem in Bohemia that was solved when the baby Ladislas Posthumus (son of Albert, King of the Romans) became King in 1440. Ladislas succeeded four years later to the Kingdom of Hungary also, when it was accepted that Ladislas v must have been killed at the Battle of Varna in 1444.

In both of the countries of which Ladislas Posthumus was King, government was in the hands of a strong regent. In Hungary, John Hunyadi (c. 1385–1456) was governor. Hunyadi, who had risen to high office because of his military ability, saw the Turks as the major threat to his country and devoted his efforts and his huge wealth to beating them. His victory over the Turks at Belgrade in 1456 removed the threat, at least for a time. In Bohemia, George of Podebrady, a moderate Hussite, was regent.

The death of Ladislas in 1457 at the age of seventeen created a new succession problem in both countries. Although several of the Hapsburgs had strong hereditary claims to both kingdoms, the nobility of both favored native

candidates. In Bohemia, George of Podebrady succeeded, and in Hungary, Matthias Corvinus Hunyadi (1458–90), son of John, was elected King at the age of fifteen. Hungary was deeply divided, and there was still some danger from the Turks; few observers gave Matthias more than a few years as King, but he proved to be a good patriot, a competent soldier and an able administrator. He formed a regular army (known from the color of its armor as "the Black Brigade"), created the Magyar Hussars, which became the best-disciplined force in Europe, and equipped his army and his fleet on the Danube with cannon. Thanks to his vigorous leadership the Turks failed to conquer Hungary, the Czechs were expelled from the north of the kingdom and the Hapsburgs from the west. Matthias patronized artists, built up a great library, and, in 1467, founded Pressburg University. His codification of the law in 1486 earned him the title "Matthias the Just."

George of Podebrady's problems were altogether different from those of Matthias. The papacy was determined to settle the Hussite problem finally. It was not successful in doing so because George could rely on widespread international support, which prevented military action, and the papacy was unwilling to make any substantial concession, which ruled out a diplomatic solution. George had so much support within the Empire that there was even a proposal that he should replace Frederick III as Holy Roman Emperor. It is doubtful whether

Hungarian drinking horn from the treasury of King Matthias.

the papacy could have relied on much support if it had not been for Matthias. Although his first wife had been George's daughter and the two men had been friends and allies, Matthias invaded Bohemia in 1464 in support of a rising of Catholic nobles. For the next seven years warfare between the two continued, but Matthias was always beaten. The struggle did, however, take its toll on George, who died in 1471. He had tried, with the assistance of the Hussite Archbishop-elect (he could not be consecrated because of the papacy's hostility) of Prague, Jan Rokycana, who also died in 1471, to continue negotiations between the Hussites and Rome. After the death of the King and the Archbishop, contacts with Rome grew rarer, and splits within the Hussite movement, in particular between the Utraquists and the more extreme Unity of the Brotherhood, more common. After George's death war broke out between Ladislas (1471–1516), son of Casimir of Poland, and Matthias Hunyadi, both of whom claimed to have been elected King, and it was not until 1478 that Matthias acknowledged Ladislas' victory. But by then the power of the crown, built up under George, had

largely been whittled away, and the Polish kings were to prove a weak dynasty.

Meanwhile Matthias was growing increasingly unpopular in Hungary, mainly because of his interference in Bohemian and Austrian affairs. Many felt that he should have continued to concentrate on opposing the Turks, and as a result, his death in 1490 was largely unmourned. He had hoped to be elected Emperor in the place of Frederick III, but these ambitions had come to naught. The nobility, having seen how weakly Ladislas of Bohemia governed his country, decided to elect him King in order to expand their own power. They were not disappointed. The strength that Matthias had given Hungary and that George had given Bohemia was thrown away by their weak successor. The desire of the nobles to enhance their own power at the expense of the crown left Europe's eastern flank open to the Turkish threat.

In Russia at this time great changes were taking place. Moscow was at last to establish its authority decisively over the surrounding regions and to throw off finally the Mongol yoke. The agent of this was Prince Ivan III.

Skanderbeg's Albanian mountain stronghold.

The End of the Golden Horde

As Grand Prince of Moscow, Ivan III conceived the ambition of "the gathering together" of Russia. After taking the holdings of the Hanseatic League and annexing the huge northern empire of Novgorod, he turned to face the Golden Horde, to which Moscow had been a vassal for two and a half centuries. The leader of the Golden Horde, Khan Ahmed, demanded that the tribute due him be paid and, relying on aid from King Casimir of Poland, invaded Russia. Casimir never arrived and, after minor skirmishes, Ahmed withdrew, only to be murdered in his tent by a rival khan. Mongol suzerainty over Russia died with him.

When Ivan III became Grand Prince of Moscow in 1462, his principality was just one of several Russian states. To the west, vast areas inhabited by Orthodox Russians were under the authority of the Grand Prince of Lithuania; these lands included most of modern White Russia and the Ukraine. Since 1385 Lithuania and Poland had been united by treaty; consequently, any attempt to expand Lithuanian territory at the expense of Russia could be supported by the Polish army. In the northwest lay the two powerful, independent city-states, Novgorod and Pskov; the Novgorodian empire extended over the whole of northern Russia. And in the south the three main Mongol states, the "Golden Horde" and the two new khanates, the Crimea and Kazan, controlled the middle and lower Volga region, as well as the Ukrainian steppes.

Ever since 1237 when Batu, the grandson of the mighty Genghis Khan, first led Tartar tribesmen into Russian territory, the Golden Horde had exercised indirect suzerainty over the whole of Russia, except Novgorod and the northeastern regions, from its headquarters at Saray on the lower Volga. By the time Ivan III became Grand Prince there had been forty-five major Mongol-Russian wars, as well as countless Mongol raids on a smaller scale and the era of the "Mongol yoke" had lasted for nearly two and a half centuries. During that period the Mongols had never attempted a policy of annexing Russian lands, or of imposing the values of an alien culture on their vassals. Pushkin's famous description of the Mongols—"Arabs without Aristotle and algebra" —suggests one major reason why the Russians did not become "Asianized" or "Tartarized" by their invaders. The Mongol khans had simply been concerned with collecting heavy tribute and levying Russian recruits to fight in their armies. By geographical necessity, the invaders had allowed the Russian princes a great deal of autonomy,

provided the princes' policies never openly clashed with the interests of the Horde. Nevertheless, Russian nobles had never been allowed to forget that they ruled on sufferance, as vassals.

Because of the indirect nature of Mongol suzerainty, and because of dissensions within the Golden Horde, certain Russian princes had managed occasionally to assert their independence, and by the mid-fifteenth century, rival khanates had begun to break away; the Khanate of the Crimea had done so in 1430, and the Khanate of Kazan in 1436. Nevertheless, if they allied, the three khanates were still sufficiently powerful to force the Muscovites to pay the symbolic annual tribute, and if their raids were supported by Lithuania, Poland or the northern Russian principalities, they could put central Russia to the sword as they had done in 1237–38. Therefore, before Ivan III could establish Moscow's ascendancy over the rival principalities, and declare the city to be the capital of the new Russian nation, it was essential that the Mongol yoke be overthrown.

From 1452 onward, Ivan's father, Basil the Blind, had refused to pay regular tribute to the Mongol khans. When he became Grand Prince, Ivan III saw no reason to revive the outdated tradition. Between 1462 and 1475, Khan Ahmed of the Golden Horde made two unsuccessful attempts to force his "vassal" to pay the symbolic protection money. In 1476 Ivan III was summoned to explain to the Golden Horde why he had stopped paying; he refused to go, and subsequently broke off all diplomatic relations with the Khan.

For the next four years both sides prepared for the inevitable, full-scale confrontation, which would finally decide the issue of whether the Grand Principality of Moscow was still a vassal state of the Golden Horde. Early in 1480 Khan Ahmed sent a final demand for tribute. He not only wanted Ivan to pay his taxes for that year, but also for "the past years"—in other words since

A Russian helmet from the armory in the Kremlin. The traditional shape with gold inlay, enamel and precious stones shows considerable Eastern influence.

Opposite A fifteenth-century icon from Novgorod with Russian cavalry being blessed before battle and then in action.

1452. According to one chronicle, Ivan refused this demand by grabbing hold of the Khan's badge of authority, spitting on it, and treading it into the ground. Whether or not this story is true, by June, 1480, news reached Moscow that the Horde's advance parties had left their headquarters at Saray in the Eurasian steppe, and had arrived at the river Oka, Moscow's natural frontier in the south. Khan Ahmed had apparently been "urged on" by King Casimir iv of Lithuania and Poland, his ally since 1473, to deliver a crushing blow to Muscovite morale, and to remind Grand Prince Ivan that the Golden Horde was not prepared to be treated in this high-handed manner.

Since the beginning of Ivan III's reign, the Horde had failed to penetrate beyond the border areas of the Muscovite state, and yet, in 1480, the Grand Prince was not in a strong position. Ivan had been negotiating for nearly eight years with Mengli Girei, the Khan of the Crimea, in an attempt to secure a firm ally in the south, and it was only in April, 1480, when rumors of Khan Ahmed's preparations for invasion were already spreading in Moscow that Ivan's ambassador managed to persuade Khan Mengli to agree to a defensive alliance against the Golden Horde. The Grand Prince had already relied on the hostility between the Girei dynasty and Khan Ahmed, when the Golden Horde raided the Muscovite borders in 1465. In 1480, he had to be certain that Mengli would continue to be hostile toward the powerful Ahmed-Casimir alliance.

To make matters worse, in February, 1480, when Ivan III was away from Moscow dealing with a rebellion in Novgorod, which he had subjugated in 1478, his two oldest brothers, Boris and Andrei, defected to the Lithuanians, taking their combined private army of twenty thousand men with them. Apparently they were disgusted with Ivan's arbitrary behavior toward his fellow princes. By the summer, they had plundered their way to the city of Velikie Luki, on the Russo-Lithuanian frontier. From this base, the brothers began to negotiate with Casimir. Ivan tried three times to dissuade them, twice using his father-confessor, Bishop Vassian of Rostov, as ambassador, but Boris and Andrei preferred to wait until Casimir made a move. One chronicle even suggests that the brothers were advising Khan Ahmed at this time, helping him plan his invasion; certainly, Ivan III later accused Andrei of "leading the Khan on to attack the Grand Prince and the Russian land." But King Casimir also preferred to wait. He made a few vague promises of protection, but refused to commit himself any further; after all, the Golden Horde was not quite ready to cross the Russian frontiers, and Ivan III was preoccupied with affairs in Novgorod and Pskov.

By the time that Boris and Andrei had decided that little was to be gained by holding out for Casimir's cooperation, the Grand Prince could afford to take a slightly firmer line. His treaty with Mengli Girei had almost been agreed upon, Casimir was clearly not in a position to accept the brothers' defection on terms which would be advantageous to both sides, and the June invasion by Mongol advance parties had proved to be simply a reconnaissance. It was only in October, 1480, when Khan Ahmed had actually entered Russian territory, that Ivan III, realizing that he might need the twenty thousand men they had taken with them, allowed himself to be persuaded to forget his brothers' treachery—for the time being at least. Nevertheless, the period from January to September, 1480, had been extremely tense; when a Mongol invasion from the southeast could have occurred at any moment, Ivan had been forced to deal with a rebellion in the northwest, a mass defection—of great propaganda value both to Casimir and Ahmed—organized by members of his own family and a diplomatic crisis in the Crimea.

In September, 1480, Khan Ahmed's advance army arrived at the confluence of two rivers, the Oka and the Ugra. The Mongols had originally made for the traditional river frontier on the Oka, but had discovered that Ivan III had already deployed his troops, under Grand Duke Ivan Ivanovich, the heir to the throne, along the river line. Ahmed had then attempted to outflank Ivan by moving westward through Lithuanian territory to the upper reaches of the Ugra. The Muscovites had countered this move, after learning from the local citizens that Ahmed's advance parties had been making enquiries about the fords across the Ugra and taking up a series of positions at likely crossing places along the left bank of the Ugra. The Mongols had failed to cross the river before Ivan's armies arrived; they now had to wait until both rivers froze over. It would be the end of October, at the earliest, before the cavalry of the Golden Horde could be certain of a safe advance.

On September 30, Ivan III, returning to Moscow for three days to convene a council of war, found the city in a state of panic. The Muscovites expected to be besieged by the Lithuanian-Polish armies at any time, and refugees from more vulnerable towns were arriving in the hundreds: "they begged the Grand Prince, with great entreaties, to stand firm."

When Ivan III returned to his front line at the beginning of October, he set up headquarters at the village of Kremenets, twenty-five miles from the Ugra; clearly, at this stage, he expected a two-pronged attack. But on October 8, Khan Ahmed decided to risk an advance at one of the heavily guarded fords across the Ugra without King Casimir's promised support. For four days the Russians on the left bank, equipped with arrows and arquebuses and led by Grand Duke Ivan Ivanovich, held the Mongols off. On October 12, Ahmed withdrew to Vorotynsk, a mile and a half west of the river in Lithuanian territory, to wait for the arrival of the Lithuanian-Polish armies. He also had to wait at least two more weeks before the rivers froze. His troops were becoming restless, and he was forced to allow them a chance to work off their disappointment in the traditional manner—looting and pillaging the towns of the upper Oka basin.

But Casimir did not arrive. He had more than enough troubles of his own. Mengli Girei had led a raiding party of Crimean Tartars into the

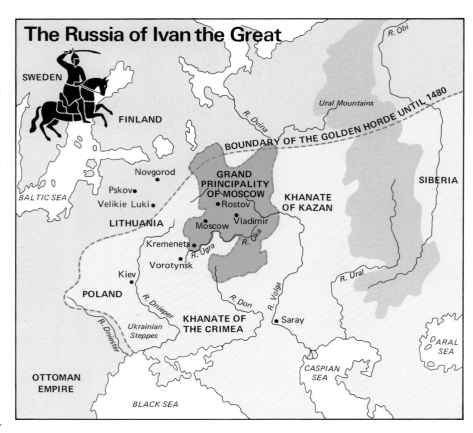

Lithuanian Ukraine at the beginning of October, "serving the Grand Prince." At the same time, three senior Russian princes in Lithuania had led a conspiracy to assassinate King Casimir. And the Lithuanian army had not received sufficient support from Poland. It may be that by allowing the Golden Horde to pillage Lithuanian territory, Khan Ahmed was getting his own back on Casimir; this was the second time he had been promised support for an invasion of Moscow (the first was in 1472), and the second time he had been let down.

While the Mongol army was waiting for Lithuanian help, the Muscovite army was waiting

Ivan III and his court from a contemporary manuscript. Ivan was the first Grand Prince of Moscow to use the titles of "Tsar" and "Autocrat."

The Annunciation Cathedral in the Kremlin. One of the fine buildings erected during Ivan's lifetime as a visible proof of the growing power and majesty of the Muscovite state and its ruler.

The contemporary Russian chronicles assess the events leading up to the final expulsion of the Mongols with chilling clarity. Both sides retreated because they were scared of each other—Ivan, because he was being badly advised and basically was a coward; Ahmed, because he thought that Ivan had evacuated the opposite bank of the river in order to lure him into a trap, and because, without reinforcements, he dared not risk an advance. Whatever the reason, neither side apparently had the stomach for a pitched battle. There are, of course, other possible explanations. Ivan III may have retreated and commenced negotiations in an attempt to play for time until Boris and Andrei arrived, and until news of the raid on Saray came through. Ahmed's actions are more understandable. Admittedly, he waited for at least two weeks after the river froze, but by the time he was certain that Casimir would not arrive, Ivan's two brothers had appeared in Kremenets, and he had heard about the Saray raid.

Perhaps the most important fact about the campaign of October, 1480, was that it was an anachronism. Clearly, Khan Ahmed was trying to model his tactics on those employed by Batu, who, in 1237–38, had mounted the only decisive winter invasion of Russia in history. Batu had managed to advance, with his extremely mobile Mongol cavalry, across a series of frozen rivers. But that had been over two hundred years before, at a time when the Mongols had been able to take full advantage of internal feuds between the Russian princes.

After 1452, as noted, Basil II had stopped paying the traditional yearly tribute to the Mongol khans, instead limiting his contribution to irregular "presents" and directing the taxes collected for payment to the Horde into his own treasury. Ahmed's invasion aimed to reestablish a tradition that had not been observed for nearly thirty years. The tribute he demanded from Ivan III during the peace negotiations of October, 1480— 4,200 roubles—was a mere fraction of the sum demanded and received by Khan Toktamish from the Grand Duchy of Vladimir in 1382— 85,000 roubles.

Khan Ahmed, in alliance with King Casimir, clearly hoped to deliver a crushing blow to Muscovite morale, and to remind Ivan III of the obligations imposed by the Mongol yoke, in one grand battle. But King Casimir consistently failed to honor his agreement with the Golden Horde, and the campaign of 1480 merely confirmed that the era of Mongol rule was over. The available sources do not tell us much about the context in which Ivan III himself placed the events of 1480. Ivan was evidently more of a statesman and diplomatist than a warrior. He preferred to exploit the potential of titles, symbols and legends as a means of cementing loyalty and entrenching his position, rather than to fight.

He was the first Grand Prince to use the titles of "Tsar" and "Autocrat" to symbolize the in-

for the reinforcements led by Boris and Andrei. Meanwhile, Ivan III sent a combined Russo-Tartar cavalry detachment to raid Saray, Ahmed's home base, and then, inexplicably, ordered a general retreat to Kremenets. There, he opened negotiations with the Khan. A Muscovite ambassador was sent, laden with presents, to persuade Ahmed to abandon his invasion and leave peacefully. In reply, the Khan threatened to return and take Ivan himself prisoner unless the Grand Prince promised to pay tribute amounting to 4,200 roubles, in quarterly instalments. But on October 20, Boris and Andrei arrived with their private armies and on November 7, although the Ugra had at last frozen over, Khan Ahmed began his long retreat to Saray. He never arrived. Early in January, 1481, Khan Ivak of western Siberia, heading an army of sixteen thousand men, managed to locate the retreating Mongols. Somehow, possibly from Ivan III, he had heard about the rich booty the Golden Horde had discovered in the towns of the upper Oka, and he took Khan Ahmed by surprise. Ivak himself met no resistance when he crept into Ahmed's white tent early in the morning, and, with his bare hands, killed the one man capable of holding the Golden Horde together. Ahmed's sons were subsequently killed in battle with the Crimean Tartars, and the Golden Horde collapsed. The fall of the Mongol yoke was complete.

dependence of the Muscovite dynasty from any Mongol master. As well as qualifying for the popular epithet "Great," Ivan was also known as "Grozni" ("the Awe-Inspiring," or, more ambiguously, "the Terrible"), like Ivan IV half a century later. From 1493 onward, his advisers styled Ivan III "Derzhavny" ("the Ruler") and "Gosudar" ("Sovereign of all Russia"). After his second marriage in 1472 to the niece of the last Byzantine Emperor, Constantine XI, Ivan adopted the Byzantine double-headed eagle as a symbol of the dynasty's authority, in addition to his own family's St. George. Ivan presumably regarded the campaign of 1480 in the light of this wider concern —"the gathering together of Russia," combined with an exultation of the power and prestige of the Muscovite dynasty.

After Ivan III's death, the Russian chroniclers evidently had difficulty describing their "Great" Prince; they could not simply list his epic battles, nor could they picture him as a mighty warrior. In the end, they created a semimythological character to match Ivan's obvious talents as a successful, but unscrupulous, politician. Ambrogio Contarini, an Italian traveler who visited Moscow in the winter of 1476–77, wrote an eye-witness description of Ivan III in his *Travels to Tana and Persia*: the Grand Prince was apparently "tall and thin and handsome." Some Russian historians and chroniclers, however, preferred to call Ivan "Gorbaty," ("the Hunchback") and to claim that the late Tsar had been so fearful to look upon that women fainted when they were forced to face him. Like Shakespeare's version of the character of Richard III of England, the Russian historians' character studies of Ivan III often stress the more grotesque aspects; he was ruthlessly calculating, basically cowardly and physically deformed. And he was apparently in the habit of drinking until he collapsed.

Perhaps Ivan's Muscovite advisers, as well as interested parties abroad, encouraged this terrifying image during the Tsar's lifetime. When the official Russian account of the deeds of Vlad the Impaler, the historical Dracula, who ruled Wallachia from 1456 to 1472, and again in 1476, was compiled in 1490, the story was substantially altered to promote Ivan III's concept of autocracy. Whereas in the German texts, Vlad Dracula impales a cowardly monk who dishonestly praises his evil deeds, and rewards a brave monk who honestly condemns them, in the *Povest' o Drakule*, the Russian version, it is the critic of Vlad's cruelty who is impaled, and the flatterer who is rewarded. The *Povest'* shows Vlad Dracula as, quite simply, a justifiably harsh father to his people. Prince Stefan of Moldavia (1457–1504) could never understand how Ivan had been so successful without behaving either as a warrior or as a tyrant: "he increased his dominions while sitting at home and sleeping."

Because of the autonomy the Mongols allowed the Russian princes, and because Muscovite scribes of the immediate post-Mongol period

A manuscript illustration of the victory of the Russians over the Golden Horde at the Battle of Kulikovo in 1380. Ivan's expulsion of Khan Ahmed was the culmination of more than a century of intermittent struggle against the Mongols.

probably altered the written sources to present their grand princes in a more glorious light, it is virtually impossible to assess the impact of the "Tartar yoke" on Russian society, politics and culture.

Recently, Russian opinion has been sharply divided on this issue. On the one hand, the "Eurasian" school presents the Muscovite Tsar and Autocracy as natural developments of the Mongol Khan and Golden Horde, and stresses the direct impact on the rebuilding of the Russian nation of the Mongol invasions, which apparently destroyed the Kievan economic and social order. It was the responsibility of the Russian princes to repair the devastation caused by the Horde in their own territories, and one major result of the Tartar yoke was a shift of population and of economic and political power to the northeast. On the other hand, the traditional "Russian" school, while admitting that the Mongols caused mass devastation, wore down Russian defenses and disrupted trade during the actual period the Golden Horde remained a powerful force, nonetheless emphasizes the continuity of cultural and political development from Kievan Russia to the rise of Moscow.

Whatever the long-term effects, at the beginning of Ivan III's reign it was still a remote possibility that the three main Mongol khanates could ally to destroy Moscow; the elimination of this possibility was an essential step in the long process of "the gathering together of Russia" as a nation.

CHRISTOPHER FRAYLING

The fall of Constantinople enabled Mehmet the Conqueror to press his attack on Eastern Europe. Believing that he was a modern Alexander, the Sultan had led his troops into Bosnia, Albania and Serbia, where John Hunyadi's heroic defense of Belgrade checked the Turkish advance. The Peloponnesus fell to the invaders, ending the rule of the Palaeologi in Greece, and in 1461 the Turks conquered the Empire of Trebizond, the last independent Greek state still in existence. Mehmet's troops then turned their attention to the Venetian and Genoese stations in the Aegean Sea, and frightened such popes as Celestine III and Pius II into preaching a crusade. But neither the conscience nor the fear of the West could effectively be aroused by such calls.

The Turkish fleet soon wrested Scutari and Euboea from the Venetians, and by 1478 their raiders had reached the outskirts of Venice. The Christians made occasional efforts to strike back; in 1472 a Venetian fleet had even attacked Smyrna and burned many buildings there. But in 1479, Venice was forced to sign a peace treaty with Mehmet that involved the surrender of lands in Albania and the payment of a substantial fee for the privilege of trading in the East. Mehmet's forces attacked southern Italy, raided the Austrian provinces of Styria and Carinthia, and unsuccessfully besieged Rhodes, which was held by the Knights of St. John of Jerusalem.

The Turks invest Rhodes.

Mehmet's death in 1481 led to disputes over the succession between his two sons. Bayazid II, the legitimate heir, and Jem. Venice attempted to take advantage of the strife between the brothers, but the drawn-out war between the Republic and the Turks from 1499 to 1503 caused little change. It did, however, prevent any immediate Turkish advance in the Balkans and removed the threat to Italy. Bayazid succeeded in overthrowing the threat from Jem, but he proved a weak ruler, and in 1512 his youngest son, Selim I, deposed him.

Classical scholarship

The effect of the printing press was felt throughout Europe. The market for books grew rapidly, as did the number of books published to satisfy the demand. New printing presses were being opened each year in Germany, France, Italy, the Netherlands and

In the Temple of Venus, printed by Manutius in 1499.

England, the most notable among them being the Aldine Press, which was established in Venice by Aldus Manutius (1450–1515). Before 1490 there were scarcely any printed Greek texts despite the demand that had been created by Humanism. Homer's ever-popular epics were almost the only Greek books available, although presses in Milan and Florence had produced a few isolated Greek texts. Aldus, who was much influenced by his friend Pico della Mirandola, therefore gathered together a band of distinguished Greek scholars— his "Academy"—to advise him on the choice of texts and to edit them. Before he died Aldus had produced the texts of twenty-eight Greek and Latin classics, of which the most important were the editions of Aristotle in 1495 and Plato in 1513. His editions

made the philosophy of the ancient Greek and Latin world available to scholars for the first time. After 1498, Aldus also produced octavo editions of the classics. After his death, the press was continued by his family.

The birth of modern diplomacy

A major change in "international relations," namely the beginning of the use of resident ambassadors, occurred during the second half of the fifteenth century. The impact this had on the relations between individual states was often enormous. Throughout the Middle Ages diplomatic activity had been undertaken by ambassadors, usually leading nobles or bishops, sent to negotiate particular treaties. After his mission was completed, the ambassador was expected to return to his own country. Two causes led to the birth of diplomacy on the modern pattern. The first was the example of the papacy and the Byzantine Empire, both of which had offices dealing with foreign affairs. The papacy, through its system of legates, who were expected to report to the pope and to conduct negotiations with the country to which they had been sent, also had a permanent diplomatic service. The second influence was the development of trade. This encouraged the Venetians to send representatives to deal with trading matters in foreign ports. In Constantinople, if nowhere else, the Venetian *bailo* had diplomatic functions in addition to his consular and trading responsibilities. Similarly, after the Medici came to power in Florence, the representative of the Medici bank was often regarded as an ambassador of the state, and was entrusted with fairly complex diplomatic activity.

But neither of these influences was the cause of the change that took place in diplomacy. The real

cause was the tension between the city-states of northern Italy, a tension that was continuous throughout the later Middle Ages. The cannibalistic wars led to a situation where the major Italian states were evenly balanced in size and strength; it was virtually impossible for any one of the major states to dominate the region entirely, because of this balance, and because there were enough of them to cut the over-ambitious down to size. North Italian politics had reached a state of equilibrium by the late fifteenth century, although it is unlikely that many contemporaries realized it.

Because of the rapid shift in alliances and the risk that yesterday's friend might be today's enemy, it became more and more important for the rulers of each of the major city-states to be well informed about life in the others, so that they would know of any impending change of plan. In the north of Europe there was no such need; the kings of France, for example, knew that the English were the enemy and they did not need a resident source of information to tell them so. In Italy hostility and friendship were more flexible. From about 1430, it became fairly normal for allies to exchange "residents." The function of the resident was twofold; to make diplomatic arrangements between the governments of the two states, and to report back regularly to his own government the behavior of the state to which he was accredited. The reports of ambassadors became, during the sixteenth century, increasingly full of descriptions of life in the states in which they were living, and are among the most valuable sources of information about contemporary life for the historian. During the period between the Peace of Lodi (1454) and the French invasion of Italy in 1494, the ambassadorial system was regularized, and the functions, responsi-

states of Italy give rise to modern diplomacy

The Arrival of the Ambassadors, by Carpaccio.

bilities and privileges of ambassadors were put on a formal basis. During the early sixteenth century, the use of ambassadors spread to northern Europe also. The use of occasional "extraordinary" ambassadors did not die out, but it gradually became less important.

The birth of modern diplomacy and the growth of the use of resident ambassadors shows how the concept of the state was developing. Until governments saw the state as an independent entity in its own right, it was merely extravagant to keep a permanent embassy abroad. The writings of authors such as Niccolò Machiavelli characterize the new attitude toward the role and meaning of the state.

Changes in warfare

The development of new fighting methods in the late fifteenth century is in many ways comparable to the birth of diplomacy, and it too depended on a changed view of the state. Infantry became much more important, and where cavalry was used it was usually only light cavalry. Heavy cavalry were too unmaneuverable and too vulnerable in an age of improving guns. In England the flower of the nobility were killed during the Wars of the Roses, largely because they were unable to get up and run away if they were knocked off their horses, as they were weighed down by their heavy armor. The quality and efficiency of guns improved rapidly throughout the century.

There were other changes even more profound. The fifteenth century was the great age of the mercenary soldier and the *condottiere* general. There have always been mercenaries, but in the fifteenth century, particularly in Italy, rulers abdicated their military functions and hired generals with their own soldiers to fight their wars. The basic cause of this was the breakdown of the old feudal responsibility to fight for a lord. In most cases this had been commuted for money payments during the thirteenth and fourteenth centuries. Many rulers could demand mass levies, but untrained and reluctant soldiers do not make efficient armies, and fifteenth-century Italians preferred farming and trading to fighting. By hiring mercenary armies, citizens of warring states were able to concentrate on the important things in life, while the professional soldiers got on with the fighting. This way of fighting wars was all right in theory, but it took no account of the ambitions of the *condottiere* leaders. They had the strength to blackmail their employers, and often did so. Many rulers had as much to fear from the armies they had hired as from those fighting on the other side.

The most highly regarded mercenaries were Swiss, and one Swiss "mercenary" force has survived into the twentieth century—the Swiss Guard at the Vatican. The fifteenth century was one of almost continual war in Switzerland as it was in Italy. The cantons were forced to fight against lords who claimed feudal rights and against each other. Although these wars did not substantially advance Swiss territory, they did result in increased freedom and in a more developed relationship with each other. The most important development was the signature by the Archduke Sigismund of Austria of the Everlasting Compact of 1474, in which he effectively renounced his claims to sovereignty in Switzerland. No new members had joined the Swiss Confederation since 1353, but the Everlasting Compact was the signal for the outbreak of a flurry of activity. Five new cantons became members between 1481 and 1515. This expansion was partly the result of unsuccessful attempts by the Emperor Maximilian to reclaim some of the rights signed away by the Everlasting Compact.

But these wars did not prevent the Swiss from building up their reputation as mercenaries, a practice that seems to have been begun by Louis XI of France, who hired Swiss mercenary help. The practice spread rapidly and the Swiss sent armies to help both sides during the invasions of Italy by Charles VIII and Louis XII. As the Swiss would not fight against each other, this sometimes created difficulties for their employers. In 1500 the Swiss employed by Ludovico Sforza betrayed him at Novara in order to avoid the necessity of fighting against the Swiss employed by Louis XII.

It was largely in order to avoid this sort of difficulty that some of the Italian states, following the lead of Florence, began to raise professional armies, a practice that was widespread by 1510.

The Wars of the Roses

Edward IV's reign continued for a dozen years after the Battle of Tewkesbury. He proved himself a strong monarch who eschewed corruption and acted much as Sir John Fortescue, Edward's Lord Chief Justice, had recommended in his tract, *The Governance of England.* But Edward had his defects. He often tended to be idle; he was somewhat spendthrift—despite the need for economy to help in his war against Louis XI in 1475; he could be cruel; and he was avaricious.

The legacy of treachery had not yet been entirely spent. Clarence, Edward's older brother, was executed in 1478 for plotting against the King, and when Edward died in 1483 his younger brother, Richard of Gloucester, dethroned Edward's son, Edward V. Richard's character has been a subject of great controversy for historians. Tudor apologists—and Shakespeare, whose *Richard III* is based on the work of one of them, Polydore Vergil—accused him of murdering Edward V and his younger brother in the Tower of London and of many other crimes. Some modern historians think that Henry VII may have been responsible for the murder of the young princes after Richard's death. Richard was certainly willing to kill in order to secure his position. Potential rebels were either assassinated or executed for treason, but, nevertheless, Richard's days were numbered.

Swiss mercenaries, a detail from the *Mass of Bolsena* by Raphael.

109

RICARDVS · III · ANG · REX ·

The Battle of Bosworth   1485

The last battle of the Wars of the Roses was fought at Bosworth, where an invading army under the Lancastrian Henry Tudor met a larger force under the usurping Yorkist King Richard III. Richard was killed and his force defeated. By marrying the Yorkist Princess Elizabeth, Henry united the warring factions, unified the country and gave England peace from civil war for the first time in a generation.

On the night of August 21, 1485, four armies converged on Redmore Plain south of the small English village of Market Bosworth, setting up their tents within a few miles of each other. The largest, numbering perhaps ten thousand men in all, encamped under the royal standards of Richard III and the banners of his two principal lieutenants, Thomas Howard, Duke of Norfolk, and Henry Percy, Earl of Northumberland. From their position on Ambien Hill on the eastern edge of the Plain, Richard's soldiers could make out—less than three miles to the southwest—the campfires of Henry Tudor's army of five thousand, a polyglot mixture of French, Welsh and Englishmen under the command of the veteran John de Vere, Earl of Oxford. To the north and south of the Tudor bivouacs lay the two smaller forces of Thomas, Lord Stanley, and his brother Sir William, recruited from the family's holdings in north Wales, Cheshire and Lancashire, poised to strike either at their King or at the "unknown Welshman" who came to challenge him.

The immediate issue was whether Richard could maintain by force the crown he had usurped two years and two months previously. When Edward IV, Richard's brother, died in 1483, it had seemed that the succession was securely vested in his oldest son, the thirteen-year-old Edward V. Richard dispossessed his nephew and seized the crown for himself, a result of a feud that existed after the death of Edward IV between the court party, led by Edward's Queen, Elizabeth Woodville, and a group of powerful magnates who looked to Richard for leadership. While Edward lived, Richard was far from court, bringing peace and order to the northern counties and the feud lay dormant. But when the King died it came to life with a vengeance. The Queen's party made the first move by trying to undermine Richard's office of Protector, of thirteen-year-old Edward V, which was sanctioned in Edward's will. Richard replied by seizing the young King. In the tense and turbulent weeks that followed Richard decided that the only way to secure his position against future reversals was to supplant Edward V as the anointed King of England. Reviving an old scandal that Elizabeth

Woodville's marriage to Edward IV was invalid, he declared all their offspring illegitimate and had himself crowned as Richard III.

The speed with which the coup was carried out and the reputation Richard enjoyed as an able soldier and a conscientious, efficient administrator brought a general measure of support for the new King from all levels of society. Only when Richard's most influential ally, the Duke of Buckingham, changed sides were the Queen's followers able to engineer an uprising. This took place in October, 1483, and was crushed promptly and without difficulty.

But Richard's initial successes could not conceal his one basic weakness. He was a usurper and his claim to the throne hung on the slender fiction of his nephews' bastardy. Once the Queen was convinced that her sons—the unfortunate princes in the Tower—would never emerge from their prison alive, she exploited this weakness in the most effective way possible. She established an alliance with the last surviving heir of the Lancastrian dynasty, which Edward IV had himself supplanted in an earlier phase of the Wars of the Roses.

The twenty-four-year-old Henry Tudor, Earl of Richmond, was at that time a refugee living at the court of Brittany and had not set foot in England since 1471. On his mother's side he traced his descent to John of Gaunt, the third son of Edward III; on his father's to the widow of Henry V, Queen Catherine, who had subsequently married Owen Tudor. The prospects of this Lancastrian claimant, who until 1483 seemed fated to spend the rest of his life in exile, were dramatically revived by the proposal that the Woodvilles now put to him. They offered him the hand of the daughter of Edward IV, Elizabeth of York. If Henry Tudor married Elizabeth of York he would command the allegiance not only of those who still believed that the crown belonged rightfully to the dispossessed Lancastrian dynasty, but also of those Yorkists who could not stomach Richard's coup d'état against the sons of Edward IV. Henry was quick to seize his opportunity, and on Christmas Day, 1483, swore a solemn oath at the high altar

Henry Tudor, who came from exile to win the last battle of the Wars of the Roses and establish his family firmly on the throne of England.

Opposite Richard III, the last Yorkist King of England. His defeat at Bosworth, caused by the desertion of part of his force, reflected the weakness of his position as a usurper.

of Rennes Cathedral that he would marry Elizabeth of York.

From that day on it was a foregone conclusion that Richard would have to defend his throne against Henry Tudor in battle. Throughout 1484 the two protagonists were locked in a war of nerves. From the base of his great castle at Nottingham, Richard toured restlessly throughout his realm, preparing his defenses, reorganizing the fleet and negotiating a truce with his troublesome northern neighbors, the Scots. A diplomatic effort to induce the Bretons to hand over his rival failed by a hairbreadth, and Henry Tudor escaped instead to the court of a more powerful patron, the King of France. In the same year Richard's prospects suffered a frightful blow from the deaths of his only son Edward and of his wife Anne. To many people, uncommitted to either side but disenchanted with the chaos and unrest of a disputed succession, a Lancastrian claimant allied to a Yorkist bride offered a better prospect of peace and settlement than a childless usurper.

For Richard III the long period of watching and waiting ended on August 11, 1485, when couriers brought word to Nottingham that Henry had landed four days earlier at Milford Haven in the Welsh county of Pembroke. As Henry marched unopposed through Wales flaunting the ancient colors of the Welsh kings, Richard summoned his captains and moved south to Leicester, guarding the road to London. Ten days later the rival armies lay camped on Redmore Plain, ready to join battle.

At first light on August 22, the Yorkist army took up a defensive position along the ridge of Ambien Hill. Norfolk's men formed the van, Richard held the center and Northumberland anchored the line in the rear. As the Earl of Oxford led the Lancastrian vanguard across the plain he saw that Richard's line could only be engaged through a frontal attack, since the southern flank of Ambien Hill was protected by marshes and the northern side was too steep to assault.

The gap between the opposing vanguards narrowed. Both Richard and Henry knew how

much the outcome would depend on the two Stanleys, who still hovered undecided in the wings. Both sent messengers to Lord Stanley demanding that he commit himself. If he refused, Richard threatened to execute his oldest son on the spot. Back came the answer that Lord Stanley had other sons and would not join the King. To Henry's appeal the reply was more courteous but still guarded—he would make his own dispositions and join the battle when the time was ripe.

This answer left Henry "no little vexed," according to his court historian, Polydore Vergil, but his troops were now too far committed to draw back. With Sir Gilbert Talbot's Shropshiremen on his right and Sir John Savage commanding the Welsh contingents on his left, Oxford planned to throw the entire Lancastrian army into the attack. Henry, who had no experience of war, would remain in the rear, protected by a screen of footmen and a single troop of horse.

As soon as the rebel troops came within range on the lower slopes of the hill, Norfolk's longbowmen unleashed a hail of arrows. Then his trumpeters sounded the charge and the royal vanguard streamed down the slopes. Oxford's formations, who had strict instructions not to stray more than a few feet from their company commanders, wavered under the shock but did not break. All around the lower slopes of Ambien Hill the two front lines locked in fierce hand-to-hand combat.

Slowly at first, Oxford's tactics began to pay off. His densely packed troops gained ground while

Above The Battle of Bosworth with Henry Tudor triumphant in the center. A stone relief from Stowe church.

Opposite left A model of the full-plate armor typical of the later fifteenth century.

Opposite right A knight being helped into his armor by a squire.

Below The arms and caparisons of knights from the counties of Suffolk, Essex and Kent from a roll painted in 1480 by the Clarenceaux King of Arms.

Talbot and Savage pressed the attack from the flanks. Suddenly disaster struck. The Duke of Norfolk was slain in the mêlée and soon his men were in full retreat up the hill. Richard gave orders for Northumberland to commit his corps of three thousand men. But Northumberland, taking his cue from Lord Stanley, had decided that he too would stand aloof until the battle was over and give his allegiance to the victor. Richard's messenger returned with the news that Northumberland would guard against a flank attack by Lord Stanley.

The situation was not yet desperate for Richard. The vanguard was badly mauled but the Yorkist center was still intact. Northumberland refused to move for Richard, but neither of the Stanleys had yet moved against him. All at once, Richard conceived a bold plan to put an end to the battle

The dragon of Wales which became the symbol of the Tudor dynasty.

without waiting for the grim slogging match on Ambien Hill to decide the issue. Less than a mile away on Redmore Plain his scouts had spotted the red dragon standard of Henry Tudor, screened only by a small rearguard. If Richard could despatch his rival, the battle would be won. More than that, Henry's death would settle forever the blood feud between Lancaster and York.

At the head of his mounted household knights and squires of the body—not more than eighty all told—Richard rode forward, skirting the battle, down the northwestern slope of Ambien Hill, and thundered out across the plain. His route took him straight across the path of Sir William Stanley's force. As Richard's cavalry crashed into Henry's rearguard, Sir William saw that now he had the opportunity to intervene decisively on the Tudor's behalf, and he ordered his men to attack. The impetus of Richard's charge carried him right through the protective screen of infantry. Making straight for his target the King slew Henry Tudor's standard bearer, Sir William Brandon, and unhorsed the bulky figure of Sir John Cheyney. For a moment success seemed within his grasp. But already Sir William Stanley's horsemen were colliding with the rear of Richard's little force. As the ring of steel closed in around him Richard was overwhelmed and battered to the ground. John Rouse, a bitter critic of Richard's life, said of his death: "if I may speak the truth to his honour, he most valiantly defended himself as a noble knight to his last breath, often exclaiming as he was betrayed, and saying—Treason! Treason! Treason!"

By treason Richard grasped the crown and by treason he lost it. After the battle his naked body was slung over a pack horse, taken to Leicester and buried without ceremony in the chapel of the Grey Friars. The tomb was destroyed in the reign of Henry VIII and Richard's bones thrown into the River Soar.

To the Tudor propagandists who later described these events, the Battle of Bosworth meant far more than the end of Richard's short career as a usurper. They saw it as the pivotal event in the history of England between 1399 and 1509. Enshrined in Shakespeare's historical plays, the Tudor interpretation has exercised a profound influence on historians ever since. Its theme is that monarchy is a sacred institution vested by divine right in the legitimate heir to the throne and that any attempt to wrest the crown from its rightful holder will be punished by God. The troubled history of England in the fifteenth century thus began in 1399 when Henry Bolingbroke deposed and then murdered his cousin Richard II and set himself up as Henry IV, the first of the Lancastrian line of kings. In Shakespeare's *Richard II* the Bishop of Carlisle warns:

If you crown him (Henry Bolingbroke), let me prophesy, the blood of England shall manure the ground and future ages groan for this foul act . . . and in this seat of peace, tumultuous wars shall kin with kin, and kind with kind confound.

The punishment for Bolingbroke's sin was visited on his grandson Henry VI, who presided over the loss of England's provinces in France, watched his realm disintegrate in the civil strife of the Wars of the Roses and finally lost his crown to the Yorkist heir, Edward IV, in 1461. Although the Yorkists enjoyed a better claim to the throne than the Lancastrians, they too stained their hands with blood. In 1471 Edward IV executed Henry VI and his son Prince Edward, and in 1478 his own brother George, Duke of Clarence. After Edward IV's death, Richard murdered his own nephews and secured the crown for himself.

The Battle of Bosworth, in this Tudor view, is not only God's judgment on Richard's villainy, it also inaugurates the reign of Henry VII who unites the warring houses of York and Lancaster and puts an end to thirty years of treachery and bloodshed. As Shakespeare has Henry declare in the last lines of *Richard III*:

> England hath long been mad, and scarred herself
> The brother blindly shed the brother's blood . . .
> All this divided York and Lancaster
> Divided in their dire division
> O! now let Richmond and Elizabeth
> The true succeeders of each royal house
> By God's fair ordinance conjoin together
> And let their heirs—God if they will be so—
> Enrich the time to come with smooth-faced peace
> With smiling plenty and fair prosperous days.

To Shakespeare's audiences, 1485 was, therefore, the dividing line between the anarchy of the Wars of the Roses and the peace and prosperity of the Tudor Age. Later generations of historians went even further. They regarded Henry as the founder, not only of a new dynasty, but of a new monarchy. The hallmarks of the new monarchy were the rigorous suppression of the aristocracy, the creation of a trained bureaucracy of professional civil servants, swift and arbitrary justice imposed by the new Court of the Star Chamber and the amassing of a large fortune that left the King free to rule without Parliament. Thus, the year 1485 has passed into history books as one of the dates that every English schoolboy remembers, marking the end of the Middle Ages and the start of modern times.

This neat and tidy dividing line has not withstood the test of scholarship. It is true that Henry VII was an able and resourceful king, but there was nothing "new" about his monarchy. Almost every innovation attributed to him has a precedent in the reign of Edward IV. The premature end of the Yorkist dynasty at Bosworth tends to obscure the fact that Edward enjoyed a long and successful reign of twenty-two years, broken only by a brief reversal of fortune in 1470–71 when the powerful Earl of Warwick, "the Kingmaker," switched his allegiance. Like Henry, Edward avoided expensive wars abroad and fostered the commercial interests of British merchants. Like Henry, he applied himself vigorously to the suppression of local

disorder, built up the crown's finances from the efficient administration of his estates and was able to dispense with Parliament during the last years of his reign. The records of Edward's government are less plentiful and more difficult to interpret than those of Henry's, but their unmistakable verdict is that the first Tudor owed a great debt to the groundwork and the example of his Yorkist predecessors. Henry acknowledged that debt himself in his choice of servants. No fewer than twenty-nine of his regular councillors, including the Chancellor, Bishop Morton, served on the council of one or other of the Yorkist kings.

The point must also be made that the Wars of the Roses were not in reality the slaughterhouse portrayed by Shakespeare. Though the ranks of the aristocracy were certainly depleted, the country as a whole was never subjected to the miseries that France experienced during the Hundred Years War. The armies that took part were small, containing few professional soldiers. They were

Elizabeth of York. Her marriage to Henry VII united the warring factions of York and Lancaster in support of the Tudors.

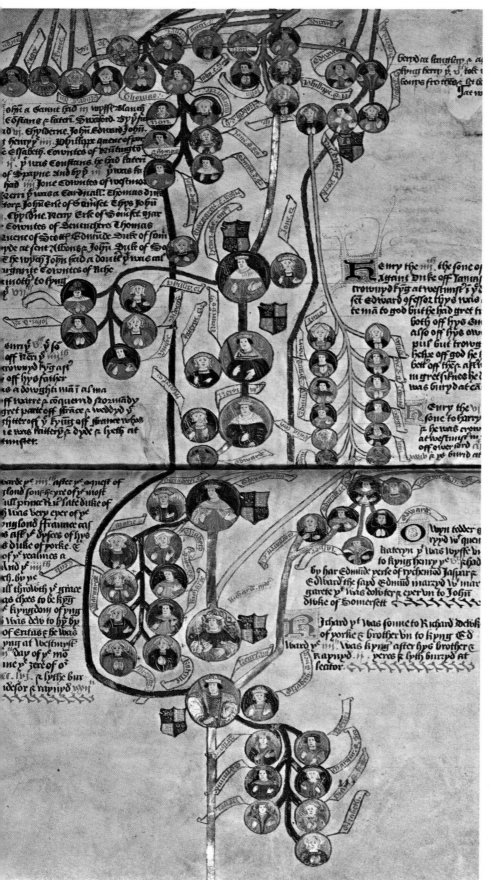

summoned at short notice and disbanded as soon as the battle was over. The whole period of campaigning between the first Battle of St. Albans in 1455 and the Battle of Stoke in 1487 (when Henry VII defeated a Yorkist invasion from Ireland) amounted to no more than thirteen weeks —in a span of thirty-two years. Moreover, most of the fighting took place between 1455 and 1461, before Edward IV came to the throne.

These arguments are a useful corrective to earlier misunderstandings, but they do not obliterate the importance of 1485 as a milestone in England's history. What distinguished the reign of Henry VII from his Yorkist predecessors was not so much his methods of government as his ability to provide a clear-cut solution to the dynastic problems of the succession. In Henry VII's cupboard there were no marital skeletons, such as the slurs on Edward IV's marriage, which had given Richard his excuse to disinherit Edward's children. As an only son, Henry had no brothers who might become a thorn in his side as the Duke of Clarence had been to Edward IV. Nor was Henry obliged to create a princely palatinate—such as Richard III had enjoyed in the northern counties—which might prove a threat to his heir.

The endowment of younger brothers of the royal house with huge estates and viceregal powers was a perennial cause of disorder and civil war in the Middle Ages. It was a dispute over the Duchy of Lancaster, the palatinate created for the cadet branch of the Plantagenet kings, that sparked off the cycle of the Wars of the Roses in 1399, after Richard II's ill-judged attempt to take the duchy away from his cousin, Henry Bolingbroke. It was the dispute between the French king and the cadet line of the dukes of Burgundy that enabled the English to step in and conquer France for Henry V. The Tudors never had to face the problems caused by a superfluity of male heirs. Henry VII was fortunate also in that the Wars of the Roses killed off most of the Yorkist claimants who might have threatened his security. Unlike Edward IV he never had to contend with a deposed king fermenting trouble in foreign courts. The best that the surviving Yorkist rebels could do after 1485 was to put up two pretenders—Lambert Simnel and Perkin Warbeck.

However Henry VII and Henry VIII after him persecuted all potential rivals with the single-minded ruthlessness prescribed by Machiavelli. Edward of Warwick was executed on a fabricated charge of treason in 1497, and in 1513 Edmund de la Pole (a son of Edward IV's sister Elizabeth) was sent to the block as a precaution before Henry VIII left the country to join his army in France.

At the same time, both Henrys took great pains to make public the legitimacy of their claims to the throne through the means of propaganda at their disposal—court festivals, plays, tournaments and pageants.

Henry VII was equally aware of the importance of establishing his dynasty in the eyes of his neigh-

The Battle of Barnet in 1471
at which Edward IV re-
established the Yorkist
dynasty on the throne.
Henry VII and his successors
were fortunate that the Wars
of the Roses had killed off
most of the Yorkist claimants
who might have threatened
their security.

bors. His canny and patient diplomacy yielded
spectacular results in 1496 when the court of Spain
recognized the House of Tudor by consenting to
a marriage treaty between Catherine of Aragon
and Henry's oldest son, Arthur. No less important
was the marriage in 1502 of Henry's daughter
Margaret to King James IV of Scotland. When
Queen Elizabeth I, the last of the Tudors, died 101
years later, it was the great-grandson of this couple
who succeeded her as James I and united the
crowns of England and Scotland. Edward IV, too,
had worked hard to arrange marriages for his
children, but when he died in 1483 not one of them
had found a partner from the courts of Europe.

The significance of Henry's vigilance and good
fortune is revealed in the fact that he died in his
bed after a reign of twenty-four years and that on
his death the crown passed without dispute to his
son. This was an event that could not have been
predicted when Henry triumphed at Bosworth
Field in 1485. Looking further ahead to the end
of the Tudor dynasty in 1603, the achievement of
its founder appears even more remarkable. For
during the sixteenth century the Tudors withstood
and survived a series of crises any one of which
could have shattered a monarchy less firmly
founded—Henry VIII's break with Rome in 1529,
the minority of Edward VI, the Roman Catholic
backlash under Queen Mary and the Spanish
Armada of Elizabeth's reign. To appreciate the
significance of the Battle of Bosworth, it must be
seen in the context of the whole Tudor age, a
period of 118 years in which the English people
reached a pinnacle of unity, self-confidence and
expansion unmatched until the reign of Queen
Victoria.   ANTHONY CHEETHAM

Opposite A genealogy made
for Henry VII which traces his
ancestry back to the biblical
Japhet, the Viking God Woden
and Rollo of Normandy. The
Tudors were always aware of
the somewhat tenuous nature
of their claim to the throne.

117

Maximilian, who was to transform, strengthen and expand the Holy Roman Empire, was born in 1459, the son of the ineffectual Hapsburg Emperor Frederick III. From 1472 Frederick saw that the power of Burgundy was no less of a threat to the Empire than it was to France. He thought that this threat could be turned to the advantage of the Hapsburgs if Mary, the only child of Charles the Bold—and certainly Europe's most eligible lady—could be married to Maximilian. Although Charles appears to have approved the plan in principle, negotiations dragged on inconclusively for years, and it was only in August, 1477 (eight months after Charles' death) that the marriage finally took place. Frederick, for the rest of his reign a feeble nonentity, had made the Hapsburgs the dominant princely family in Germany. But the new Hapsburg possessions had to be fought for. Louis XI of France was determined to get at least the French areas while the Count of Lorraine was determined to recover the whole of his former territory. It was only in 1479, after a battle at Guinegate —known as the Battle of the Spurs because of the hasty retreat of the French cavalry—that Maximilian could rely on widespread recognition. He was still not accepted everywhere, and had to put down a rising in the Netherlands province of Gelderland in 1480. The death of Mary in 1482 was the signal for a further outbreak of trouble. Some of the Dutch states refused to acknowledge Maximilian as regent for his baby son Philip and in 1482 Maximilian was forced to agree to the Treaty of Arras, which arranged a marriage between his daughter

The Emperor Maximilian with his family.

Margaret and the Dauphin. As dowry, Maximilian was forced to give Artois and Franche Comté, and to leave all the French regions in the hands of Louis XI. It was only in 1486 that Maximilian was able to subdue the remaining Burgundian possessions—and even then not finally, for Maximilian was imprisoned by the city of Bruges in 1488. In 1486 Maximilian was crowned King of the Romans and took over much of the administration of the Empire from his father. The next few years were spent in quelling rebellion in Germany. In order to provide the Empire with an army, the leading nobles, bishops and towns of Swabia were summoned to a conference at Esslingen in 1487. With the support of the army of the Swabian League, Maximilian forced his cousin Sigismund, Archduke of Austria, to grant him the County of Tyrol.

The death of Matthias of Hungary in 1490 gave Maximilian a further opportunity to expand his possessions. He tried to be elected King of Hungary, but was beaten by the King of Bohemia. He did, however, regain part of the Hapsburg possessions in Austria, which Matthias had conquered five years before, and, by the Treaty of Pressburg (1491) was given a good opportunity to succeed to the Hungarian throne.

Maximilian was forced to divide his efforts between East and West. He was betrothed to the Duchess of Brittany, but Charles VIII married her in 1491, and at the same time sent Maximilian's daughter home in defiance of the Treaty of Arras. The King of the Romans could do nothing to avenge this insult, as he was busy fighting the Turks, whom he defeated at Villach in 1492, and sorting out quarrels between his father and the electors. Maximilian accepted the return of the Counties of Artois and Franche Comté by the Treaty of Senlis of 1493, instead of going to war with France.

The death of Frederick III in 1493 at last left Maximilian with a free hand, but it also left him with an Empire weaker in many ways than it had been when Frederick had become Emperor. The princes had reduced Germany to an unorganized federation of independent states, held together in name only by the Emperor, who had been deprived of all effective

power. On the borders of the Empire there had been territorial losses—the Swiss cantons were independent, Holstein had been lost as had the lands of the Teutonic Knights. Maximilian saw his task as the creation of a monarchy that would be able to govern. The need for unity was paramount, and he applied all his efforts to achieving it. He was to be only partly successful in his ambitions.

Outside the Empire, Maximilian turned his attention southward. He handed over the government of the Netherlands to his son Philip, who was now of age. Maximilian married Bianca, daughter of Galeazzo Sforza, Duke of Milan. He supported Charles VIII's invasion of Italy, hoping to make territorial gains at the expense of Venice. But Charles' success soon led Maximilian to change his mind and oppose his Italian ambitions. In order to pay for an army to fight in Italy, the *Reichstag*—a parliament representing the different municipalities and principalities of Germany— voted Maximilian a general tax. But this early success was followed by continuous quarrels between Maximilian and the Reichstag. It was not until 1505 that Maximilian crushed his princely enemies— who favored the particularism that the Emperor opposed—and this largely occurred as a result of the death of their leader, Berthold of Henneberg, Elector of Mainz.

Maximilian's success against his enemies led him to indulge in grandiose dreams of power. He saw himself as the ruler of a worldwide empire, but was not even content with that. Soon after being crowned Holy Roman Emperor by Julius II in 1508, he quarreled with the Pope; he seems to have considered deposing him and having himself elected instead.

His power in reality was considerable. He held substantial lands in Germany. His son Philip ruled the Burgundian Netherlands. Philip would inherit the Empire, while his wife, Joan, would inherit Aragon and Castile from her parents, Ferdinand and Isabella. But the death of Philip in 1506 spoiled Maximilian's more elaborate dreams, and further quarrels with the German princes added to his difficulties. But he soon transferred his ambitions to his grandson, Charles, the child

Maximilian and his kinsmen on the heavenward ladder.

of Philip and the mad Joan. Charles would succeed to the whole of the Hapsburg inheritance. Maximilian's great achievement was to create an inheritance for his family that was to make it by far the most powerful family in Europe, as well as the richest. He also ensured that the Empire would become one of the Hapsburg possessions. He turned all his efforts toward the end of his life to making certain that his grandson would succeed to the Empire, which Maximilian had made a Hapsburg fief.

Persia

Timur's death did not lead to the immediate collapse of his family's power. In parts of what today is Iran and Soviet Central Asia they retained power as late as the sixteenth century. But the dynasty's possessions were broken up into several states, of which the most important were Herat, Khurasan and Transoxiana. From about 1450 the first two were threatened by migrant invaders. The rival Turkoman dynasties of the White Sheep and the Black Sheep had been given land by Timur, in return for their support. The White Sheep, from their base in Armenia, became a threat in the middle of the fifteenth century, after they thought that they had been insulted by the Timurids of Herat. They invaded Herat and conquered it in 1447.

The next decades are confusing. The Timurids found a strong ruler in Abu-Said, who was able to unite Khurasan and Transox-

Ismael attacking the fort of Rustam Shah.

iana. The leader of the White Sheep, Uzun Hasan, whose capital was at Tabriz, held most of the rest of Iran. The death of Abu-Said in 1469 allowed Uzun Hasan to seize most of the area around Khurasan. He became Sultan of Persia. During the following years he allied himself with European states, such as Venice, in order to help them by attacking the Ottoman Empire from the rear. This was not successful, and the White Sheep were decisively defeated. From the time of Uzun Hasan's death in 1479 until 1500 there was anarchy, as the White Sheep possessions split up into independent warring states.

In 1499 a young Sufi prince, Ismael (1487–1524), whose family had been killed by the White Sheep, raised an army and set up a state with its capital at Baku. In 1502 he swept southward and occupied Tabriz, and in 1503 Fars. By 1508, having overcome the many small states in the region, he was the master of Iraq and most of western Iran.

The possessions of Timurid Khurasan fell in 1500 to a Turkoman group, but there were religious differences between Ismael and the Turkomans— Ismael was Shiite Moslem and the Turkomans were orthodox Sunni Moslems—that led to war. In 1510 Ismael beat the Turkomans in a decisive battle near Merv and took over the whole of Khurasan. Iran was now united under a new ruler, whose dynasty, the Savafids, was to remain in power for over two centuries.

Exploration continues

The death of Henry the Navigator in 1460 had been followed by a decline in Portuguese interest in discovery. However, it was inevitable that the western kingdoms of Europe would again take up the search for a sea-route to India. Ships were improving rapidly during the fifteenth century. Rigging particularly was improved, and for ocean-going boats a combination of the old square-rigged sails with the latteen-rigging that the Spaniards and Portuguese had learned from the Arabs of North Africa became common. This allowed greater flexibility and speed than would have been possible with either system alone. Although boats were small and uncomfortable, the caravels of the Portuguese and Spaniards were built for safety in the rough Atlantic seas. Enormous improvements in cartography helped exploration, and within a few years of a discovery, reasonably accurate maps were produced, despite the difficulties of measurement involved in mapping land masses when exploration had been confined to the coast. Another difficulty for cartographers was that the Portuguese government insisted upon great secrecy in order to discourage outsiders.

Under John II of Portugal (1481–95) the crown began once again to patronize voyages of discovery. John, whose enthusiasm for discovery was certainly as great as Henry's, was the real founder of Portuguese navigational efforts. As soon as he came to the throne he showed his determination to keep exploration largely in Portuguese hands by decreeing that foreign ships found off the Guinea coast should be sunk and their sailors thrown to the sharks. He arranged the foundation of a second African settlement, at Benin on the Gold Coast, and this soon became a flourishing trading center for gold and, in the sixteenth century, slaves. Ships were also sent to explore the coast farther south, and one captain, Diego Cão discovered the Congo in 1482 and reached Southwest Africa three years later.

Although the hope of finding a Christian state in Africa was part of the motivation for the voyages of John's reign, the real driving force was the determination to find a sea-route to India. Cão's discoveries were soon surpassed by those of Bartholomew Dias (1450–1500). The west coast of Africa had seemed endless to Cão and his men, and hopes of finding a sea-route to India were diminishing, when, in 1488, Dias rounded the Cape of Good Hope and reached the Indian Ocean. After this it was obvious to the Portuguese that the sea-route to India lay open, but internal difficulties prevented John from making immediate arrangements to take advantage of it. Columbus' American discoveries, so important for the world's future, were at first of little significance to the Portuguese. They realized that wherever it was that Columbus had reached, it was not India.

Magellan's route around the world, by Battista Agnese.

1492 Landfall at San Salvador

The patent from Spain's Catholic Kings gave the Genoese sea captain the mission to "discover and acquire islands and mainland in the Ocean Sea." When he set out across the unknown Atlantic, Christopher Columbus was seeking to establish the western route to Japan and China—the Cipangu and Cathay of Marco Polo's tales. Most men recognized that the earth was round; from various sources one could calculate the distance to Japan as only 3,000 miles (it is actually 10,000 miles); and no one—least of all Columbus—suspected the presence of an intervening continent. Thus, the historic landfall of October, 1492, was not immediately recognized as the great discovery it was—and Columbus died believing he had reached the Orient. Columbus' error was soon detected, of course, and the impact of Europe on America— and America on Europe—was profound and enduring.

A ship, thought to be Columbus' *Santa Maria*.

Opposite Christopher Columbus, the discoverer of America.

According to popular myth and many textbooks, Christopher Columbus, a Genoese in the service of the Spanish court, sailed with three ships from the River Odiel, crossed the Atlantic, and discovered America in 1492. In truth, Columbus' voyage revealed to contemporary Europe the existence of islands and a continent that were already inhabited —and had been for many centuries by peoples who had crossed the Pacific.

Of the people who first migrated to the Americas from Asia by crossing the Bering Strait, we know next to nothing. They were, no doubt, primitive hunters and gatherers who carried very little in the way of cultural baggage with them. They almost certainly developed their characteristic cultures independently in the Americas. They may, conceivably, have been reinforced by subsequent transpacific migrations, but there is no real evidence.

Thus, Columbus was not the first man to land in the Americas. In fact, he was not even the first European commander to land in the Americas: Icelanders and Greenlanders preceded him by nearly five hundred years, and it is possible that fishermen from English west-country ports, fishing off Newfoundland, may have sighted land before 1492. Columbus, then, did not discover a new world; he established contact between two worlds, both already old.

The significance of historical events, nevertheless, must be measured by their consequences. The discoveries of the Norsemen were all but forgotten by 1492, and those of the Bristol fishermen, genuine or not, got no publicity; but all Europe heard about Columbus. He made his voyage at a time when recently developed ships and navigating instruments made it possible to maintain contact with the discovered lands. His expedition was the first transatlantic voyage to have immediate, significant and permanent results; from that time, people, plants and animals flowed in a steady stream from the world of Europe to the world of America. Christopher

Columbus—not Leif the Lucky or some nameless fisherman from Bristol—made the voyage that brought the Americas firmly within the range of European action.

The precise objects of Columbus' first voyage have never been satisfactorily resolved. By the terms of his agreement with the Spanish monarchs, Columbus was to "discover and acquire islands and mainland in the Ocean Sea " This standard formula would obviously include the legendary island of Atlantis or Antilla, if such a place existed; but the phrase "islands and mainland" was almost certainly also understood to mean Cipangu and Cathay, the names by which Marco Polo had described Japan and North China some two centuries earlier.

In theory, at least, there was nothing fantastic about a proposal to reach eastern Asia by sailing west. Men recognized that the earth was round, and no one suspected an intervening continent; getting to Asia was a matter of winds, of currents and above all of distance. Could a ship, her crew and the stores she carried endure so far? Columbus apparently thought they could. What he proposed to do if he actually reached Cathay, he never explained. His ships were almost unarmed, carried few trade goods and no presents for princes. He bore a letter for the "Great Khan," but once Columbus arrived in what he believed to be the general neighborhood of Cathay, he made no serious attempt to find and enter its harbors. Instead, he wandered among the islands looking for gold and eventually, having lost his flagship, set sail for home.

Columbus returned to Spain in 1493, convinced that he had found outlying islands in the archipelago of which Japan was supposed to form a part and such an archipelago is indicated on the German cartographer Martin Behaim's 1492 globe. Columbus supported his contention by combining Marco Polo's estimate of the east-west extent of Asia—which was an overestimate—and Polo's

OLOMBVS   LYGVR·NO

RBIS ·   REPTO

Insula hyspana

Woodcut of Columbus' landing on what he thought was the coast of Cathay.

A practicable western sea route to Asia not only promised an immensely valuable trade in silk and spices—it also evoked a wide range of cherished dreams.

Was Columbus to be believed? The King of Portugal and his advisers, who knew more about exploration than most people, apparently thought not. Had they believed Columbus, they could have made more diplomatic fuss than they did. They were already deeply committed to an attempt to reach India by the route around Africa, and so therefore had strong motives for discrediting Columbus. On the other hand, they also wanted to keep the Spaniards out of the eastern Atlantic, and were delighted to see them pursuing chimeras to the west. The Portuguese therefore kept their own counsel; they laid half-hearted claims to Columbus' discoveries, but made no trouble.

Columbus' arguments were not entirely implausible; they were supported by—or, with a little ingenuity, could be reconciled with—respectable and respected authorities. Columbus himself was a self-taught and extremely persuasive geographical theorist, a capable sea commander and a careful, although somewhat old-fashioned, navigator. He had also shown himself to be a hard-headed negotiator—to picture him as an impractical mystic is mere caricature.

Spain's regents, Ferdinand and Isabella, were sufficiently impressed by Columbus and his reports to undertake a considerable outlay in money and diplomatic effort. The Bull of Demarcation of 1493 assured them of papal support, and the Treaty of Tordesillas, signed by Spain and Portugal in 1494, guaranteed Portuguese acquiescence, at a price which—as later appeared—included the renunciation by Spain of both the eastern route to India and all claim to Brazil. Meanwhile, Columbus was sent off again with a powerful fleet and a numerous company to settle Hispaniola and its gold "mines"— and to pursue his search for Cipangu and Cathay.

Thus early, and as a result of Columbus' arguments, there appeared an ambiguity in Spanish colonial policy: were the new "Indies" to be developed as possessions, valuable in themselves—or were they to be treated as ports-of-call in a maritime drive to reach the commercial centers of the East? Columbus' insistence, after his second voyage, that Cuba was actually a promontory of mainland Cathay, deceived no one. Subsequent voyages—by Vespucci, by Columbus himself and by many lesser discoverers —revealed a landlocked Caribbean to the west of Cuba, and a great continental land mass to the south. Nowhere, on islands or mainland coast, were there kingdoms remotely resembling those described by Marco Polo or his fellow Venetian, Niccolò de' Conti.

The new territories had their attractions for settlers, however: free land, abundant labor, gold in the islands and on the Isthmus and pearls off Cumaná. And as the settlements grew, so did the revenue that accrued to the crown. Maritime expeditions in search of Asia by a westward route, on

report of the distance from Japan to the Asian mainland—1,500 miles, another overestimate—with Ptolemy's estimate of the circumference of the earth, which was an underestimate. Columbus next assumed the length of an equatorial degree of longitude to be 10 per cent shorter than Ptolemy had taught— or 25 per cent shorter than the true figure. By this calculation, the westward journey from Spain to Japan was less than 3,000 nautical miles (the actual great circle distance is 10,000 nautical miles). Thus, according to Columbus' reasoning, Hispaniola and Cuba were near to where Japan ought to be, and the east coast of the mainland of Cathay was within reach. Columbus clung to this belief with passionate insistence to the end of his life.

Long-lived Christian legends—such as those of Prester John and of St. Thomas in India— appealed to those who sought an ideal of Christian perfection, now lost in Europe, that had existed long ago and might be found again, surviving far away.

the other hand, were costly in lives and money—and for many years produced nothing but disappointment. There seemed to be no way of sailing round, or breaking through, the vast barrier that men now called "America." Spanish attempts to reach Cathay were consistently disastrous; meanwhile the Portuguese were fighting and trading in all parts of the Orient, and making Lisbon one of the greatest spice markets of Europe.

The events of 1519–21 posed this Asia-American dilemma in clear and unmistakable terms. In 1519 Magellan left Spain on his great voyage around the world, in the course of which he proved that an all-sea western route to Asia was feasible—but long, dangerous and scarcely economic. Magellan's expedition also revealed that the South Pacific was no mere gulf, but an ocean wider than the Atlantic.

In the same year that Magellan established a long-coveted Spanish outpost in the Moluccas, or Spice Islands, Cortes set out from Cuba to conquer Mexico. The Aztec Empire was unlike any the Spanish had encountered in the New World, and its immensely greater population and sophisticated culture and economy made Mexico a prize that was seriously comparable with the kingdoms of the East. The riches of the Aztec nation invited systematic campaigns of conquest instead of random marauding.

Cortes hoped, in the Columbus tradition, to

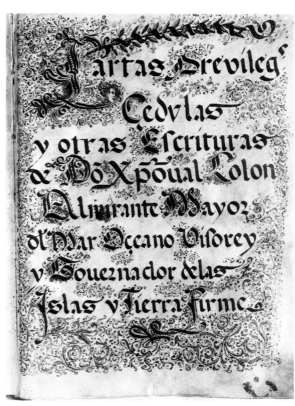

The beginning of the *Book of Privileges* granted to Columbus by Ferdinand and Isabella of Spain, and Columbus' coat-of-arms as Admiral of the Ocean.

Amerigo Vespucci, after whom the American continents are named.

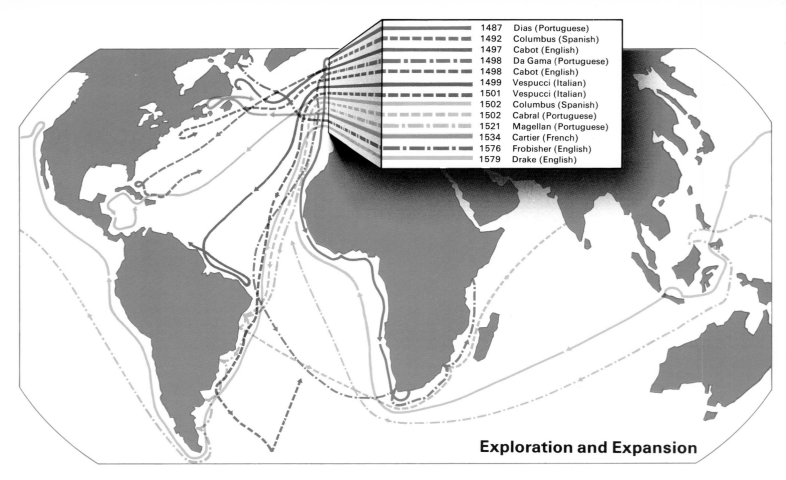

1487	Dias (Portuguese)
1492	Columbus (Spanish)
1497	Cabot (English)
1498	Da Gama (Portuguese)
1498	Cabot (English)
1499	Vespucci (Italian)
1501	Vespucci (Italian)
1502	Columbus (Spanish)
1502	Cabral (Portuguese)
1521	Magellan (Portuguese)
1534	Cartier (French)
1576	Frobisher (English)
1579	Drake (English)

Exploration and Expansion

Opposite The Virgin of the Navigators, to whom sailors prayed for protection from the dangers of the sea.

A mid-sixteenth-century Genoese map showing contemporary ideas of the world.

pursue the search for Eastern trade, in ships built on the Pacific coast. But in 1527—six years after Cortes delivered Mexico to Spain—Charles v decided to abandon Spain's claims to the Spicery. The distances and the hazards were too great, and the Portuguese were locally too strong. In 1529, by the Treaty of Saragossa, Charles sold out to the Portuguese.

Fresh developments in the "Indies" seemed to confirm the wisdom of his decision. During the 1530s, a second and greater native empire—the Inca, in Peru—was discovered, conquered and laid under tribute. In the 1540s, immensely productive silver veins were found both in Mexico and in Peru. Within a decade, streams of bullion were flowing into Spanish coffers, and the pepper profits of Portugal seemed insignificant by comparison. By mid-

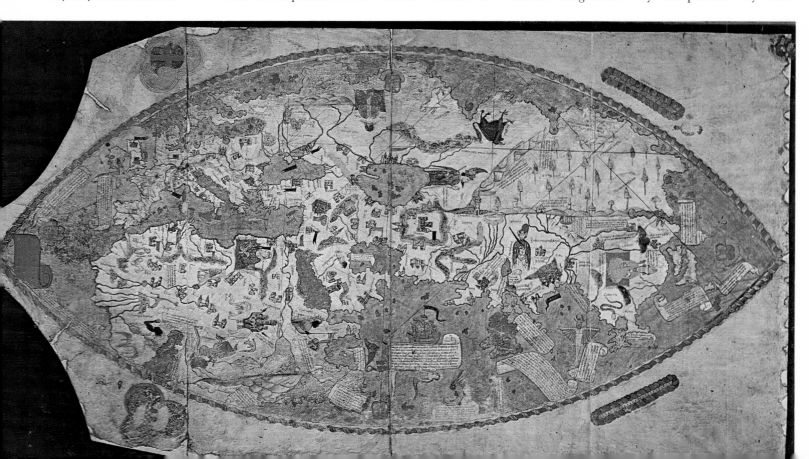

century, the decision seemed final. Spain's overseas interest was to be concentrated on an empire of territorial dominion, tribute and mineral exploitation in the New World—not on an empire of commercial profit in Asia.

Spain's initial settlements in America had been outposts in the race to reach the East; Spain, in losing the race, gained an empire. Spheres of influence had been delimited, a sensible, strategic withdrawal had been made, and a fair compensation had been received. Yet the interwoven stories of the European colonization of the East and West Indies were not so easily separated. The Treaty of Saragossa, backed by Portuguese pugnacity, kept Spaniards away from the Moluccas, but the Portuguese made no particular protest when Miguel López de Legazpe landed in the Philippines in 1564 and seven years later founded Manila as a Spanish colony. Chinese junks and Portuguese ships from Macao were soon trading there, and Manila became a unique back door to the closed, self-sufficient, xenophobic half-world of late Ming dynasty China, linking a society in which silver was in high demand with one in which it was cheap and plentiful. The Spanish ships that carried silver from Acapulco to Manila returned with silk, porcelain, jewelry and drugs—some for sale in Mexico, some for transshipment to Peru (the source of much of the silver),

Cardinal Cisneros lands in Africa; the conquest of the New World and North Africa was seen in religious terms.

some for reexport to Europe. At its height, the Manila trade equaled in value the official transatlantic trade of Seville. The Manila galleons maintained their hazardous but profitable sailing until 1815—a long-lasting reminder of the world-encircling visions of Columbus and Cortes and other explorers.

In another and more general sense, the stories of the East and West Indies were also connected, for in the course of the seventeenth century, the Portuguese monopoly of European-Asian trade was invaded—and the volume of that trade greatly increased—by Dutch, English, French and other European trading companies. Since few European goods were salable in the East, the companies exported silver to pay for their purchases of spices, silks, calicoes and, later, coffee and tea. Much of this silver came directly or indirectly from America, and the impact of American silver upon the monetary and price systems of Western Europe is well known: it made Spain, for a time, the economic envy and commercial terror of Europe. The use of American silver outside Europe is not as well known, and its effect is often overlooked. It is noteworthy, therefore, that throughout much of the seventeenth and all of the eighteenth centuries, Spanish or Mexican *piasters*, or pieces of eight, were the coins most commonly used and most readily accepted in business dealings between Asians and Europeans throughout the Orient. Piasters flowed to the East not only across the Pacific and through Manila, but also across the Atlantic and around Cape Horn, having played their part in European commerce on the way. Without this flow of silver, the successes of the various East India companies would have been difficult, perhaps impossible. Columbus and Cortes were intuitively right, in ways that they could not have dreamed of—for the exploitation of the New World was a necessary condition of the eastward spread of European trade and influence in the Old.

Silver was not the only New World product that altered the course of Old World history. European settlers used the apparently limitless land of the Americas to raise the products with which they were familiar—sugar, wheat, cattle—and in so doing vastly increased the world's supply of food. At the same time, traders brought native American crop plants to Europe, Africa and Asia, and some of these took root and spread. Potatoes, originally grown in a limited area in the high valleys of the Andes, became an indispensable staple throughout temperate Europe. Maize, which originated in Central America and spread both north and south in the centuries before Columbus' arrival, quickly established itself in southeastern Europe, West and Central Africa, and—perhaps most significantly of all—in China. It was an essential factor in the rapid growth of the Chinese population in the eighteenth century, particularly in inland provinces where rice could not flourish. Even the humble cassava, an insipid staple of the native peoples of northern South America and the Antilles, was carried to West Africa by slavers, where it became the chief food of millions of natives. Thus, the establishment of transatlantic contacts—which in the Americas led to demographic catastrophe and the destruction of whole civilizations—made possible the support of immensely greater populations in Europe, Africa and Asia.

Along with new food crops, Europe acquired new luxuries and new social habits from America. Cacao —chocolate—had been a royal food and drink, a means of exchange, and the basis for social ritual in ancient Mexico. In seventeenth-century Europe, it became a fashionable fad, and Venezuelan planters made fortunes growing cacao beans in the eighteenth century for the European market.

Tobacco too had a profound impact on the Old World. An indigenous American plant, it was used by the natives in almost all the known ways— powdered as snuff, infused, and smoked in pipes, cigars, and cornhusk cigarettes. It made the circuit of the world within a century of Columbus' landfall, and aroused choruses of curiosity, enthusiasm or indignation wherever its use became prevalent. Vice or solace, drug or poison, it has probably made more men's fortunes than all the silver of the Indies.

The impact of all this upon the economic fortunes of Europe can hardly be exaggerated. It began to be felt within a few years of Columbus' first voyage. Moreover, the impact of discovery was not only economic, but intellectual and imaginative as well.

In the space of a hundred years, European seamen achieved an enlargement of geographical knowledge that was unparalleled in its extent and in the speed of its discovery.

In addition, those explorers had encountered curious animals, unfamiliar plants, and strange natural phenomena in such variety that the purveyors of fabulous tales were suddenly unable to compete with the truthful narratives of sober adventurers. The knowledge they brought home, which was subsequently spread by the new device of printing, affected every aspect of European life and thought. Geographical exploration is the most empirical of all forms of scientific inquiry, the most dependent upon eyewitness experience. Practical navigators put the theories of revered authorities in cosmography to the test, and often proved them wrong. Inevitably, men of inquiring mind were encouraged to question, by observation and experiment, accepted authorities in other fields of knowledge. Unknown lands, and the social behavior of their supposedly simple inhabitants, caught the imagination of philosophers, poets and painters.

This new appreciation of the number and diversity of human societies led Europeans to look with fresh and critical eyes at their own society and institutions. Slowly, hesitantly, the idea grew in the minds of a few outstanding men, that there might be a new realm of learning and understanding beyond the horizon of the classics, ancient philosophy and the teachings of revealed religion. Magellan, contemplating the immensity of unknown oceans, prepared the way for Kepler, to whom the round earth itself was "of a most insignificant smallness, and a swift wanderer among the stars." J. H. PARRY

Above Natives looking for gold. The search for precious metals was the major lure which drew Spanish and Portuguese explorers to the New World.

Left A map on oxhide showing Europe and the west coast of Africa which is said to have been used by Columbus.

The monarchs of Spain and England

The helmet of Boabdil, last Moslem King of Granada.

The expansion of the Spanish kingdom was not confined to America. Indeed it was no coincidence that Columbus should have sailed in 1492, for in that year Granada fell. The Reconquista was complete. During the first half of the fifteenth century little progress had been made by Christian Spain toward the extinction of the Moslem Kingdom of Granada. But the fall of Constantinople and the marriage of Ferdinand and Isabella led to a revival of crusading hopes and a number of unsuccessful attempts to capture Granada were made between 1455 and 1464. Then, from 1482 on, a series of campaigns gradually whittled away the Moorish kingdom, as much the result of dynastic difficulties affecting the royal House of Granada as the military genius of the Spaniards. From 1482 to 1483, Granada was split between two rival kings, Abu-al-Hassan (1461–85) and his son Boabdil (Muhammad XI, 1482–92). Even though Abu-al-Hassan was deposed in 1485, civil war continued between his successors, his brother Muhammed XII, and Muhammed XI. The Spanish helped Muhammed XI against his uncle, and by 1487, most of the western part of the kingdom—the part that supported Muhammed XII—had fallen to the Christians, including the important city of Málaga. In 1489 Muhammed XI broke his treaty with the Spanish monarch, whom he had promised to support, but by then little more than the city of Granada itself was left to Muhammed, and the huge Christian army encamped outside the city spread fear within it. At the beginning of January, 1492, Muhammed surrendered and Moslem rule in Spain was entirely ended. By the terms of the surrender the Moors were allowed to practice their own religion, but the Archbishop of Toledo, Cardinal Jiménez de Cisneros, ignored the agreement. Many Moors were forced to become Christians, and, as a result, there were several risings during the 1490s, and the population of Granada was only gradually assimilated. A similar intolerance was shown toward the Jews, who were forced to accept Christianity or leave Spain.

The borders of the Spanish kingdom were pushed forward in other directions too. In 1493, by the Treaty of Barcelona, Charles VIII of France ceded the County of Roussillon to Spain, although the Kingdom of Navarre on the slopes of the Pyrenees still looked to France rather than Spain. Meanwhile the conquest of the islands off the Spanish coast was completed by the capture in 1492 of Palma and in 1496 of Tenerife.

The final success of the Reconquista allowed the Spanish to extend their empire westward across the Atlantic.

Poland

In 1471 Ladislas, the oldest son of Casimir IV, became King of Bohemia. This had led to a long conflict between Poland and Hungary, and only in 1478 was Ladislas' claim allowed. In 1490 he succeeded to the Hungarian throne, which he claimed through his mother. In 1492 Casimir died and his second son, John Albert, succeeded to the throne of Poland and the Grand Duchy of Lithuania.

John Albert was determined to crush the power of the great nobles, and sought support from the lesser nobility to do so. In 1496, by the Statute of Piotrkow, the rights of towns were reduced. They were banned from buying rural land, and the peasants, even harder hit, were virtually reduced to serfdom. This attempt to win the support of the lesser nobles failed in its main intention; it was royal power and the influence of the towns, rather than the power of the great nobles, that suffered. The crown began to be increasingly dependent on the support of the nobility, and throughout the sixteenth and seventeenth centuries the crown was forced to grant more and more concessions to the aristocracy.

Poland was hard-pressed by Ivan III's Russia in the late fourteenth century. In 1492, Ivan invaded Lithuania. John Albert succeeded in repulsing the attack, but after his death in 1501, the Russians again invaded the Grand Duchy. The new King, Alexander, brother of John Albert, was forced to conclude a treaty in 1503 that gave Moscow much of the land on the eastern bank of the Dnieper.

The weakness of the crown, which had been so well illustrated by Alexander's failure to repel Ivan, led the nobility to demand further privileges in 1505. This led to a national Diet—under the control of the nobility—which took over supreme legislative power. After Alexander's death his brother, Sigismund I (1506–48) was forced to make further concessions, including the formal establishment of serfdom.

Tudor power consolidated

Henry VII was not accepted as King of England without challenges. Within a year of his accession, Henry was almost killed in Yorkshire in an ambush, organized by a Yorkist peer, Lord Lovell. In 1486 Lovell, who had escaped after the failure of his previous rising, put forward a pretender to the throne. Lambert Simnel, the eleven-year-old son of an Oxford tradesman, was described as the Earl of Warwick, the son of the murdered Duke of Clarence. Other Yorkist leaders, such as John de la Pole, Earl of Lincoln, and many of the English nobility in Ireland supported his claim. Simnel was crowned as Edward V in Dublin, was brought to England and Lovell and Lincoln led a mercenary army toward London. A battle was fought with Henry VII's forces near Newark. The Yorkists were decisively beaten, their leaders killed in the fighting, and Simnel captured. Henry made the young "king" a kitchen scullion. A further rising took place in Yorkshire in 1489, when villagers refused to pay taxes. The Earl of Northumberland was killed, and only after the King marched north with an army did the rising subside.

John Albert, King of Poland and Lithuania.

consolidate their power

Perkin Warbeck, the second pretender against Henry VII.

A far more serious rising was that of Perkin Warbeck in 1491. This seventeen-year-old Fleming was put forward by the Irish earls of Kildare and Desmond—who had both played a prominent role in the Simnel rising—as the younger son of Edward IV. Margaret, Duchess of Burgundy. Edward IV's sister, accepted Warbeck's claim. Other enemies of Henry such as James IV of Scotland, Charles VIII of France and Maximilian, King of the Romans, were persuaded to support him. Several small invasion attempts financed by Scotland and the Empire were made, but found little popular support in England. Henry saw that Warbeck could most easily be dealt with by removing his royal support. He invaded France in 1492, and Charles—more concerned with his Italian ambitions than with a pretender to the English throne—agreed by the Treaty of Étaples to expel Warbeck from France. Pressure on the Flemish merchants led to the signing of the Magnus Intercursus, a treaty which forced Margaret of Burgundy to give up her support for the pretender. In 1497 Scotland and England made a treaty, by which James IV gave up his support for Warbeck. The pretender was captured the same year and hanged in 1499. Only in Ireland had Warbeck found widespread support, and this had been energetically put down by the Lord Deputy, Sir Edward Poynings (1459–1521). Poynings thought that the independence of the legislature in Ireland was the cause of the rising in Ireland, and the Irish Parliament was forced to pass Poynings' Law, which gave the Westminster Parliament control over that of Ireland. Although there were later risings such as

that of the Earl of Suffolk in 1501, they did not present serious challenges to the throne.

Security against rebellion was only one part of Henry's consolidation of power. In 1486 he married Elizabeth, daughter of Edward IV, thus combining the Yorkist and the Lancastrian lines. Legislation was used in order to strengthen Henry's hold over the country. In 1495 Parliament passed the Statute of Treason, which declared that to serve a king—even if his claim to the throne was based purely on force—could not later be interpreted as treason. In this way, Henry won the support of those who feared that they might later be tried for treason for having served Richard III, and at the same time persuaded some that they could serve the Tudor monarchy, even if its legitimacy was in doubt.

Henry tried to win acceptance of the Tudor dynasty by following a policy of dynastic marriage. As early as 1489 he sought a marriage alliance with Ferdinand and Isabella, which came to fruition in 1501 with the marriage of Henry's oldest son, Prince Arthur, to Catherine of Aragon, youngest daughter of the Catholic monarchs. Henry was so determined that this alliance should be kept that when Arthur died in 1502, his younger brother, the future Henry VIII, was made to marry his widow. Margaret Tudor, Henry's daughter, was married to James IV of Scotland, and it was from this marriage that the future Stuart royal line was descended. After the death of his wife Elizabeth, Henry sought to make a further marriage, either with the Spanish or the Imperial Royal House, neither of which succeeded.

Henry saw the necessity of rebuilding the economy of his shattered kingdom. His minister, Cardinal John Morton, raised "benevolences," supposedly freewill offerings, and introduced the system which came to be known as "Morton's Fork." Those who spent money freely were heavily taxed while those who lived in poverty were held to be misers who could easily afford to pay high taxes. Two royal councillors, Richard Empson and Edmund Dudley, were in charge of taxation. Their efficiency made Henry financially secure, although at the price of popularity.

Charles VIII of France

France lacked a ruler of importance comparable to Maximilian, Ferdinand and Isabella or Henry VII. Charles VIII, son of Louis XI, was born in 1470. He was not brought up at the royal court, but at the Loire château of Amboise, and as a child was not involved in government at all. When Louis died in 1483, Charles was too young and inexperienced to take the reins of government, and his sister, Anne of Beaujeu, became regent. She followed a cautious policy of centralization in government, and built up the royal exchequer. Even after Charles came of age, Anne and her husband Pierre of Beaujeu continued to govern. Like other major European monarchies, France became involved in the dynastic marriage game, made necessary by the closely guarded independence of the Duchy of Brittany. Just as Louis XI supported rebels against Henry VII of England, so the English King encouraged Brittany to follow its

independent line. In 1487 Brittany rose, and was only put down with difficulty by the French army. At the Treaty of Sablé, which followed the suppression of the rising in 1488, it was agreed that the twelve-year-old Duchess of Brittany, Anne, would not marry without France's permission. This clause was ignored, and Anne married Maximilian—though only by proxy—in 1490. This marriage was set aside, and Anne was forced to marry Charles instead. Charles made separate treaties with the allies of Brittany: Senlis with Maximilian; Étaples with England; while Spain was bribed with the grant of Roussillon and Cerdagne.

Charles failed to see that the success of French policy was largely due to his sister's careful government. She had followed Louis XI's policy of reducing the power of the great ducal houses of Burgundy and Brittany, and at the same time had managed to shake off the need for summoning the Estates General. Influenced by a favorite, Étienne de Vesc, Charles threw aside the Beaujeu and began to rule alone in 1492.

Anne of Beaujeu, sister to Charles VIII and regent of France.

Charles VIII Invades Italy 1494

Ill-equipped in mind, body or training for the role of monarch, Charles VIII of France resolved to march through Italy and conquer the Kingdom of Naples. From there he would mount a crusade, expel the Turks from the Holy Land and assume his hereditary—if empty—title of King of Jerusalem. His successful entry into Naples only united the squabbling Italian states against him and he was forced to fight his way back to France where he died shortly thereafter. The garrison he left in Naples was soon expelled. The major result of his blundering enterprise was a dynastic marriage between Spain and the Holy Roman Empire that would virtually encircle France with Hapsburg power from Flanders in the northeast to the Bay of Biscay in the southwest.

In September, 1494, Charles VIII of France led an army of some 20,000 men over the Col du Mt. Genèvre into Italy, and was welcomed in Turin, capital of the Duchy of Savoy, by a splendid display of pageantry. He proceeded to Asti, a possession of his cousin the Duke of Orleans, where he was met by a committee including Cardinal Giuliano della Rovere, the Duke of Ferrara and Ludovico Sforza, ruler of the Duchy of Milan.

Charles' objective was the conquest of the Kingdom of Naples, one of the five major powers on the Italian peninsula, to which the French had a long-standing claim of sorts. At Asti, Charles suffered a fever—perhaps smallpox—and for several days his life hung in the balance. It was not until the end of October that he had recovered sufficiently to decide how to proceed and ordered his troops to advance on Florence.

Charles' illness was not the only cause of a delay that might have proved fatal to his enterprise had the halcyon weather broken with the heavy rains usual in an Italian autumn. The King's council was far from unanimous in supporting the endeavor. Some members were convinced of its folly, others were dissuaded by Italian bribes, and the Duke of Orleans argued that the army would be far better employed in asserting his claim to the Duchy of Milan. Charles himself, ill-favored both in mind and body, was a prey to indecision; it was said that he would immediately adopt the most recent advice, only to reject it as soon as he heard an opinion to the contrary.

Born in 1470, Charles had begun his personal rule in 1492. Since the death of his father, Louis XI, in 1483, France had been ruled by Charles' sister, Anne of Beaujeu. Her firm regency had preserved the authority of the French monarchy in the face of rebellions by the great peers. The outstanding issue was the conquest of Brittany. With no son to succeed him, the last Duke, Francis II, was pushed by his subjects into courses designed to preserve Brittany's autonomy. Foreign rulers—Henry VII of England, Ferdinand of Aragon and Maximilian of Austria and Flanders—had furthered these efforts in order to prevent a new access of strength to the French throne. The Regent Anne thwarted their schemes, and Breton independence ended with the marriage of Charles to the Duchess Anne in 1491. An English invasion followed, but Henry VII soon settled for peace with a pension in the Treaty of Étaples.

The young Charles had been poorly trained for monarchy. His sickly childhood had not permitted a rigorous education in the arts of kingship. His principal reading had been in tales of chivalry, and his mind was obsessed with romantic ambitions to pursue glory. Charles entertained the typically medieval desire to lead a crusade against the Infidel, to expel the Turk from Constantinople, restore in his own person the Christian Empire of the Greeks and recover the Holy Places. He held, after all, the somewhat empty title of King of Jerusalem.

This, among other unfulfilled titles, Charles had inherited by the bequest of Réné of Anjou to Louis XI. Louis had contented himself with absorbing Réné's County of Provence, thus gaining the French monarchy a Mediterranean coastline. Réné had also bequeathed his claim to the Kingdom of Naples. Possession of southern Italy would give Charles a springboard for his conquest of the Levant.

Charles had ample encouragement for his fantasies for the younger nobility shared his chivalrous ambitions, if not for the crusade, at least for the Italian adventure. Foreign war was a recipe for domestic peace—until the cost became intolerable, which would not occur if the war were successful.

At the close of the fifteenth century, France had recovered from the devastations of the Hundred Years War. Her economy was self-sufficient and

Charles VIII of France. His invasion of Italy was one of the supreme blunders of French history. Poorly executed and serving only to strengthen France's enemies, it was nevertheless of importance in disseminating Italian culture throughout Western Europe.

Opposite Monument to a *condottiere.* Commutation of military service for cash marked the decline of the Italian citizen militia and the consequent dependence on these mercenary captains. In the event the *condottieri* proved no match for the French *compagnies d'ordonnance.*

Charles VIII holding a council of war: an engraving by Hans Burgkmair.

Compté in the northeast to Maximilian. This ended the protracted struggle over the remains of Charles the Bold's Burgundian empire. But if Charles believed that Ferdinand and Maximilian would now show indifference to his Italian project, he was deluding himself anew. His attempt to buy their neutrality at the price of territory inside what we tend to regard as France's natural frontiers demonstrates the intensity of his ambitions in Italy—and beyond.

Italy's fragmented condition offered strong inducements to a belligerent neighbor. In 1454 the Peace of Lodi had provided a framework for harmonious relations among its five major powers —the papacy, the Kingdom of Naples, the Duchy of Milan, and the republics of Florence and Venice. This peace had been broken by occasional wars. However these had been curtailed by the diplomatic skill of Lorenzo de' Medici, ruler of Florence, whose policies have won him the reputation of inventor of the theory of the balance of power.

In addition to these larger powers, there were lesser principalities. The Marquess of Mantua was independent, the Duke of Ferrara was nominally a vassal of the papacy but effectively as sovereign as that other papal vassal, the King of Naples. Inside the frontiers of the Papal States numerous little states enjoyed virtual autonomy—the Bentivoglio family ruled Bologna; other cities of the Romagna had their own despots; there was a celebrated ducal court at Urbino; and nearer Rome republican institutions survived in some towns while the countryside was dominated by such baronial families as the Colonna and Orsini. In the Neapolitan kingdom the intransigent barons waged a continuous duel with their despotic monarch. The latest round had ended in 1487 with a peace treaty, despite which the King, Ferrante, arrested the baronial leaders, completing their bloody liquidation on Christmas Day, 1491.

The political condition of Italy was thus unstable. However, Italian warfare might best be described as "civilized." The *condottieri* who hired themselves out to belligerent powers were skilled in cavalry tactics, but as professional warriors were not ardent protagonists of their employers' causes. Their engagements were notoriously half-hearted because, their detractors alleged, captains were reluctant to endanger the lives of the soldiers whose service was their source of income. In consequence, *condottiere* warfare was not particularly destructive and did not threaten Italian prosperity. Italy's thriving industries, trade and agriculture thus escaped devastation, as the architecture and other arts of the Renaissance amply testify. These splendors were evident and French envoys and scholars could report to their countrymen that Italy was a land rich in treasure but poor in the means of self-defense. The *condottieri* would be no match for the *compagnies d'ordonnance*.

History also attracted France to Italy. Charles of Anjou, brother of St. Louis of France, had

expanding, her population increasing. She had the resources for war. The measures taken by Charles VII to expel the English in the 1440s were still in force, providing the King with the largest standing army in Western Europe. Its core was the *compagnies d'ordonnance* of some 9,000 heavy cavalry recruited from the nobility. To their native *élan* was added the discipline of regular training. French artillery was also the most formidable of the day, its fire power enhanced by the use of iron balls, instead of stone. It was also mounted on carriages, enabling it to move at a speed that did not delay the army. The mediocre quality of French infantry was overcome by hiring the Swiss Confederation's uniquely disciplined companies of pikemen. Payment for these forces came from a well-organized tax-system.

An essential preliminary to Charles' Italian expedition was the securing of France's other frontiers. English neutrality had already been guaranteed by the Treaty of Étaples. In 1493 Charles made territorial concessions to his two strongest neighbors. To Ferdinand of Aragon he ceded Roussillon and Cerdagne, tiny provinces north of the Pyrenees which Louis XI had occupied in 1475, and he abandoned other conquests of Louis with the cession of Artois and Franche

conquered the Kingdom of Naples after its grant to him by the Pope in 1265. Two of Charles' descendants, Joanna I (d. 1382) and Joanna II (d. 1435), were childless and adopted as their heirs the contemporary heads of a new ducal house of Anjou, descended from John II of France (d. 1364). The Angevin claimants invaded Naples, but although they gained some support from the fractious nobility were unable to withstand rival contenders. King Alfonso V of Aragon had won the succession to Joanna II, and on his death in 1458 he was succeeded in Naples by his illegitimate son Ferrante.

It was this Angevin claim to Naples that Charles VIII put forward. Its legality was dubious. The papacy, Naples' feudal overlord, recognized the Aragonese dynasty. Italian enemies of the King of Naples had occasionally invoked the Angevin claim, but hitherto the kings of France had not responded and its invocation had simply become a ploy in Italian politics. Its employment prompted other native powers to settle any dispute quickly to avoid French intervention. The tragedy for Italy was that Charles VIII took the Angevin claim in earnest.

Fugitives from Ferrante's savage suppression of the Neapolitan baronage were the first to urge Charles to expel the Aragonese tyrant. Another Italian who, perhaps less seriously, encouraged Charles was Ludovico Sforza of Milan. That duchy's most persistent fear had been the Venetian Republic, with whom she shared possession of Lombardy. The westward expansion of Venice had been held in check by the policy of Lorenzo de' Medici to preserve an alliance of Florence, Milan and Naples.

This policy was now in ruins. Lorenzo's heir Piero had none of his father's statesmanship and Milan's internal affairs antagonized the King of Naples. The latter was able to claim the duchy as an heir of the last Visconti duke, who died in 1447, but he had sufficiently reconciled himself to the new Sforza dynasty to marry his granddaughter Isabella to Duke Gian Galeazzo in 1489. For the last ten years Gian Galeazzo's uncle Ludovico had ruled Milan as regent, and although his nephew was now of age Ludovico kept him in a state of tutelage, to the natural resentment of Isabella and her parents.

Ludovico, moreover, having married a daughter of the Duke of Ferrara and begotten a son, wanted the duchy in his own right. The title had been assumed by the Sforzas without imperial authority and in 1493 Ludovico had applied to Maximilian for a grant of the duchy to himself, backing his petition with an offer of the hand of his niece Bianca Maria and a cash payment which the impecunious Emperor found irresistible.

Ludovico knew that Charles was intending to invade Naples and had in fact received a request to assist him. When the French army was in the Duchy of Milan, Ludovico received Maximilian's warrant to assume the title of Duke. By a coincid-

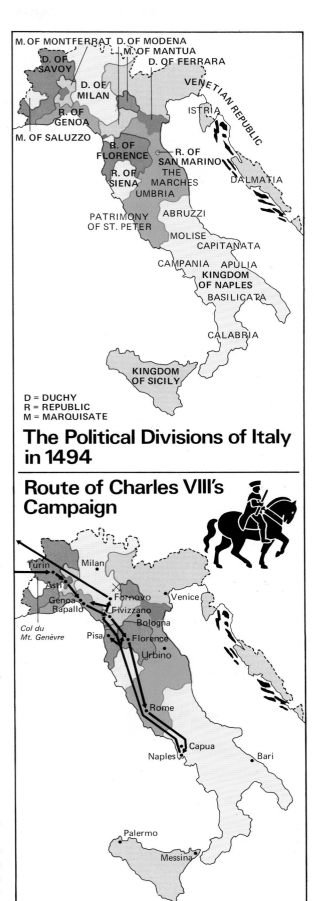

The Political Divisions of Italy in 1494

D = DUCHY
R = REPUBLIC
M = MARQUISATE

Route of Charles VIII's Campaign

Charles VIII's entry into Florence, by Granacci. The combined effects of the French trade embargo and the apocalyptic preaching of Savonarola induced the Florentines to submit to Charles and to drive out Piero de' Medici, but they subsequently abandoned the French alliance.

ence, which Ludovico's enemies inevitably attributed to poison, Gian Galeazzo died on October 21, 1494, and Ludovico immediately received his title by popular acclaim. This ambition achieved, Ludovico was anxious to speed the French from his lands and against the parents of Isabella of Naples and her disinherited children.

Charles was attended from June, 1494, by another important Italian anxious to direct him south to Rome. Giuliano della Rovere had been made a cardinal by his uncle, Pope Sixtus IV, to whom nepotism was the major instrument of a policy designed to strengthen his temporal authority in the Papal States. Della Rovere's family connections with the barons of the Campagna made him an enemy of Naples and thus a friend of France and Charles had supported his candidacy in the papal election of 1492. The victor in this corrupt event was Rodrigo Borgia, a cardinal of statesmanlike qualities but scandalous morals. As Pope Alexander VI he, too, practiced nepotism for political ends. He allied with Naples for protection against della Rovere's baronial kinsmen and the Cardinal fled to France.

Alexander had also antagonized Charles by rejecting his claim to Naples and investing Alfonso as King in succession to his father Ferrante in 1493. Charles' response followed the precedent set for facing papal hostility. He formed a commission to plan the reform of the Church and threatened to call a general council to depose Alexander—another pope might be more amenable in the matter of Naples. Cardinal della Rovere was naturally an interested supporter of this program and the Italian expedition took on the further character of a crusade against the Pope.

Between Milanese territory and the Papal States lay the Tuscan dominions of Florence. Despite the republic's traditional alliance with France, Piero de' Medici intended to support Naples and had refused a free passage for Charles' army. Charles retaliated by expelling Florentine merchants from France and putting an embargo on their trade. This led to unemployment in the Florentine cloth industry, and caused unrest. To discontent with the Medici government was added

fear, as news arrived of the brutal sack and slaughter at Rapallo and Fivizzano, small walled towns that had resisted the French and were battered by artillery and taken by assault. The Florentines had already been prepared for doom by the fiery, evangelistic preaching of Friar Girolamo Savonarola, whose packed audiences were importuned to renounce their luxurious lives and turn to penitence.

In a desperate gamble to avert revolution, Piero de' Medici secretly made for the French camp and put himself at Charles' mercy. He accepted all the terms for French protection—surrender of fortresses, free passage and a huge loan. Notwithstanding, the Florentines rose against him, and when Charles entered the city on November 17, its cheering inhabitants had a new government. It showed more resolution in negotiating with Charles, but his passage through Tuscany was nonetheless clear.

Virtually all Italian resistance was now at an end. Charles entered Rome on December 31, and the city of Naples on February 22, 1495. Everywhere cities and castles opened their gates rather than risk bombardment and sack; the fragile loyalties of papal and Neapolitan barons easily succumbed to fear of French atrocity. This almost unopposed procession reputedly caused Alexander VI to observe that the French came into Italy with chalk to mark their lodgings, rather than with swords to fight.

On reaching Rome, Charles abandoned his plan to reform the papacy and instead negotiated with the Pope. He was anxious to press on to Naples, and trying to depose Alexander would have led to limitless international repercussions as well as time-consuming difficulties. Alexander had no choice but to negotiate—he had no means to resist. He contrived, however, to avoid conceding the most critical French demand, papal investiture of Charles as King of Naples. He agreed that his son, Cesare Borgia, should accompany the French army, but two days after it had left Rome the hostage escaped by a prearranged design. With his son safe, Alexander's opposition to the French invasion was stiffened by Spanish offers of aid.

Although only a year had passed since Ferdinand of Aragon had promised neutrality toward France, he easily found a pretext to claim that Charles had violated their treaty. As he was also the ruler of Sicily, Ferdinand was alarmed, and probably surprised, at the French conquest. He sent envoys to urge the Italian states to unite in defense of their independence and in February and March of 1495 ambassadors of the Pope, Germany, Spain and Milan and other north Italian principalities gathered in Venice. On March 31, they concluded the League of Venice, all the parties agreeing to provide forces for the defense of Italy and the preservation of their own states.

Despite the formation of the League, Charles showed little sense of urgency or fear of being trapped in Italy. Having entered Naples in great

VENECIE

A panorama of Venice, from a
fifteenth-century manuscript.
By the League of Venice the
various north Italian
principalities and allied
powers united to expel the
French invaders.

pomp, he remained there celebrating until May 20, when he finally departed, leaving about half of his force behind as a garrison. Moving northward in a leisurely manner, he detached a part of his forces for a fruitless attack on Genoa, at the urging of Cardinal della Rovere. He also left a garrison at Pisa, to keep that city from falling under Florentine control. Then he prepared to cross the Apennines. Fortunately for him, the forces of the League were slow to assemble. Charles was even able to transport his cannon through the undefended pass across the Apennines.

Once across the mountains, the French entered the valley of the Taro, a north-flowing tributary of the Po River. As the forces of the League were on the right bank, the French proceeded up the left, planning to continue until they were met in battle or made good their escape. They were met at Fornovo on July 6. The forces of the League, however, were forced to cross the swollen Taro, and their numerical superiority was further squandered when the Venetian light-horse elected to loot the French baggage train rather than attack the French rear. The battle was fierce and bloody, and victory—if anyone could claim it—went to the French. The object of the League had been to annihilate Charles' little army which instead was able to complete its retreat into France.

The formation of the League had forced Charles to take the major part of his army with him from Naples to protect his person. Hardly ten thousand troops remained under his viceroy, Gilbert de Montpensier. No attempt had been made to entice the Angevin barons of Naples to the French cause. Charles instead had favored Frenchmen in his grants to office and their greed and license quickly earned them popular hatred. Cut off from France by want of sea power, lacking in supplies and desperately short of money, the French garrison in Naples could only stave off its final reduction by superior fighting discipline and harsh measures, which only served to increase its unpopularity.

Alfonso of Naples had abdicated when his authority crumbled before Charles' advance. His son Ferrantino, from his base in Sicily, now led the movement for the recovery of his kingdom. On July 6, the day of Fornovo, he sailed into the Bay of Naples. The city immediately rose in his favor. Spanish troops under Gonzalo de Cordoba—"the Great Captain"—and other forces supplied by Venice helped to reduce French strongholds. Montpensier finally surrendered on July 20, 1496.

The purpose of the League of Venice had been achieved—the expulsion of the French from Italy. But the League itself was already falling apart. First to secede was Ludovico Sforza of Milan, who made a separate peace with Charles. Soon other powers—the Pope, Venice, even Ferdinand of Aragon—were suggesting that he return, to assist their schemes. Charles remained in France. With difficulty he repaid the enormous cost of his great adventure, but the means to finance another were not found before his early death on April 7, 1498.

The Italian powers had not learned that unity was essential to deter would-be foreign conquerors. Charles' successors, Louis XII (formerly Duke of Orleans) and Francis I, could claim an hereditary title to Milan as well as Naples. Ferdinand of Aragon, determined to exclude the French from Italy, made a marriage alliance in 1496 with Maximilian. This was to unite Spain and the German Empire under the Hapsburg Charles v.

Charles VIII's invasion of Italy was one of the supreme blunders of French history. Events proved that he and his immediate successors had inadequate resources to pursue their campaigns of conquest over the enormous lines of communication from France to Naples. Without Mediterranean sea-power they could not contend with Spanish opposition. Earlier French kings had contented themselves with acquiring and exploiting legal claims to sovereignty over lands closer to Paris. Charles VIII had sufficient grounds to allow him, if he chose, to absorb Flanders and Calais. Their conquest would have been an immeasurable addition to France's wealth and security. Instead, as a consequence of Charles' obsession with Italy, Flanders remained in the hostile hands of the expanding Hapsburg Empire.

The legacy of Charles' passage over the Alps was that Flanders became the "Cockpit of Europe." It was to be a forward base for Spanish and German invasions of the Île de France. Alternatively, it was to be the target of aggressive French kings, like Louis XIV. As Hapsburg power declined, England was to intervene to preserve Flanders from France and safeguard the Channel. The situation unwittingly created by Charles VIII ended in such famous battles as Blenheim, Waterloo and Ypres.

ROBIN STOREY

135

The death of Lorenzo the Magnificent in Florence in 1492, removed from the Italian scene the one ruler capable of maintaining peace, and was a major cause of the French invasion in 1494. The election of Rodrigo Borgia, Lorenzo's longtime rival, as Pope, also in 1492, ensured that Italy would be plunged into turmoil. Earlier popes throughout the fifteenth century had already weakened the papacy's moral authority by promoting their nephews in order to strengthen their territorial power and control over the Papal States. Sixtus IV and Innocent VIII were mere corrupt nonentities, but Cardinal

Pope Alexander VI Borgia.

Borgia's election as Alexander VI—achieved through wholesale bribery—opened the most scandalous chapter in papal history.

Alexander VI swiftly established Borgia rule in central Italy by securing sinecures for the various children—he had at least six—borne him by a succession of mistresses. His second son, Cesare, became an archbishop at the age of sixteen and a cardinal two years later, although he later threw over his high ecclesiastical office to marry the sister of the King of Navarre. Alexander's daughter, Lucrezia, changed her husbands as policy dictated. By sheer ruthlessness, the head of the Church subdued the great houses of Orsini and Colonna in Rome. Moved by the murder of another of his sons, the Duke of Gandia, Alexander appointed a committee of cardinals to plan reforms, beginning with the Curia itself, but he soon abandoned the idea.

Living in great splendor at Rome as a secular monarch, Alexander spent a fortune patronizing the arts. He decreed that the year 1500 was to be celebrated as a jubilee year of the Church, and the pilgrims who flocked to

Rome—to be fleeced by papal tax collectors—saw for themselves the level to which the Church had been reduced by the House of Borgia.

Savonarola

The most outspoken critic of Alexander VI was Girolamo Savonarola (1452–98), who became prior of San Marco in Florence in 1491. In sermon after sermon Savonarola denounced the corruption of the papacy, the immorality of the clergy, the shortcomings of Medici rule in Florence and the paganism of the Renaissance. When the Florentines banished Piero de' Medici in the aftermath of the French invasion of 1494, they turned to Savonarola, of whose criticism of the Medici and favor for France they approved. He refused an office in the Christian Republic whose constitution he devised, but remained nonetheless its guiding spirit. The administration of justice was remodeled and poor-relief introduced. Savonarola was a rigorist in his religious views, and opposed Humanism and much contemporary art as immoral and irreligious.

Alexander summoned Savonarola to Rome to explain his curious prophetic views, and, when the friar refused to come, excommunicated him. Savonarola then demanded that the Augean stables of Rome be cleansed; he insisted that Alexander call a general council to reform the Church, but his demand went unheeded. Savonarola, because of his extremism, became unpopular and Alexander was able to persuade the Signory of Florence, who resented him anyway, to execute him.

Savonarola, by Fra Bartolomeo.

Machiavelli

Niccolò Machiavelli (1469–1527) was the son of a Florentine lawyer. After becoming a civil servant at the beginning of the Republic, he rose gradually in the public service, taking part in many embassies, including one to the court of Louis XII in 1500. After the fall of Savonarola, the Florentine Republic decided to base its constitution on the oligarchic system that had stood the Venetians in such good stead. In 1502 a new constitution was adopted and a leading civil servant, Piero Soderini, was elected for life as *gonfaloniere* (standard bearer)—a post which carried much influence but little direct power, similar to that of the Doge in Venice. This increased Machiavelli's involvement in public life for Soderini became his patron. In 1503 Machiavelli produced a speech for Soderini advocating the formation of a professional militia instead of relying further on *condottieri*, who had proved so unreliable in the past. The arguments that Machiavelli put forward were largely historical, showing that he was already using political arguments based on history. His case was accepted and during the next few years he was made responsible for organizing the militia. In 1508 he was sent as ambassador extraordinary to the court of the Emperor.

In 1512 Soderini was deposed and the Medici returned to Florence. Machiavelli was imprisoned for several months and on his release devoted himself to writing.

His diplomatic missions had brought him in contact with Cesare Borgia, the tyrant of the Romagna. Machiavelli admired Borgia's political realism without qualification—and indeed it is Cesare who is the hero of the Florentine's book, *The Prince*.

The Prince taught rulers the means of maintaining themselves in power, and the author's name came to have an unfortunate meaning in most European languages as a synonym for duplicity, intrigue and cunning.

Although *The Prince* became Machiavelli's most famous book, other works including *The Discourses On the First Decade of Titus Livy* also were popular, and his

Bronzino's portrait of Machiavelli.

play *Mandragola* is often regarded as the first modern comedy. *The Prince* and *The Discourses* are often seen as the foundation of modern political science. Indeed, Machiavelli's vision of politics was so all-embracing that he tended to forget that man might be anything but a political animal.

For all his useful advice to rulers, Machiavelli proved unable to win back even his old position in Florence. Instead he was commissioned to write a *History of Florence*, a work left unfinished at his death that proved to be important historiographically. Machiavelli did not chronicle the city's history, but tried to explain why events had happened. As a result, he is sometimes seen not merely as the father of political science and an important dramatist, but also as the first modern historian. Along with his close friend Francesco Guicciardini (1483–1540), author of the influential *History of Italy*, Machiavelli had a decisive impact on historical writing. Together they managed to widen the application of Humanist ideas to history and establish the importance of the study of institutions and the reasons for institutional change.

Louis XII continues the Italian wars

Upon Charles' death in 1498, his cousin the Duke of Orleans—last of the direct line of the House of Valois—succeeded him as Louis XII. He safeguarded his position within France by marrying Charles' widow, Anne of Brittany (thereby also securing the Duchy of Brittany for the crown). Influenced by the Archbishop of Rouen, George d'Amboise, who hoped to be elected pope, Louis launched a second invasion of Italy. He laid claim to Milan as the grandson of Valentina Vis-

Venetian influence in northern Italy

Louis XII plays cards with the Doge of Venice and a Swiss; the European powers look on.

conti, and with Spanish help succeeded in driving Ludovico Sforza out of Milan in September 1499. Ludovico briefly regained control of the Duchy with the help of Swiss and German mercenaries, but he was soon captured and taken to France as Louis' prisoner. Louis united the Orleanist claim to Milan with the French crown's claim to Genoa and Naples.

Louis XII next made a treaty with Ferdinand of Aragon for the partition of Naples, but the allies subsequently fell out over the division of the spoils, and Spain was able to regain control of Naples in 1504. For another half-century the Italian peninsula was to remain a battleground for the great powers.

The decline of Venice

While Europe's western states, and in particular Spain and Portugal, rejoiced at their new-found transatlantic wealth and at the opportunity for vastly expanded trade, Venice, Europe's greatest trading state, faced a real threat of extinction at the end of the fifteenth century. Venetian galleys were not equipped for the rough Atlantic weather. The acquisition of Cyprus in 1488 scarcely equaled the Venetian losses in Greece, and the Turkish threat had not been overcome. In vain Venetian ambassadors protested at Western courts that Venetian sea power and wealth alone protected Christendom from Moslem conquest. Venice saw

itself in the same role that for centuries had been forced on Constantinople—a shield against the Turks, but also a useful victim of aggression from the West. Venetian successes inland in Lombardy had created jealousy and fear throughout north and central Italy and even in the south, and Venice was widely regarded by the other Italian states as a troublemaker.

Venice had opposed Charles VIII, but supported Louis XII's invasion in return for the promise of territory in the north of Italy. These ambitions failed because the Turks attacked Venetian possessions in Yugoslavia. Venice was forced to concentrate on defense, but even so the navy was defeated at Sapienza, and a Turkish army was able to threaten Venice itself.

The death of Alexander VI in 1503 and the election of Julius II

as Pope resulted in a change in the balance of power in Italy. By 1508 Julius was able to persuade the Emperor Maximilian, the kings of Spain, France and Hungary, and the dukes of Savoy and Ferrara to join in an alliance against Venice. The League of Cambrai, as this alliance came to be known, was designed to destroy what the treaty described as "the insatiable cupidity of Venice." In battle at Agnadello the Venetian army was routed, and the whole mainland empire of the Serene Republic seemed ready to crumble away. But Julius did not want Venice to be utterly defeated by France and the Empire, and in 1410 destroyed the League and allied the papacy with Venice. France now became the common enemy. Venice's land empire was recovered, but the League had shown that Venice's strength was not what it had been. Venice was still a major commercial power and had an important role to play in the defense of Europe from the Turks, but Venetian influence in north Italy never recovered from the War of the League of Cambrai. Italian politics were now the concern of France, Spain and the Empire, and Venice was forced to play a largely passive role.

Other blows affected Venetian morale during this period. A fire had destroyed the Doge's palace in 1479, and the most grandiose plans for rebuilding it had been put forward. The present palace—only half as large as that originally proposed—was regarded as a modest compromise, forced on the Republic by financial considerations. The magnificent works of art glorifying Venice's

great past that lined the walls of the Doge's palace were executed in a period of decline, and at a time of great self-doubt in Venice.

One of the causes of Venice's lack of confidence was the rise of piracy along the coast of the Adriatic Sea. Venetians regarded the Adriatic as their sea—the theme of dominion over the sea and of marriage to the sea constantly recurred in Venetian literature. Throughout the sixteenth century, Venice was desolate in the knowledge that shipping in the Adriatic was no longer safe and that pirates could even occupy whole towns. They pretended only to attack the Turks, but Venetian trading ships were more valuable and more vulnerable targets than the few Turkish ships that ventured into the Adriatic.

The papacy defeats France

The regeneration of the papacy owed much to Julius II (1503–13), a determined enemy of the Borgia family. He destroyed Borgia influence in central Italy and exiled Cesare. As a soldier, Julius led an army against Perugia in 1506 and, with French aid, conquered Bologna. As a diplomat, he was largely responsible for the formation of the League of Cambrai, organized for the express purpose of dismembering Venice and her holdings. He was able to benefit by the French victory at Agnadello by gaining Rimini and Ravenna. And by changing sides, he was able to influence Milan into surrendering, and came to be known as the "Deliverer of Italy."

St. Ursula setting forth on pilgrimage, from the series by the Venetian Carpaccio.

Frescoes for Pope Julius

Insisting that he was a sculptor, not a painter, Michelangelo Buonarroti reluctantly mounted the scaffolding that his assistants had erected inside the Sistine Chapel and began the task of covering more than one thousand square yards of plaster with frescoes. For more than three years, from late in 1508 until 1512, Michelangelo labored under the Sistine's vaulted roof. Working almost singlehandedly, he covered the vast ceiling with some three hundred Biblical figures. The task was a staggering one, and took its toll: in a letter to a friend, Michelangelo complained in verse that "the brush endlessly dripping onto my face has coated it with a multi-colored paving." When he finished, the Florentine was, by his own description, "bent as a Syrian bow"—but his masterwork was lauded as a triumph of Renaissance art.

A portrait of Michelangelo by Jacopino del Conte.

Opposite Adam and Eve are dismissed from the Garden of Eden after eating of the fruit of the Tree of Knowledge of Good and Evil; one of Michelangelo's paintings from the Sistine Chapel.

When he yielded to Pope Julius II's insistent pleas and returned to Rome in 1508 to paint the frescoes on the vaulted ceiling of the Sistine Chapel, Michelangelo Buonarroti was accepting a unique and hazardous artistic challenge. The thirty-three-year-old Florentine was already recognized as the foremost sculptor of the age. His *Pietà* had been on display in St. Peter's in Rome for nearly a decade and his colossal *David* had dominated a central square in Michelangelo's native Florence for four years. And although he had worked on a number of paintings—including the *Doni Tondo* (the Holy Family) and the *Battle of Cascina*—Michelangelo had always preferred sculpture to painting. (Months later, when he was totally absorbed with his work in the Sistine Chapel, the artist complained "I am neither working in a pleasant environment, nor am I a painter").

After resolving a longstanding quarrel with Julius, Michelangelo returned to Rome in the spring of 1508. At that time the sculptor still hoped to be given permission to start work on the gigantic mausoleum that he and the Pope had planned several years earlier. Michelangelo intended to ornament Julius' tomb with a series of powerful figures—slaves, victories and prophets—and he had already begun work on several of those statues. But now the Pope had another scheme in mind; he wanted Michelangelo to paint the vaulted Vatican chapel named for Pope Sixtus IV. That ambitious project had been suggested to Julius by the treacherous Bramante, the architect in charge of the reconstruction of St. Peter's.

Bramante disliked Florentines in general and he was particularly jealous of Michelangelo. The latter's return to Rome acutely displeased the architect, and he did his best to provoke another quarrel between Michelangelo and the Pope by persuading Julius to ask the Florentine to paint the Sistine ceiling. The cunning architect suspected that Michelangelo would refuse, and he knew that the sculptor's refusal would exacerbate the already

precarious truce between the two men. If, on the other hand, Michelangelo accepted the commission, Bramante felt sure that he would botch it, since the project was alien to the sculptor's temperament. Such a failure would almost certainly force the Florentine artist to leave Rome—and Bramante had already arranged to have his friend and distant relation, Raphael, take over the work on the Sistine Chapel.

The professional risk that Michelangelo was taking in accepting Julius' offer was compounded by the fact that Raphael was just beginning to paint a series of frescoes in a number of smaller rooms in the Vatican. It was inevitable that the Florentine's Sistine frescoes would be compared with Raphael's *stanze*. Moreover, his work would have to compete with the scenes from the life of Moses and Christ—painted by the finest fresco artists of the quattrocento—that already decorated the walls of the Sistine Chapel and were much admired.

Michelangelo had every reason to refuse the commission; instead, he accepted Julius' offer with apparent relish—and immediately set about complicating his task. He discarded the Pope's rather unpretentious plan to add the twelve apostles to the arch-stones of the vault while decorating the central section with grotesques, and he obtained Julius' permission to replace it with a far more ambitious composition consisting of three superimposed schemes. That revised design called for a series of panels depicting the Biblical story of Genesis. To them, Michelangelo planned to add portraits of Christ's blood ancestors, and the prophets and the sibyls who announced his coming on Earth. The third element of Michelangelo's composition was to be a series of *Ignudi* (nude youths), whose function was to provide a dynamic link between the Biblical scenes and the intermediate panels.

Not surprisingly, Michelangelo soon found himself faced with several significant problems. He arranged to have a number of his students come south from Florence to assist him, but he soon realized

The Temptations of Jesus: one of Botticelli's paintings in the Sistine Chapel.

A detail from Perugino's *Baptism of Christ* from the Sistine Chapel.

that they were not equal to the task. He sent some of them back to Florence and employed the others at menial tasks, while undertaking most of the painting himself. In addition, the already overtaxed artist was obliged to contend with the Pope's impatience to see the work finished and to deal with the ambitions of Raphael, who longed to take Michelangelo's place. Moreover, he ran into technical trouble, particularly with mildew. These dilemmas were minor ones, however; the artist's greatest problem was that he had to paint three hundred figures and roughly one thousand square yards of plastered surface while lying curled up under the ceiling. Michelangelo described the curious torture that he endured while carrying out his task in a poem to a friend:

> My stomach is thrust towards my chin,
> My beard curls up towards the sky,
> My head leans right over onto my back,
> My chest is like that of an old shrew,
> The brush endlessly dripping onto my face
> Has coated it with a multi-colored paving.
> My loins have retreated into my body,
> And my buttocks act as a counter-weight.
> I tread blindly without being able to see my feet,
> My skin stretches out in front of me
> And shrinks in folds behind.
> I am as bent as a Syrian bow.

Apart from anything else, Michelangelo's feat was one of sheer physical endurance. The Florentine began work on his frescoes at the end of 1508 or the beginning of 1509, and did not finish them until November of 1512.

Michelangelo's frank and generous character led him to adopt a totally different approach to fresco painting from that taken by his predecessors, who had sought to camouflage the shape and mass of the vaults they were painting. In contrast, Michelangelo deliberately emphasized the massive appearance of his figures by framing them with painted *trompe-l'oeil* architecture. Within those monumental structures, the artist created a vast, interlocking masterwork that so overwhelmed the other fine murals decorating the walls of the Chapel that they were completely forgotten.

The natural manner in which the human figures were portrayed, the high quality of the drawing, the use of perspective and the outstanding combination of coherence and movement embodied in Michelangelo's Sistine frescoes so enchanted contemporary critics that for centuries observers failed to realize that Michelangelo had shown himself to be a very fine colorist as well. Unfortunately, subsequent restorations—undertaken in 1565, 1625, 1710, 1903–5 and again in 1935–36—have dimmed the freshness of the original frescoes. During the eighteenth century, the panels were varnished with glue in a well-intentioned attempt at restoration that deadened the frescoes' colors. The accumulation of dust, the infiltration of water and the smoke from wax candles have also contributed to the ceiling's deterioration—to the extent that today they are darkened and cracked. Nevertheless, a careful

St. Peter's Montorio, Rome, designed by Bramante.

Chronology of the Renaissance

1300	Giotto working in Assisi
1304-21	Dante Alighieri publishes *Divine Comedy*
1348-51	Black Death devastates Europe
1360	Boccaccio publishes *Decameron*
1405	Aretino translates Plato
1416	Donatello casts statue of St. George
1420-43	Brunelleschi builds cupola of Florence Cathedral
1440	Nicholas of Cusa publishes *On Learned Ignorance*
1450	Gutenburg perfects moveable type
1452	Piero della Francesca paints murals at Arezzo
1452	Alberti publishes *On Architecture*
1469	Lorenzo de' Medici becomes ruler of Florence
1478	Botticelli paints *Primavera*
1481-83	Leonardo paints *Virgin on the Rocks*
1480	Beginning of Spanish Inquisition
1492	Columbus discovers America
1494	Aldus Manutius prints first pocket books
1495	Leonardo paints *Last Supper*
1498	Execution of Savonarola
1506	Bramante begins to rebuild St. Peter's
1508	Michelangelo paints ceiling of Sistine Chapel
1509	Raphael paints frescoes in Vatican
1511	Erasmus publishes *In Praise of Folly*
1513	Machiavelli publishes *The Prince*
1514	Castiglione writes *The Book of the Courtier*
1518	Titian paints *The Assumption of the Virgin*
1533-35	Rabelais publishes *Gargantua* and *Pantagruel*
1534	Luther publishes German Bible
1543	Copernicus' book on Astronomy
1548	Council of Trent begins
1548	Tintoretto paints *The Miracle of the Slave*
1550	Vasari publishes *Lives of Painters*
1568	Mercator's world projection
1580	Montaigne publishes *Essais*

The *Pietà*. Michelangelo preferred sculpture to painting, and was reluctant to paint the Sistine Chapel for Pope Julius.

Medal of Pico della Mirandola, expressing the philosophy of love in the words "Beauty, Love and Pleasure."

examination of the Chapel ceiling reveals richly orchestrated colors that are a far cry from the stony, monotonous palette so often attributed to Michelangelo.

From the beginning, Michelangelo was faced with an esthetic and theological dilemma that was as great as any of his technical quandaries: his frescoes clearly had to relate both in theme and order to the two series on the lateral walls. Those works, painted by the great artists of the quattrocento, represented the history of humanity *sub lege* (that is, under the law of Moses) and *sub gratia* (during the life of Christ). Michelangelo decided, therefore, to concentrate

mainly on the history of the world *ante legem* (before Moses received the Ten Commandments)—and he filled the center of the vault with nine great Biblical scenes. To illustrate the announcement of the coming of Christ through the ages Michelangelo added the ancestors of Jesus, starting with Abraham, and the soothsayers.

Michelangelo also had to take into consideration the fact that his predecessors, in accordance with an ancient Christian tradition, had started painting their frescoes from the altar and worked their way toward the main door. Consequently, the same chronological order had to be preserved in the ceiling

Love, Sacred and Profane by Titian.

Left Michelangelo's
Universal Guide, from
the Sistine Chapel.

Below The Creation of Man.

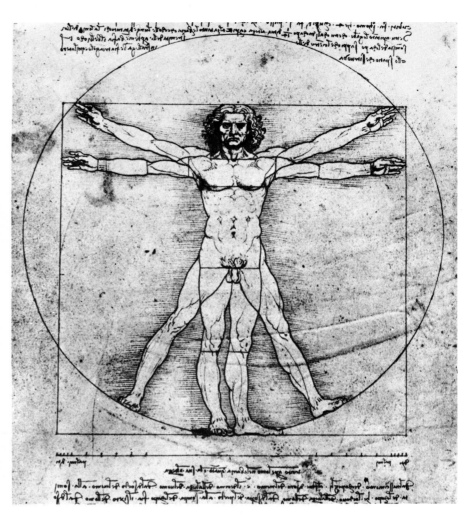

Above right Leonardo da Vinci's Vitruvian Man.

Above A poem by Michelangelo, with a drawing of himself painting the Sistine Chapel.

Right The title page of Marsilio Ficino's treatise *On the Immortality of Souls*.

frescoes, which began with a scene depicting the first day of Creation (*God Dividing the Light from the Darkness*), painted above the altar, and ended with the *Drunkenness of Noah* at the far end of the Chapel.

That constant reference to the Scriptures lent a strong Christian flavor and religious fervor to the Sistine frescoes, one that is not apparent in Michelangelo's earlier works. The Christ of the St. Peter's *Pietà*, for example, is depicted as a kind of Apollo put to death, while the *David* looks more like a beautiful Greek youth than the ancestor of Jesus. The naked fauns lurking behind the Holy Family in the *Doni Tondo*, like the figures in the *Battle of the Centaurs*, Michelangelo's first work, reveal the esthetic and artistic influence of the Greeks and Romans—not the Bible—upon Michelangelo's early work. The paintings on the ceiling of the Sistine Chapel, on the other hand, are grounded in the concept of Original Sin and represent an impassioned call to the Redeemer.

The theme of the Fall of Man was not a uniquely Christian one, however, and Michelangelo's fervor may have been aroused as much by his Neoplatonic background as by his heightened Christian awareness. Indeed, Michelangelo spent his formative years in Florence at a time when Neoplatonism was rapidly becoming the favorite philosophy of the

intellectuals. He was profoundly influenced by that trend and at least one eminent scholar has called Michelangelo the only Renaissance artist "to adopt Neoplatonism in its entirety, and not just certain aspects of it."

It is, in fact, possible to interpret the Sistine frescoes in Platonic terms, starting from the main door instead of from the altar. According to that interpretation, the first scene to be observed, the *Drunkenness of Noah*, represents the imprisonment of the soul within the body and the fetters of an earthly existence. The next painting, the *Deluge*, symbolizes the despair of humanity enslaved by the passions of a mundane world, and the panel that follows it, the *Sacrifice of Noah*, reveals the moment when the soul first becomes aware of its own existence and tries to communicate with God by offering Him a gift. That awareness of self implies an awareness of sin—which is illustrated in the next painting, the *Fall of Adam and Eve*. When studied in inverse order, the other Biblical scenes on the ceiling—the *Creation of Eve*, the *Creation of Adam*, *God Dividing the Waters*, the *Creation of the Sun, Moon and the Planets*, and *God Dividing the Light from the Darkness*—illustrate the ascent of the human soul from earthly, material existence to a final state of grace.

Neoplatonism is one of the keys to understanding the apparent paganism of many Renaissance art works, for despite their outer charm and pagan worldliness, most of those works are grounded in asceticism. Indeed, an invitation to asceticism can be found at the core of Platonic philosophy. According to Neoplatonist doctrine, the soul can remember only God and can attain grace only by breaking the chains that bind man to the earth. Ficino's *Theologia platonica*, one of the classic books of the Renaissance, states that "the life of the body is a sickness of the dreaming, tortured soul. All our movements, actions and passions are nothing more than the twisting and turnings of sick people, the nightmares and delirium of the insane." It is essential, the author insists, to banish all temptations produced by the senses. "The desire of the senses, which draws us towards everything that is material, massive, dull and shapeless . . . is not love but merely a pointless, stupid hunger,

degrading and hideous." That doctrine, which permeated the whole of the Renaissance, rejects all sensual pleasure but glorifies earthly beauty, which is seen as the first step up the "miraculous ladder" that ascends to God. Thus, Michelangelo's *Ignudi*, which created something of a stir when the Sistine ceiling was unveiled on August 14, 1511—and which led to the aforementioned accusations of paganism— were in fact symbols of truth and purity. (Michelangelo also expressed the Neoplatonic creed in one of his poems. "My eyes which are in love with beauty and my soul which is in love with salvation," he wrote, "can only ascend to heaven by the contemplation of all the beauty surrounding me.")

It is vitally important to appreciate the degree to which the Renaissance evolved its own philosophy of art—for if the Renaissance had not developed its uniquely "religious" and fundamentally optimistic conception of beauty, many superb works of art might never have been produced. Neoplatonism equated beauty and goodness with godliness. Its disciples maintained with absolute assurance that beauty was the "flower of goodness," and that it was through beauty that goodness was revealed to us. "We would not know the meaning of goodness," wrote Ficino, "nor would we seek it, since it is so well concealed, if we were not guided to it by the signs and marks of beauty and of love which accompanies it." Some fifty years later, in 1528, Castiglione took up the same theme in the *Cortegiano*:

It is very rare for an evil soul to inhabit a beautiful body. For outer beauty is the true sign of inner goodness . . . Beauty and goodness are more or less the same thing. This particularly applies to the beauty of the human body, whose main function, it seems to me, is to reflect the beauty of the soul. The latter, aware of the true beauty, which is that of God, glorifies and beautifies everything it touches.

In the light of these—and other—fervent declarations, it is not surprising that the Renaissance produced such poetic wealth and artistic originality. Or that Michelangelo produced such exuberant, inspiring, and fundamentally Christian frescoes for the ceiling of Julius' renovated Chapel.

JEAN DELUMEAU

145

At the height of the Renaissance, a decline

Leonardo da Vinci was perhaps the most characteristic of the giants of the Renaissance—a "universal man" who took all knowledge as his province. He combined superb artistic skill as a painter and sculptor with remarkable scientific insight to a degree that no individual had ever achieved. Born at Vinci in the Arno valley in 1452, he joined the artists' guild of St. Luke in Florence and trained under Verrocchio before moving to Milan, where his many-sided genius developed under the patronage of Ludovico Sforza. Leonardo made elaborate drawings for a bronze equestrian monument to Francesco Sforza, Ludovico's father, during this period, but his project never advanced beyond the clay model stage.

After painting the *Virgin of the Rocks*, Leonardo painted the *Last Supper* on a wall of the refectory of the Convent of Santa Maria delle Grazie at Milan. Working on the plaster in oil instead of fresco, Leonardo created an entirely original painting, which became for Christians the world over the standard representation of Christ with his disciples. When Louis XII saw the finished work in 1499, he was so moved by it that he asked whether it could be removed from the wall and transported to France.

Throughout these years, Leonardo filled his notebook with meticulous drawings which showed his power as a creative thinker. These sketches exemplified his acute observations of nature, his inventive genius and the extraordinary range of his interests. He drew daring flying machines, a helicopter which he developed from his studies of birds in flight, armored fighting vehicles and a submarine. He studied anatomy and optics and the formation of rocks, and his head was full of ideas for constructing irrigation works and fortifications. In his

paintings, he put into practice his theories of perspective and of light and shade, which he had worked out in his journals.

For most of Leonardo's active life, Italy was the cockpit of war. He spent a season with Cesare Borgia in the Romagna as a military engineer, and in 1507 was appointed painter and engineer-in-ordinary to the King of France. He ultimately settled in France.

The arts in Italy

Although Leonardo stands out because of his versatility, and Michelangelo because of the brilliance of his Sistine achievement, the early years of the sixteenth century saw a flowering of art probably unequaled in Europe's history. Raphael, who was a generation younger than Leonardo and eight years younger than Michelangelo, received numerous papal commissions, and rapidly became the leading exponent of the High Renaissance. While Michelangelo was completing the ceiling of the Sistine Chapel, Raphael was working on the frescoes in the Stanza della Segnatura at the Vatican, and painting the *Sistine Madonna*. Sandro Botticelli (1445–1510), highly influential at the end of the fifteenth century, was still painting, although his work was regarded as antiquated by both Leonardo and Michelangelo. More in keeping with their approach was the work of Andrea del Sarto (1486–1531), whose use of color was influenced by Michelangelo.

The Bellini brothers, Gentile (1430–1507) and Giovanni (c. 1430–1516), were the most distinguished Venetian artists of the time. Gentile did much work in the *Scuole* (religious foundations) of the city, while Giovanni became chief painter to the Republic in the 1490s, and was responsible for the artistic work in the rebuilt Doge's palace after the fire of 1479—although little has survived due to a further fire in 1577. Titian (1477–1576) attempted to become the chief painter to the Republic during Bellini's lifetime, but was appointed to the post only after Bellini's death. The main artistic influence on Titian was Giorgione (1476–1516) who brought a somewhat impressionist approach to painting.

A very different exemplar of High Italian culture in literature was Ariosto's *Orlando Furioso*, which was published in 1516 after a dozen years of steady composition. That poetic romance, which deals with the epic struggles of the Christians and the Saracens, has two secondary themes: Orlando's madness and his eventual cure, and the love between Ruggero and Bradamante.

Rebuilding St. Peter's

Just as Leonardo and Michelangelo dominated the artistic scene, so Bramante (Donato d'Angeli Lazzari, 1444–1514)—despite his hostility for Florentines—held a similar position in architecture. After carrying out small commissions for various cardinals, he

was commissioned by Alexander VI to build new offices for the papal Chancery. Julius II commissioned him to build the galleries in the Chancery and the Belvedere, and he quickly became the Pope's architectural consultant. His greatest work was the design for the rebuilding of St. Peter's, which Julius saw as the centerpiece of his rebuilt city. Earlier popes had realized that substantial rebuilding would be needed if the basilica was not to fall into ruin. Bramante proposed to build a huge dome over the foundation of the old Constantinian basilica. Although after his death many changes were made on his original plan, Michelangelo tried to preserve as much as possible of Bramante's design and it was only in the seventeenth century that the present shape—a Latin cross—replaced the Greek cross that Bramante had designed.

Three young kings

While developments in art were changing the visual face of Europe, death was changing its political face. In England, France, Spain and the Empire the old guard was changing, and Europe was soon dominated by three youthful kings. In England, Henry VIII succeeded his father in 1509 at the age of eighteen, and in 1515, the nineteen-year-old Duke of Angoulême succeeded Louis XII of France and became Francis I. Charles of Ghent inherited the throne of a united and prosperous Spain in 1516, when his maternal grandfather, Ferdinand I, died. The three young monarchs were personal rivals. Each had been brought up with an ideal of Renaissance kingship in mind, and each saw himself as the embodiment of Renaissance chivalry. All three were to be candidates at the imperial election in 1519. The relations of these three with the papacy were to be the dominant feature of European politics for the next thirty years. Italy ceased to be the political center of Europe, and became little more than the battleground over which the new monarchies fought.

The unification of Spain and the discovery of vast wealth in its American colonies, the reduction of the great feudal nobles in France and the centralized state

Ludovico Sforza by da Vinci.

Leonardo's study for the Sforza monument.

in Italy's political fortunes

The Michelangelo dome of St. Peter's, Rome.

introduced into England by Henry VII had created a new type of monarchy.

For the first two years of his reign, Henry VIII took little interest in government, preferring to leave it in the hands of Richard Fox (c. 1448–1528), and William Warham (c. 1450–1532), Archbishop of Canterbury. Fox and Warham pursued a quiet domestic policy, following in the footsteps of Henry VII and avoiding potentially expensive commitments abroad. The rise of Thomas Wolsey as Henry's minister resulted in a more dynamic and energetic policy. Although Wolsey, the son of an Ipswich butcher, became Bishop of Lincoln in 1512, of Tournai in 1513, Archbishop of York in 1514 and Cardinal and Lord Chancellor in 1515, he was beginning to influence the King as early as 1510. Wolsey was responsible for England's reentry into European politics in 1511, when Henry joined the Holy League of Pope Julius II, which

Pietà, by Giovanni Bellini.

was intended to drive the French out of Italy.

Henry, previously only interested in sport and building up the power of the Royal Navy, on whose reform and consolidation he had spent much time, now began to interest himself in politics. He saw the value of control of the English Channel and frequently sent small expeditions to burn French coastal villages. In 1513 he signed an offensive alliance with Emperor Maximilian and Ferdinand of Spain that called for an invasion of France. The King led his army out to join the Emperor's troops, but in so doing, he missed the only large engagement of this short campaign, the Battle of the Spurs at Guinegate. Henry did, however, take part in the successful siege of Tournai and in a few small skirmishes.

Francis I, whose love of sport was no less great than Henry's was brought up, like Henry, to admire chivalry. His early exploits were described by his sister, Margaret of Navarre, in her *Heptameron*. Francis married the daughter of Louis XII in 1515. His character was like Henry's: an outward veneer of brilliance and charm that often vanished leaving only selfishness and arrogance.

The Battle of Marignano

In the summer of his accession, Francis I set out for northern Italy with an army of 110,000 men. His immediate objective was to capture the Duchy of Milan, but he expected to subdue all Italy and sweep onward speedily to Con-

stantinople. So he marched into Italy and routed the Milanese at Villafranca. A few days later, the Swiss infantry attacked Francis' camp at Marignano. They pressured the French relentlessly, but Gian Trivulzio, the French commander, maintained his ground, and when reinforcements arrived was able to defeat the Swiss. The battle was the end of an epoch in European warfare—until that clash, Swiss troops had been all but invincible.

One immediate result of Francis' first campaign was the signing of the Concordat of Bologna in 1516. The Concordat entitled Francis to appoint French bishops and abbots and freed the French Church from close papal control. In return it called for the payment of annates to Rome—a system called the "Gallican liberties"—which were not abolished until the nineteenth century.

Charles' accession to the Spanish throne completed the trio. It was soon clear that the first real contest among them would be the imperial election that would follow Maximilian's death. The scene was already set for the struggles to come. Charles and Francis were the main contestants for the dominance of Europe, while Henry could not be ignored and his support seemed essential for the success of either.

Educational changes in the north

The revival of an interest in learning spread far beyond Italy and was not confined to Latin scholarship. Greek as well as Latin began to be taught in

schools. When John Colet (1467–1519), Dean of St. Paul's Cathedral, London, founded St. Paul's School, he insisted in the statutes that the headmaster should, if possible, know both Latin and Greek. Schooling from the age of eight was made compulsory by the Scottish Parliament for the sons of "substantial householders," although it is doubtful that this law had any effect outside the cities.

New universities were founded at Aberdeen (1494), Wittenberg (1502) and Marburg (1527), and university attendances rose steadily—although in Germany the intake of students was to be seriously affected by the difficulties of the Reformation era. Perhaps more significant than the foundation of universities was the setting up of new colleges within established universities. At Louvain the Collegium Trilingue was set up in 1517 with the specific purpose of improving the quality of teaching in Greek and Hebrew. At Oxford, Richard Fox founded Corpus Christi College as a center of Humanism in 1517, and in 1525 Cardinal Wolsey set up Cardinal's College with the same object in mind. At Cambridge, Jesus (1496), Christ's (1505) and St. John's (1509) all reflected Humanist interests. Lady Margaret Beaufort, mother of Henry VII, was the foundress of Christ's and St. John's, and also set up professorships of divinity in both Oxford and Cambridge in 1502.

The main cultural influences in the north were still Italian. It was only with Erasmus that the Northern Renaissance began to strike an independent note.

Francis I defeats the Swiss infantry at Marignano.

148

Erasmus and the New Learning

The greatest scholar of his age, Erasmus of Rotterdam, leader of the Christian Humanists, helped usher a new spirit of inquiry into scholarship and bring about a rebirth of learning. Although his call for the moral renewal of society and for religious toleration was doomed to failure, the seeds he sowed came to fruition two centuries later in the Age of Enlightenment.

In 1516 the greatest scholar of the age reached the peak of his academic career. "The name of Erasmus will never perish," claimed John Colet, one of his English admirers. The fifty-year-old scholar of Rotterdam had already made a name for himself in intellectual circles through his earlier writings, but that year saw the publication of his most important work—the first printed Greek edition of the New Testament, with commentary by him. This text, and especially the commentary, won high praise throughout the academic world. Even Pope Leo x welcomed it, ". . . not only because you have dedicated it to Us but because it contains a new kind of science." But the fame of Desiderius Erasmus had spread far beyond the confines of the universities. In his homeland, the Netherlands, he was recognized wherever he went and applauded in the street. Ordinary folk bribed his servants to let them peep through a keyhole at him while he slept, while others fought for the stubs of his candles to keep as souvenirs. He was showered with offers from European kings and princes of a professorship, or a wealthy ecclesiastical appointment, if only he would make his home in their land or at their court. Leo x himself wanted Erasmus by his side at Rome.

Yet the year 1516 marked even more than the high point in this remarkable man's career. It saw the triumph of a new philosophy, of which Erasmus was a forceful advocate. This philosophy had won support not only in the universities, but in the courts of kings, in the highest ranks of churchmen and in the printers' workshops that had recently been set up in Western Europe. In the same year another famous book was published that also reflected these new ideas—Thomas More's *Utopia*. This new philosophy has been called New Humanism, or Christian Humanism, and this latter title gives a clue as to its origin. The ideas of the new Humanists were similar to those of the Italian Humanists of the Renaissance, but had been given a new, specifically Christian, slant.

All these thinkers were devout Christians, and so were certainly not humanists in the modern sense of the word. A fifteenth- or sixteenth-century thinker described as a Humanist was interested in the "new learning" which had first begun in Italy in the late fourteenth century. At that time, there had been a revival of interest among Italian scholars in the works of Greek and Latin philosophers, poets and other writers. Many manuscripts that had been completely unknown to the Middle Ages were unearthed and were studied carefully. At first, interest centered on Latin works, but from the middle of the fifteenth century Byzantine scholars had settled in Italy and had taught their fellow scholars Greek. The works of the thinkers of classical Greece then became equally well known.

As more and more copies of classical manuscripts were discovered, a new kind of scholarship developed to deal with them. Scholars began to take a keen interest in the original languages of these documents—classical Latin, Greek and even Hebrew—so that they could understand the writer's exact meaning. They began to compare different texts of the same work and to find alternative readings, discrepancies and errors and thus were able to date the different copies and determine the most accurate reading. Once a reasonably accurate manuscript had been found it could be safely preserved for future generations in a printed edition. However, it was not the documents that interested these scholars so much as the ideas of the thinkers of classical antiquity, and the ways in which these ideas were expressed. The new Humanists began to copy their style and adopt their ideas. They felt sure that a rebirth of learning was taking place before their eyes.

Certainly this "new learning" was in complete contrast to medieval Scholasticism, which had dominated all education for so long. Whole new areas of learning opened up before the new Humanists—history, literature, the arts—whereas medieval learning had been restricted to law, medicine and particularly theology. A wealth of new ideas were available in the classical writers; the medieval thinkers had not had access to the ideas of any Greek philosopher, except through a poor translation of Aristotle's *Metaphysics* and a fragment of

The title-page of Erasmus' *Enchiridion Militis Christiani* —a plea to return to simple, essential Christianity by referring to the teachings of the Bible and the Early Church Fathers.

Opposite Erasmus by Holbein. The forceful advocate of the New Humanism saw its triumph in 1516, the year he published his annotated Greek edition of the New Testament.

Plato. The Humanists also had some idea of how to treat manuscripts; their medieval predecessors were notoriously uncritical, accepting forgeries as well as the genuine. Also, in emulation of the classics, the new learning was acquiring a rich, elegant and flexible Latin in which to express its ideas.

Medieval Latin had a limited vocabulary and a rigid structure suitable only for certain kinds of argument. Moreover, as there had been no standard rules of spelling or pronunciation, it was a rather inexact means of communication. There was also a striking contrast in spirit between the new learning and the old. The Humanists had an inquiring approach. They felt free to explore any area of human thought, to adopt any philosophy they chose, whether it be the paganism of their classical forbears, or the ideas of Plato, which they were certain could be reconciled with Christianity. Medieval learning had been rigidly controlled by the Church; schoolmen, such as Thomas Aquinas, had been concerned with building up watertight philosophical systems that left no room for questioning. In fact, well before the end of the Middle Ages, the Scholastics had succeeded in producing two totally irreconcilable philosophies, Nominalism and Realism, and much time was devoted to violent but fruitless debate between advocates of the two. To the medieval scholar, learning was a matter of memorizing the Scholastic arguments rather than understanding them; anyone who did not want to learn, must be compelled to do so. For the Humanist, learning was a matter of conveying enthusiasm, persuading and arguing until things were understood.

The new learning gradually spread from Italy during the fifteenth century. Some scholars, attracted by the new ideas, went to Italy to study and carried an enthusiasm for the new learning home with them. Italian scholars also traveled to other European universities, where they were sometimes invited to lecture on Greek and Latin poets. By the beginning of Erasmus' life (c. 1466) there were groups of Humanist sympathizers in

many European countries. They had not ousted medieval Scholasticism from the universities, and both systems existed side by side.

In Germany, the new learning had been adopted in several schools and universities including Heidelberg and Basel, and Germany had produced an outstanding Hebrew scholar in the person of Johann Reuchlin. An equally famous German, Beatus Rhenanus, was editing classical texts, and several cities, notably Strasbourg and Nuremberg, had literary societies or other groups of Humanist sympathizers while Basel had become a center of Humanist printing. There were other followers in the courts of various princes and bishops.

In France, Italian scholars had made an impact at the Sorbonne where they greatly influenced men like Robert Gaguin and the University librarian who, in 1470, had installed a secret press to publish Humanist works. Later, other Italian Humanists, including Fausto Andrelini and Aleandro, made their home in Paris, and in 1476 a Greek, George Hermonymos, settled there and taught men like Jacques Lefevre D'Etaples and Guillaume Bude who themselves became famous Humanist scholars. Humanist ideas were also popular in court circles; Louis XII had brought, as prisoner from his Italian wars, a famous Italian, Johannes Lascaris, and there were other Humanists in favor at the French court.

In England, foreign Greek scholars had visited both Oxford and Cambridge, and several English scholars had spent time in Italy. William Grocyn

who, having learned Greek in Italy, returned to teach, among others, Thomas More at Oxford. Thomas Linacre used his Greek to make an intensive study of Greek medicine and John Colet, somewhat late in life, studied in Rome. Although Colet did not learn Greek, he began to adopt a Humanist approach to the text of the New Testament. English Humanism also had its share of wealthy patrons, including, at one stage, William Warham, Archbishop of Canterbury, the bishops of London and Winchester, Lady Margaret Beaufort, Henry VII's mother, and others in court circles.

Spanish scholars had also visited Italy and taken the new learning to their homeland, especially Castile. The University of Salamanca boasted an outstanding Humanist scholar, Nebrÿa, and Cardinal Ximenes, Archbishop of Toledo, founded a new university at Alcala, specifically, for the study of Greek, Hebrew and Aramaic. Humanist ideas were also gaining ground at the court of Ferdinand and Isabella.

Humanism was still strong in Italy at the end of the fifteenth century, even in the papal court. There were several Humanists among the cardinals, especially those related to the Medici family. There were also Humanists in papal service in other parts of Europe, such as Andrea Ammonio, who resided in England. The first decades of the sixteenth century saw several popes who were sympathetic to the new philosophy—Leo X, Adrian VI, who had been the tutor of the Emperor Charles V, and Clement VII.

In the Netherlands, also, were men who had been influenced by the Italians. Among them were Alexander Hegius, a lover of classical literature who, in the 1480s, headed a school at Deventer, and Rudolf Agricola, who had been to Italy, became proficient in Latin, Greek and Hebrew and now gave a weekly Sunday lecture on Humanism at the school. Among the audience sat the young Erasmus; it was his first introduction to Humanist ideas.

During his career, Erasmus was to come into contact with large numbers of these European Humanists; many of them acclaimed him as their leader, and saw in his writings the finest expression of their own ideas. But there was another influence, apart from Italian Humanism, which affected Erasmus and his fellow thinkers—a religious movement grown strong in Germany and the Netherlands. (A similar movement also took place in Spain.) It was called the *devotio moderna* and was a call for reform of the Church, for a return to simple, essential Christianity. Its followers stressed that true religion was a matter of inward sincerity and pious devotion, rather than an outward fulfillment of ceremonies and ritual. It influenced Erasmus more than he realized, and under his leadership the new Humanism "began to put forward a plan of religious and moral reform."

Erasmus' career did not have an auspicious beginning. It is not even certain when he was

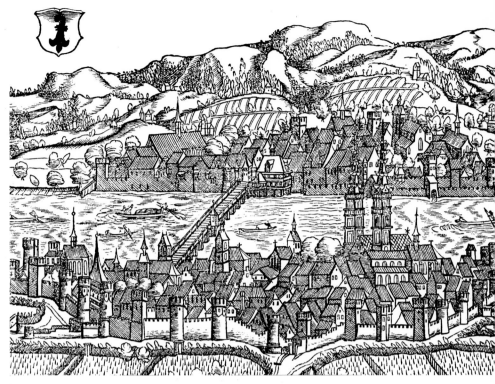

A woodcut of sixteenth-century Basel, a center of Humanist printing.

born—1466 or 1469—but he was known to be the illegitimate son of a Dutch priest, a stigma he spent much of his life trying to overcome. His mother sent him to the school at Deventer run by the Brethren of the Common Life, the *devotio moderna* movement. By modern standards, the teaching was barbaric, but Erasmus came to share his teacher's enthusiasm for Latin literature. He was not an outstanding scholar, and when his parents died in 1484 he was not sent to a university by his guardians as he wished, but to an even less enlightened Brethren school at 'sHertogenbosch. Even here, he had access to Latin literature and acquired a fairly fluent Latin style. As there was little money to provide for his future, and as he had never enjoyed good health, Erasmus' guardians put pressure on him to enter a monastery, and reluctantly he entered the Augustinian monastery at Steyn.

Erasmus always claimed that he hated his six years at Steyn, but he learned much during his stay there. The monastery had an excellent library, where he immersed himself in the works of the Early Church Fathers, medieval Scholastic writers and Latin poets and philosophers. He met Plato's ideas for the first time, and was introduced to the writings of such Italian Humanists as Volla and Poggio. His writings at this time show that he had developed a Latin style of his own which, though it owed much to classical writers, was adapted to the needs of his own time. It was just this proficiency in Latin that earned him his escape from Steyn. A neighboring bishop wanted a secretary skilled in Latin and Erasmus was granted leave to enter his service in 1492.

In 1495 the bishop agreed to send Erasmus to

Paris to study for a doctorate in theology, and he enrolled at the College Montaigu. Erasmus hated the theology faculty, which was dominated by the old Scholastic approach, and felt much more drawn toward the Humanist circle, especially to Robert Gaguin. The latter introduced him to Fausto Andrelini with whom he became close friends. Gaguin also gave Erasmus a chance to make himself known by allowing him to write an introductory letter to his own *History of France*.

While at Paris, Erasmus was always in financial difficulties, and his patrons being unreliable, he started taking pupils. This gave an impetus to his ideas on education and he began to write textbooks. This remained one of his main concerns; throughout his life he was continually revising his educational books which he insisted be sold cheaply enough to enable many people to buy them. His most important educational book was the *Adages*, a collection of sayings and proverbs from classical authors, useful material for illustration and argument. His pupils also introduced him to English Humanists, and in the summer of 1499 he went to England at the invitation of a young English peer, Lord Mountjoy.

Erasmus found a warm welcome in England. It was an important visit in many ways, for it saw the beginning of a close friendship with Thomas More, and it introduced Erasmus to the ideas of the Neoplatonists. He watched Colet applying a Humanist approach to the New Testament, looking for the exact meaning of the original in its historical context. Erasmus determined to learn Greek so that he could apply those same methods not only to the

New Testament but to the works of the Early Church Fathers, especially St. Jerome. He could not afford to go to Italy to learn Greek, so he returned to France, where he sold his coat to be able to purchase Greek books.

A work published at this time, *The Dagger of a Christian Soldier*, shows the direction of Erasmus' thought. A guide to practical piety for the layman, it preached the importance of inward sincerity and piety as a way of life for all Christians, not just for monks and clerics, and recommended that the layman should read the classical authors, the Scriptures and the Early Fathers and make them his guide in life. The book was welcomed by fellow Humanists, particularly Guillaume Bude and Beatus Rhenanus. It became a topic of discussion in Spanish ecclesiastical circles and at the courts of Mantua and Hungary, for although written in Latin, it was translated into many languages.

In 1506 Erasmus finally had an opportunity to go to Italy, accompanying the sons of the physician to Henry VII. He took his doctorate of divinity at Turin and went on to visit Florence, Venice, Bologna and Rome. He met several Italian Humanists, the most important being Aldus Manutius, the world-famous Venetian printer of ancient Greek and Latin texts. Erasmus seems to have spent most of his time collecting additional material for his *Adages*, which he persuaded Aldus to print, and he wrote an introduction to it that reflected his criticism of existing institutions and his concern for a moral renewal of society.

Erasmus was becoming better and better known and spent much of his time traveling from one academic center to another. His satire *In Praise of Folly* had been an instant success, and in 1514, he made a triumphant procession up the Rhine, heralded and honored in every city. By 1516 he had fulfilled two of his main ambitions; he had published both his annotated Greek version of the New Testament and the works of St. Jerome. The Greek version had inaccuracies and Erasmus revised it many times, but what made an impact on the world were the criticisms of ecclesiastical abuse, ritual and superstition included in the commentary.

Another deep concern of Erasmus and the new Humanists was peace. This comes out most clearly in Erasmus' *Complaint of Peace*, in which he makes concrete suggestions as to how peace can be achieved—by recognizing unalterable boundaries and having international laws about succession. Erasmus also felt equally strongly about the need for religious toleration; some of the new Humanists followed him in this, but conservatives like More and Fisher remained staunch in their orthodoxy.

The year 1516 marked the height of the new Humanism. With the support of the Pope and a large number of European princes, it looked as if the reforms they advocated could come about. Both Church and State might be persuaded by rational argument to change their ways. But the hopes of 1516 were shattered in 1517 when Martin

Luther nailed his ninety-five theses to the door of the church of Wittenberg. Although Erasmus' ideas still gained support, for example in Poland, Hungary, Spain and Portugal in the 1520s, there was little hope of their being put into effect. Luther's defiant stand against the Pope made any request for reform sound like heresy, and religious wars were soon to wreck the peace Erasmus so prized.

Erasmus spent the rest of his life fighting for moderation and religious toleration and failed, except in two insignificant areas of Europe—Poland and Transylvania, where his ideas of peace and toleration were successfully implemented. But his philosophy did not die—the seeds he had sown came to fruition two centuries later in the Age of Enlightenment. HEATHER SCEATS

The English Humanist John Colet who greatly admired Erasmus.

Opposite above A self-portrait of Dürer, whose works reflect the spirit of Humanism. His studies and treatises greatly influenced the development of techniques in the graphic arts.

Opposite below Sir Thomas More with his family. Erasmus' visit to England saw the beginning of a close friendship with More.

1400   1415

1415
The Battle of Agincourt
By his victory at Agincourt, England's
Henry V, "the last medieval king,"
rekindles the Hundred Years War

1415
Heretic or Martyr?
John Huss' execution identifies
religious reform with Bohemian
nationalism, splitting the Empire in
the Hussite Wars

Wenceslas IV 1361—1419
    Holy Roman Emperor   Murad II 1403-51 *Ottoman Sultan*

    Martin V *Pope* 1368—1431   Charles VII 1403-61 *King of France*
Sigismund 1308—1437
    Holy Roman Emperor   Giorgio Castriota (Skanderbeg) 1403-67 *Albanian prince*

John Huss 1369-1415 *Czech religious reformer* Constantine XI Palaeologus 1404-53 *Byzantine Emperor*

    Joanna II 1371-1435 *Queen of Naples* Pius II 1405-64 *Pope*

    Filippo Maria Visconti ?—1447 *Duke of Milan*   Richard Duke of York 1411-60 *Pretender to English throne*

    Cardinal Beaufort 1375-1447 *Chancellor of England*   Joan of Arc (St.) c. 1412-31 *French national heroine*

    Jan Žižka c. 1376-1424 *Czech military leader*   Sixtus IV 1414-84 *Pope*

    Filippo Brunelleschi 1377-1446 *Florentine architect*   Frederick III 1415-93 *Holy Roman Emperor*

    Lorenzo Ghiberti 1378-1455 *Florentine sculptor*   Henry VI 1421-71 *King of England*

    Calixtus III 1378-1458 *Pope*   Bartolomeo Platina 1421-81 *Vatican librarian*

    Thomas à Kempis (St.) c. 1380-1471 *German monk*   William Caxton c. 1421-91 *English Printer*

    Eugenius IV 1383-1447 *Pope*   Louis XI 1423-83 *King of France*

    Jan van Eyck 1385-1441 *Flemish painter*   Ferdinand I 1423-94 *King of Naples*

    Donatello c. 1386-1446 *Florentine sculptor*   Casimir IV

    Gian Galeazzo Storza ?—1479 *Duke of Milan*   Richar

    Henry V 1387-1422 *King of England*   Mehmet II

    Cosimo de' Medici 1389-1464 *Ruler of Florence*

    John Hunyadi 1390-1456 *Hungarian national hero*

    Henry the Navigator 1394-1460 *Portuguese prince*

    Philip the Good 1396-1467 *Duke of Burgundy*

    Nicholas V 1397-1455 *Pope*

    Paolo Uccello 1397-1475 *Florentine painter*

    Rogier van der Weyden 1400-64 *Flemish painter*

    Johann Gutenberg c. 1400-68 *German printer*

    Guillaume Dufay c. 1400-74 *Composer*

    Masaccio 1401-29? *Florentine painter*

    Francesco I Sforza 1401-66 *Condottiere of Milan*

1414-77 ●
Council of Constance : end
of Great Schism

1427 ●
Portuguese discovery
of the Azores

● **1402**
Turks defeated by
Timur at Ankara

● **1415**
Portuguese take Ceuta,
initiating policy of expansion
on African mainland

● **1419-35**
Hussite Wars

● **1409**
Sicily annexed by Aragon

● **1420**
Treaty of Troyes

● **1410**
Baghdad captured by Turks
(from Timurid Mongols)

143
Turks capture Saloni

31
aid of Orleans — Saint or witch, a peasant
om Orleans sways a nation — and is burned
stake for fulfilling her mission

1434
A Ferment in Florence — Cosimo de'Medici,
leading Florentine statesman, helps ignite
the cultural explosion known as the
Renaissance

1434 Conquest of the "Bulging Cape" — The
rounding of Cape Bojador by the Portuguese
opens the sea-route to Africa and ultimately
to India

1450
A Service to Men of Learning — The rise of
Humanism coutributes to the founding of
the Vatican Library by Pope Nicholas V

1453
The Fall of Constantinople — The inexorable
advance of the Ottoman Turks spells the end
for the once-brilliant Roman Empire of the
East.

1455
Gutenberg's "Right Worthy Art" — With the
printing of Gutenberg's Bible civilization
enters a new dimension

Bramante 1444-1514 *Italian architect*

Lorenzo de'Medici (the Magnificent) 1449-92 *Florentine ruler*

John Cabot c. 1450-98 *Italian explorer for England*

Bartholemew Dias 1450-1500 *Portuguese navigator*

Francisco de Almeida c. 1450-1510 *Portuguese admiral*

Aldus Manutius 1450-1515 *Venetian printer, Humanist*

Isabella I 1451-1504 *Queen of Castile and León*

Christopher Columbus c. 1451-1506 *Italian discoverer*

Ludovico Sforza "Il Moro" 1451-1508 *Duke of Milan*

Amerigo Vespucci 1451-1512 *Italian discoverer*

Richard III 1452-85 *King of England*

Girolamo Savonarola 1452-98 *Italian religious reformer*

Ferdinand V the Catholic 1452-1516 *King of Aragon*

Leonardo da Vinci 1452-1519 *Italian artist and inventor*

Alfonso de Albuquerque 1453-1515 *Portuguese admiral*

Lithuania and Poland

Earl of Warwick, "Kingmaker"

Henry VII 1457-1509 *King of England*

an Sultan

Maximilian I 1459-1519 *Holy Roman Emperor*

Bellini 1430-1507 *Venetian painter*

Jacob Fugger 1459-1525 *German merchant prince*

ni Bellini 1430-1516 *Venetian painter*

Alexander VI 1431-1503 *Pope*

Charles the Bold 1433-77 *Duke of Burgundy*

Marsilio Ficino 1433-99 *Florentine Humanist*

Andrea del Verrocchio 1435-88 *Florentine sculptor*

Ivan III the Great 1440-1505 *Grand Prince of Moscow*

Edward IV 1442-83 *King of England*

Matthias I Corvinus 1443—90 *King of Hungary*

Julius II 1443-1513 *Pope*

Sandro Botticelli c. 1444-1510 *Florentine painter*

● **1434**
Colonna proclaim Rome
a republic

● **1439**
Council of Florence:
attempt to end East-West
schism

● **1455-85**
Wars of the Roses

1452 ●
University of Glasgow
founded by Pope Nicholas V

●
1435
Rebellion in Sweden and
Denmark

● **1456**
Turks checked by
Hungarians at Belgrade

●
1453
Castillon: end of Hundred
Years War

● **1431-35**
Council of Basel

● **1435**
Treaty of Arras: alliance
of Charles VII and Philip
of Burgundy

●
1450
Cade's rebellion

1460

1475

1477
Louis XI Overthrows Burgundy — Louis XI's annexation of Burgundy strengthens the French monarchy but the power struggle for predominance in Europe continues

1469
Ferdinand Marries Isabella — The marriage of the heirs of two minor Spanish principalities transforms the history of Spain and of the world

1480
The End of the Golden Horde — Ivan III's defeat of the Golden Horde ends Mongol suzerainty over Russia

1485
The Battle of Bosworth — The last battle of the Wars of the Roses ends England's thirty years of civil war

Anne of Beaujeu 1460-1522 *Regent for Charles VIII of France*

Charles, Duke of Bourbon 1480-1527 *Constable of France*

Vasco da Gama c. 1460-1524 *Portuguese navigator*

Christian II 1481-1559 *King of Denmark, Sweden, N*

Louis XII 1462-1515 *King of France*

Raphael 1483-1520 *Italian painter*

Pico della Mirandola 1463-94 *Italian Humanist*

Baber 1483-1530 *Founder of Mogul Em*

Elizabeth of York 1465-1503 *Queen of England*

Francesco Guicciardini 1483-1540 *Ital*

Montezuma 1466-1520 *Mexican Emperor*

Martin Luther 1483-1546 *German relig*

Desiderius Erasmus c. 1466-1536 *Dutch Humanist*

Ghirlandaio 1483-1561 *Florentine pain*

John Colet c. 1467-1519 *English Humanist*

Ulrich Zwingli 1484-1531 *Swiss r*

Selim I 1467-1520 *Ottoman Sultan*

Catherine of Aragon 1485-

Paul III 1468-1549 *Pope*

Thomas Cromwell c. 1485

Niccolò Machiavelli 1469-1527 *Florentine statesman*

Hernando Cortes 1485-15

Charles VIII 1470-98 *King of France*

Andrea del Sarto 14

Francisco Pizarro 1470-1541 *Spanish conquistador*

Atahualpa ?-1533

Piero de'Medici 1471-1503 *Ruler of Florence*

Albrecht Dürer 1471-1528 *German artist*

Thomas Wolsey c. 1472-1530 *English cardinal and statesman*

Lukas Cranach 1472-1553 *German painter*

James IV 1473-1513 *King of Scotland*

Nicholas Copernicus 1473-1543 *Polish astronomer*

Ludovico Ariosto 1474-1533 *Italian poet*

Leo X 1475-1521 *Pope*

Michelangelo 1475-1564 *Italian sculptor and painter*

Cesare Borgia c. 1476-1507 *Italian ruler*

Giorgione 1476-1516 *Venetian painter*

Titian 1477-1578 *Venetian painter*

Clement VII 1478-1534 *Pope*

Thomas More, Sir 1478-1535 *English Humanist and statesman*

Ferdinand Magellan 1480-1521 *Portuguese navigator*

● **1478**
Inquisition established in Spain

1489
Venice annexes Cy

● **1487-88**
Dias round Cap
Good Hope

● **1465**
League of the Common Good founded

● **1479**
Venetian-Turkish peace treaty

● **1474**
Treaty of London, splitting France between Charles the Bold and Edward IV

1492
Landfall at San Salvador — Seeking the elusive Orient, Chistopher Columbus happens upon America and opens a new world to Europe

1512
Frescoes for Pope Julius — Michelangelo's triumphant achievement in painting the ceiling of the Sistine Chapel marks a high point of the Italian Renaissance

1494
Charles VIII Invades Italy — Charles VIII's misguided invasion of Italy succeeds in only increasing the Hapsburg threat to France

1516
Erasmus and the New Learning — With his new spirit of inquiry into scholarship Erasmus sows the seeds of the Age of Enlightenment

Louis II 1506-25 *King of Hungary*

Edward Seymour Duke of Somerset 1506-52 *Lord Protector of England*

Francis Xavier (St.) 1506-52 *Jesuit missionary*

Fernando, Duke of Alva 1508-82 *Spanish general, Regent of Netherlands*

Humayun 1508-1556 *Mogul Emperor*

John Calvin 1509-64 *French Potestant leader*

Gerard Mercator 1512-94 *Flemish cartogapher*

Mary of Guise 1515-60 *Wife of James V of Scotland*

f England   Mary I 1516-58 *Queen of England*

statesman   Henry II 1519-59 *King of France*

conquistador   Francis of Lorraine 1519-63 *Duke of Guise*

alian fresco painter   Gaspard de Coligny 1519-72 *French Protestant admiral*

Peru   Catherine de'Medici 1519-89 *Queen of France*

r 1489-1556 *English prelate*   Sigismund II 1520-72 *King of Poland*

natius Loyola (St.) 1491-1558 *Spanish founder of Jesuits*   Sixtus V 1521-90 *Pope*

enry VIII 1491-1547 *King of England*   Ali Pasha ?—1571 *Ottoman general*

William Tyndale 1492-1536 *English Humanist and reformer*

Paracelsus c. 1493-1541 *Swiss physician*

Francis I 1494-1547 *King of France*

François Rabelais 1494-1553 *French satirist*

Suleiman I the Magnificent 1494-1566 *Ottoman Sultan*

Gustavus I Vasa 1496-1560 *King of Sweden*

Philip Melancthon 1497-1560 *German Humanist*

Charles V 1500-58 *Holy Roman Emperor and King of Spain*

John III 1502-57 *King of Portugal*

Ferdinand I 1503-64 *Archduke, then Holy Roman Emperor*

John Knox c. 1505-72 *Scottish religious reformer*

Pius V 1505-72 *Pope*

● **1495-98**
Leonardo's *Last Supper*

● **1502**
University of Wittenberg founded

League of Cambrai founded
1508
●

1516-17 ●
Turks conquer Syria and Egypt

1527 ●
University of Marburg founded

da taken: Moors and xpelled from Spain
● **1492**

● **1497**
Cabot discovers Newfoundland

1509 ●
Battle of Agnadello: French defeat Venetians

1516 ●
Ariosto's *Orlando Furioso*

1494 ●
rsity of Aberdeen lled

● **1497-99**
Vasco da Gama discovers sea-route to India

1509
●
Eygptians and Indians routed by Portuguese in Indian Ocean off Diu

1513
Battle of the Spurs: French defeated by Maximilian I and Henry VIII

1519 ●
Magellan's circumnavigation

● **1495**
Diet of Worms abolishes private warfare in Germany

1515 ●
Marignano: Francis I takes Milan

1494 ●
Treaty of Tordesillas divides world between Spain and Portugal

● **1499-1503**
War between Venetians and Turks

1516 ●
Sir Thomas More's *Utopia*

Acknowledgments

The authors and publishers wish to thank the following museums and collections by whose kind permission the illustrations are reproduced. Page numbers appear in bold, photographic sources in italics:

12 *Editions Laffont*
13 British Museum, London
15 (1) British Museum (2) Victoria and Albert Museum, London
16 British Museum
17 British Museum
18 Lambeth Palace Library
19 British Museum
20 National Museum of Prague: *Antonin Blaha*
21 *Foto Marburg*
22 National Museum of Prague: *Antonin Blaha*
23 National Museum of Prague: *Antonin Blaha*
24 (1) Rosgarten Museum, Constance: *Jeannine Le Brun* (2) Kunsthistorisches Museum, Vienna
25 British Museum
26 (1) Universitätsbibliothek, Göttingen (2) Staatliche Museen, Berlin
27 Rosgarten Museum
28 (1, 2) *Giraudon*
29 (2) *Giraudon/Lauros*
30 Bibliothèque, Nantes: *Giraudon*
32 (1) *Giraudon* (2) Louvre, Paris
33 Bibliothèque Nationale, Rouen: *Giraudon*
34 (1) British Museum (2) Bibliothèque Municipale, Lille: *Photo Bulloz* (3) *Michael Holford*
35 (1, 2, 3) Bibliothèque Nationale, Paris: *Photo Bulloz*
36 (1, 2) *Giraudon*
37 (1) Bibliothèque Nationale, Paris: *Giraudon* (2) *Mansell Collection*
38 (1) *Hulton Picture Library* (2) *Barnaby's* (3) *Mansell Collection*
39 (1) Edinburgh University Library (2) Universitätsbibliothek, Basel
40 *Scala*
41 *Scala*
42 *Scala*
43 *Scala*
44 (1, 2) *Scala*
45 *Scala*
46 *Mansell Collection*
47 (1) *Mansell Collection* (2) *Alinari*
48 Museo de Arte Antiqua, Lisbon: *Photo Mario Novais*
49 Museo Cozaro, Madrid: *Foto Mas*
50 Bibliothèque Nationale, Paris
51 (1) National Maritime Museum, London (2) Biblioteca Universitaria, Bologna
52 (1) Archiv für Kunst und Geschichte, Berlin (2) Bibliothèque Nationale, Paris: *Aldus Books*
54 British Museum
55 Bibliothèque Nationale, Paris
56 (1) *Scala* (2) Victoria and Albert Museum (3) *Mansell Collection*
57 (1) *Scala*
58 *Scala*
59 Vatican Library
60 *Alinari*
61 *Mansell Collection*
62 *Scala*
63 (1, 2) *Scala*
64 (1) Vatican Library (2) Uffizi, Florence
65 *Scala*
66 (1) *Giraudon* (2) *Photo Bulloz* (3) *Mansell Collection*
67 (1) *Novosti* (2) Chester Beatty Library, Dublin
68 *Foto Mas*
69 British Museum
70 Elea Buchall
71 (1) *J. Allan Cash* (2) *Ian Graham*
72 Palazzo Medici-Riccardi: *Scala*
73 National Gallery, London
74 (1) *Giraudon* (2) National Portrait Gallery, London (3) Centrale Bibliotheek, Ghent
75 (2) India Office Library: *Fleming*
76 British Museum
77 *Mansell Collection*
78 (1, 2) *Ludwig Richter*
79 Victoria and Albert Museum
80 (1) *Ludwig Richter* (2) British Museum
81 Victoria and Albert Museum
82 (1) *Scala*
83 (1) National Gallery of Art, Washington; Samuel H. Kress Collection (2) *Gabinetto Fotografico, Florence* (3) *Foto Mas*
84 *Foto Mas*
85 *Foto Mas*
86 (1, 2) *Foto Mas*
87 *Foto Mas*
88 *Foto Mas*
89 *Foto Mas*
90 (1) *Nordiske Pressefoto* (2) *A.C.L.*
91 (1, 2) *Photo Bulloz*
92 *Giraudon*
93 Rijksmuseum, Amsterdam
94 (1) National Gallery, London (2) Musée des Beaux Arts de Dijon
95 *Giraudon*
96 (1) Bibliothèque Nationale, Paris (2) Musée des Beaux Arts de Dijon
97 Musée de Berne: *Editions Laffont*
98 *Giraudon*
99 *Giraudon*
100 (1) National Portrait Gallery, Scotland (2) Japanese Cultural Office
101 (1) Royal Geographical Society, Copyright Reserved (2) *Interfoto M.T.I., Hungary*
102 *Novosti*
103 *Novosti*
104 (1) *Novosti*
105 (2) *H. Roger Viollet*
106 *Novosti*
107 *American Heritage*
108 (1) *Mansell Collection* (2) Victoria and Albert Museum (3) British Museum
109 (1, 2) *Scala*
110 National Portrait Gallery, London
111 National Portrait Gallery, London
112 (1) Crown Copyright Reserved (2) *Pierpont Morgan Library*
113 (1) *Peter Clayton* (2) British Museum
115 *Mansell Collection*
116 British Museum
117 Centrale Bibliotheek, Ghent
118 (1) Kunsthistorisches Museum, Vienna (2) Österreiches National-bibliothek
119 (1) Chester Beatty Library (2) Biblioteca Ambrosiana, Milan
121 Museo Civico, Como: *Scala*
122 *Mansell Collection*
123 (1, 2) Naval Museum, Pegli: *Gabinetto Fotografico* (3) *Giraudon*
124 British Museum
126 Toledo Cathedral: *Foto Mas*
127 (1) Bibliothèque Nationale, Paris (2) Bodleian Library, Oxford
128 (1) *Foto Mas* (2) Polish Library, London
129 (1) *Hulton Picture Library* (2) *Photo Bulloz*
130 *Scala*
131 *Giraudon/Lauros*
132 *Hulton Picture Library*
134 *Scala*
135 *Scala*
136 (1) *Gabinetto Fotografico Nazionale* (2, 3) *Mansell Collection*
137 (1) Bibliothèque Nationale, Paris: *Photo Foliot* (2) *Mansell Collection*
138 Uffizi, Florence
139 *Rizzoli-Editore*
140 (1) *Alinari* (2) *Anderson*
141 *Anderson*
142 (1) *Scala* (2) *Gabinetto Fotografico Nazionale* (3) *Scala*
143 (1) *Anderson* (2) *Gabinetto Fotografico Nazionale* (3) *Alinari*
144 (1) *Gabinetto Fotografico Nazionale*
145 (1) *Scala* (2) Society of Antiquaries, London
146 (1) *Mansell Collection* (2) Royal Library, Windsor
147 (1) *Scala* (2) National Gallery, London (3) *Giraudon*
148 Kunstmuseum, Basel: *Colorphoto Hinz*
149 Gemeentbibliotheek, Rotterdam
150 (1, 2) Staatsbibliothek, Berlin
151 Archiv für Kunst und Geschichte, Berlin
152 (1) Alte Pinakothek, Munich (2) National Portrait Gallery, London
153 Mercers Company, London: *B.P.C. Library*

Managing Editor: *Jonathan Martin*
Assistant Editors: *Geoffrey Chesler, Francesca Ronan*
Design Consultant: *Tim Higgins*
Art Director: *Anthony Cohen*
Picture Editor: *Judith Aspinall*

Index